E-Commerce & Information Technology In Hospitality & Tourism

E-Commerce & Information Technology In Hospitality & Tourism

Zongqing Zhou, PhD

Associate Professor
College of Hospitality and Tourism Management
Niagara University

THOMSON
DELMAR LEARNING

Australia Canada Mexico Singapore Spain United Kingdom United States

E-Commerce and Information Technology in Hospitality and Tourism
by Zongqing Zhou, Ph.D.

Vice President, Career
Education SBU:
Dawn Gerrain

Editorial Director:
Sherry Gomoll

Senior Acquisitions Editor:
Joan M. Gill

Editorial Assistant:
Lisa Flatley

Production Director:
Wendy A. Troeger

Production Manager:
Carolyn Miller

Production Editor:
Matthew J. Williams

Marketing Director:
Donna J. Lewis

Channel Manager:
Wendy E. Mapstone

Cover Image:
Brand X Pictures

For permission to use material from this text or product,
contact us by
Tel (800) 730-2214
Fax (800) 730-2215
www.thomsonrights.com

Library of Congress
Cataloging-in-Publication Data

Zhou, Zongqing
   E-commerce and Internet technology in hospitality and tourism / Zongqing Zhou.
      p. cm.
   ISBN -7668-4140-5
   1. Hospitality industry—Data processing.
2. Tourism—Data processing. 3. Internet.
4. Electronic commerce. I. Title.
   TX911.3.E4Z46 2003
   647.74' 0285--dc21   2003009190

NOTICE TO THE READER

Publisher does not warrant or guarantee any of the products described herein or perform any independent analysis in connection with any of the product information contained herein. Publisher does not assume, and expressly disclaims, any obligation to obtain and include information other than that provided to it by the manufacturer.

The reader is notified that this text is an educational tool, not a practice book. Since the law is in constant change, no rule or statement of law in this book should be relied upon for any service to any client. The reader should always refer to standard legal sources for the current rule or law. If legal advice or other expert assistance is required, the services of the appropriate professional should be sought.

The Publisher makes no representation or warranties of any kind, including but not limited to, the warranties of fitness for particular purpose or merchantability, nor are any such representations implied with respect to the material set forth herein, and the publisher takes no responsibility with respect to such material. The publisher shall not be liable for any special, consequential, or exemplary damages resulting, in whole or part, from the readers' use of, or reliance upon, this material.

Contents

9

A NEW PARADIGM FOR INTERNET RESEARCH   173

10

THE FUTURE OF HOSPITALITY AND TOURISM E-COMMERCE AND INFORMATION TECHNOLOGY   190

GLOSSARY   209

INDEX   223

Preface

It is just past 11:00 at night, and Mr. Mike Jones, age 76, receives a phone call from his friend that he is to fly to a neighboring city the next day to join a group of World War II buddies for a reunion. He turns on his computer, connects to the Internet, and goes to his favorite airline Web site. A few clicks later, he has his e-ticket, paid through his credit card. He then checks in at the same Web site, obtaining his seat number. Mission accomplished. He is pleased and gets ready to go to bed.

What Mike Jones has just gone through is a simplification of what has come to be called electronic commerce, or e-commerce. It is the result of the accumulation of over 100 years of advancement in information technology, resulting in a new phenomenon called the Internet. When America completed the first transcontinental railroad, transportation and commerce were revolutionized as business expanded into a previously unreachable national market. The telephone, perhaps the greatest breakthrough ever in information technology, brought an instant means of communication to everyone in American society. The development of the highway system in the early 1920s enabled all Americans to travel distances never thought possible. The emergence of airline travel opened up a new world of possibilities as people and information began to travel faster and more efficiently—and the new era of globalization was born.

This book is the result of several years of research and teaching in the field of information technology and Internet commerce. Over the years, I have been searching for a book that reflects the increasing role of the Internet as an agent of change in hospitality and tourism information technology and commerce. The contents of this book represent a systematic approach to information technology and the Internet as a force that shapes the hospitality and tourism enterprises in their business decision making, meeting the needs and wants of consumers as well as the goals of companies.

AUDIENCE

This book is intended for students at all levels, from community colleges and technical schools to universities. Students who have little systematic background in information technology and the Internet other than what they obtain in the course of personal experience and/or from courses related to the topics will benefit from this book. Since this book is written with the hospitality and tourism industry in mind, it is especially suitable for programs at all levels that offer hospitality and tourism courses in information technology and e-commerce. In addition, this book will be helpful to people in the hospitality and tourism industry who need to understand the changing role of technology and the Internet as a channel of communication and commerce.

WRITING STYLE

My students have told me that they enjoyed reading the manuscript for this book because it explained technical jargon with nontechnical terms and analogies. That is exactly what I intended this book to accomplish: to provide a wealth of information in simple, easy-to-understand English. Such feedback told me that this writing style suits students at all levels since it contains both needed technical terms and simple, vivid explanations that everyone can understand.

This writing style facilitates students' reading of the book and therefore better prepares students for classroom discussion, saving the instructor time explaining complex concepts in the classroom. Both the student and the instructor will benefit from using this book.

HIGHLIGHTS

As mentioned at the beginning of this preface, this book is based on my teaching experience and research efforts. Accordingly, the materials are presented in a logical, building-block fashion. Words and terms are defined and explained when they are first introduced. Examples are used as a foundation and then expanded with more detail. By the end of the book, the student will have an excellent understanding of the subject.

This book takes an outside-in approach to its subject. Concepts and terms are explained in clear, simple language. All the examples, references, and case studies come from real-life settings and illustrate the impact of the Internet on e-commerce and information technology in the hospitality and tourism industry. The student will learn how the Internet works and what kind of impact it has exerted on this industry.

The travel information distribution sector has seen many changes since the advent of the Internet. I have devoted a whole chapter to discussing the changes this sector has undergone. This chapter should be particularly useful and interesting to those two-year colleges whose traditional curricula center on travel agents and information distribution.

One of the major themes running through this book is that customer service and marketing communication are the driving forces behind the importance of the Internet for the travel and hospitality industry. Concepts, ideas, and technologies in this book are discussed within the context of better serving the customers and improving marketing communications. For this reason, this book can also be used for those teaching Internet marketing courses, either as the main text or as a supplementary reading.

■ ORGANIZATION OF THE BOOK

This book has been organized to cover the Internet as an agent of change that impacts various sectors of the hospitality and tourism industry. It begins with an overview of the impact of the Internet and ends with a discussion of the future directions and issues in the hospitality and tourism industry in terms of information technology and e-commerce. The following outlines the organization of the chapters.

- ❏ Chapter 1 provides an overview of the subject matter, including a brief history of the Internet. It leads students to understand that the impact of the Internet on the information technology in the hospitality and tourism industry is probably far more reaching than they realize. It also conceptualizes the functions of the Internet as an agent of change.
- ❏ Chapter 2 discusses the fundamentals of the Internet. Basic Internet terms are introduced and explained. This chapter lays the foundation for a more detailed discussion of these terms in later chapters.
- ❏ Chapter 3 continues to discuss one particular aspect of the Internet: how to connect to the world. It aims to provide an introduction to Chapter 4, which discusses e-commerce fundamentals.
- ❏ Chapter 4 follows up on discussions in Chapter 3 and details how e-commerce works. Additional issues in e-commerce are introduced, including reliability, privacy and security.
- ❏ Chapter 5 introduces various platforms of Internet communication. It covers Internet communication tools, such as Intranet and Extranets. It also outlines four basic types of e-commerce models: B2B, B2C, C2B, C2C.
- ❏ Chapter 6 examines a set of Internet marketing and information distribution tools. The concepts of push and pull marketing are introduced and discussed. This chapter attempts to provide a comprehensive overview of the available marketing schemes and strategies used by various sectors of the hospitality and tourism industry.
- ❏ Chapter 7 discusses in greater detail the impact of the Internet on different sectors of the hospitality and tourism industry. Sectors discussed include airlines, hotels, car rentals, cruise lines, bed and breakfasts, travel agencies, brochure distribution, online travel stores, and other types of related businesses.

❏ Chapter 8 examines a special sector of the hospitality and tourism industry: the travel agency, pointing out reasons that travel agencies need special attention. It examines the factors that impact the travel agencies most and suggests strategies for such agencies in dealing with the Internet phenomenon. A historical perspective is also provided.

❏ Chapter 9 looks at the Internet as a research tool for marketing, customer service, and other business decisions. It shows students how to do research on the Internet and describes measurements used to determine marketing effectiveness.

❏ Chapter 10 provides a glimpse of future directions and issues faced by the hospitality and tourism industry in their adoption and management of information technology. It concludes by emphasizing the fact that the Internet and traditional information technology are becoming more integrated. The convergence of technologies will lead the trend in the 21st century.

PEDAGOGICAL FEATURES

This book contains many pedagogical features designed to assist both the student and the instructor.

❏ A set of objectives appears at the beginning of each chapter, outlining what the student should learn.

❏ A case study at the end of each chapter illustrates how the concepts and techniques have been applied by a real company. Questions have been added to stimulate students' thinking about the real world of Internet applications.

❏ Many Internet links (URLs) have been added throughout the text and in references to direct the student to those Web sites where they may find the most current information or do additional research.

❏ An extensive list of key words and terms at the end of each chapter serves as a checklist of important concepts and ideas within each chapter.

❏ A comprehensive glossary of terms appears at the end.

SUPPLEMENTAL MATERIALS

Also available from Delmar Learning are the following supplements to aid in the instruction and student learning processes:

❏ Instructor's Manual/Test Bank. Written by the author of this text, the Instructor's Manual is designed to assist instructors with lesson plans, review questions, chapter tests, and other teaching tools.

❏ Online Resource. Visit our Web site at www. hospitality-tourism. delmar.com and click the Online Resource tab to gain access to additional resources for both students and instructors.

Acknowledgments

A rapidly changing field, such as the Internet and information technology, presents tremendous challenges to write a textbook for it. Without the help and input from many people, this book would not have been possible. Therefore, I would like to thank the following individuals for reviewing the manuscript and for their comments, input, and suggestions: Liping A. Cai, Purdue University; Ronald J. Cereola, James Madison University; Cihan Cobanoglu, University of Delaware; Reed Fisher, Johnson State College; Roger Gerard, Shasta College; Jim Murdy, University of New Haven; Mary Jo Ross, University of Central Florida; Mairanna Sigala, University of Strathclyde.

Special thanks go to my daughter, Juan Zhou, who is the best proofreader I could ever find. Her input on my writing style has greatly impacted how I chose my diction and presented the materials. I can never underestimate her contribution to the completion of this book. I can not complete the list of acknowledgement without thanking my son, William Zhou, whose wit, smiles and A's from his school provided me with the best stress relief and writing inspiration every day.

I am also very grateful to Gary Praetzel, Dean of the College of Hospitality and Tourism Management at Niagara University, whose brotherly support came in abundance throughout the production of this book.

And finally, I want to thank all my students who have read the manuscripts and provided valuable feedback, especially those who help with the research on some of the case studies in this book.

Z. Q. Zhou
Feb. 1, 2003

1

OVERVIEW

LEARNING OBJECTIVES

After you complete your study of this chapter, you should be able to:

- Understand the rapid growth of the Internet.
- Explain why the hospitality and tourism industry, as well as its consumers, are at the forefront of Internet usage.
- Explain how the Internet can be used for different communication and business purposes.
- Understand the impact of the Internet on the many sectors of the hospitality and tourism industry.
- Explain why it can be difficult to maintain up-to-date Internet knowledge.

▌1.1 THE GROWTH OF THE INTERNET

The growth of the Internet can only be described as breathtaking, if not revolutionary. This is seen from the increased number of Internet users in recent years. In 1994 in the United States, there were only 25 million Internet users (Verity and Hof 1994), but this number increased to 40 million in 1997 (Cortese 1997) and to 95 million in 2001 (Figure 1.1).

The ability to communicate with one another instantaneously, without geographical limitations, and without time constraints, captures the imagination of millions worldwide. The total online population was estimated to be 619 million in 2002 and will reach 940 million in 2004 (Global Reach 2003). This is not surprising. Countries, both large and small, are seeing the Internet not only as a means of communication, but also as a new area of economic growth. China, for instance, has invested billions of dollars in developing its Internet infrastructure and is projected to own the most Internet users by 2006. Table 1.1 presents a brief overview of the number of Internet users according to languages spoken.

FIGURE 1.1
Online past-years travelers, 1996–2001.

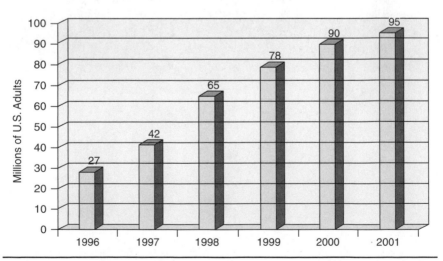

Online Past-Year Travelers, 1996-2001

SOURCE: Travel Industry Association of America, *Travelers' Use of the Internet,* 2001 Edition.

	TABLE 1.1		
	Worldwide Internet Users by Language		
LANGUAGES	INTERNET ACCESS, 2002 (1,000s)	WORLD ONLINE POPULATION (%)	2004 ESTIMATED POPULATION (1,000s)
English	230	36.5	280
European (non-English)	224	35.5	328
Asian (including Chinese)	179	28.3	329
Chinese	68	10.8	170
Total world	619		940

SOURCE: Compiled by the author, from Global Reach, www.glreach.com (2001).

1.2 THE INTERNET AND THE HOSPITALITY AND TOURISM INDUSTRY

The hospitality and tourism industry has always been among the first to capitalize on new technology. Because it is an information-rich industry, it depends heavily on finding and developing new means to distribute travel and hospitality products and services, marketing information to consumers, and providing comfort and convenience to travelers. Similarly, consumers are constantly seeking new sources of information to help them make decisions before purchasing travel services to make their trips more satisfying. It is not surprising that travel and hospitality e-commerce is among the top four growth categories, second only to finance and insurance services.

Use of the Internet by travelers to plan and book their trips continues to grow at a rapid rate. In the United States, according to the Travel Industry Association (TIA 2003), about 64 million online travelers used the Internet in 2002 to get information on destinations or to check prices and schedules, growing about 400% over three years. From 1999 to 2002, online booking showed a remarkable double-digit growth for four consecutive years, with a spectacular 58% growth in 2001, followed by a 25% growth in 2002. It is estimated that online leisure travel sales totaled $20.4 billion in 2002 and that hotel reservations booked online reached $3.8 billion (Forrester Research 2002).

Statistics also suggest that online travelers are a very attractive group of people. They tend to be under the age of 55, have an annual household income above $75,000, are college educated, and work in a professional/managerial occupation. The average spending by frequent online travelers was about $3,200 in 2000 (TIA 2001). As a whole, online travelers spent over $13 billion in 2000, buying travel and related services over the Internet. With the Internet evolving so rapidly, these statistics will soon become outdated. There is strong evidence to suggest that this trend will continue in the years to come.

In Canada, Buhasz (2001) has also shown that travelers are increasingly turning to the Internet for travel planning and booking, bypassing travel agents and making fewer phone calls to airlines, tourism offices, hotels, and car rental agencies. The general consensus is that compared to other **online transactions,** such as retail shopping or banking, online travel booking will be the number one growth area for the Internet in the following years.

The demand for travel products and services from the Internet is still growing despite the **dot-com** bust that took place beginning with the last quarter of 2000. This is when the NASDAQ plummeted from more than 5,000 points to under 2,000 points in early 2001 and to under 1,500 points in 2003, a loss of almost 70% from the peak. Some well-known travel sites, such as Expedia (www.expedia.com) and Travelocity (www.travelocity.com), are still going strong, and new sites are being added. In late 2000 and early 2001, a new travel site, Orbitz (www.orbitz.com), received a $50 million investment fund from some of the major airlines in the United States. Among the founders of the site, we see some of the largest airlines, including American, Continental, Delta, Northwest, and United. The Orbitz site promises to use new technology to help consumers find the best available fare. In Europe, it is predicted that the online travel market will more than triple in size, from an estimated $2.9 billion worth of gross bookings in 2000 to more than $10.9 billion in 2002.

1.3 CHARACTERISTICS OF THE INTERNET

The exponential growth of the Internet is due in large part to its unique capabilities. The first characteristic is its **peer-to-peer system.** This means that everyone on the Internet can communicate and function as an equal with anyone else. Anyone with an **IP** (Internet Protocol) address can host server functions from their own computer and offer these to anyone else on the Internet. Theoretically, therefore, every business in the hospitality and tourism industry can offer and market their services and products directly to customers. Information about these services and products can be updated instantly around the clock.

The second characteristic is that the Internet is an interconnected network and thus has the capability of interaction. Its peer-to-peer design allows users, including customers, merchants, and financial institutions, to interact with each other. This has resulted in a real-time online reservation system—a direct electronic distribution system accessible through the Internet to the general public. This characteristic can also be used to gather customer feedback to help plan or design customizable new products or services or to test-market new products or services.

The third characteristic of the Internet is its **hyperlink** capability. Unlike the traditional print publication, the Internet allows text and information to be linked in such a way that a simple click will lead you to the next level of text or information. It is truly a web of information. This characteristic makes the Internet a great research tool and an instant information finder.

The fourth characteristic is that the Internet embodies a key underlying technical idea: that of **open architecture networking.** In this approach, the choice of any individual network technology employed by individual companies and organizations is not subject to a central control. In an open architecture network, each network can be designed according to the specific environment and user requirements of that network. However, this can create a situation in which different communication hardware and software compete with one another and may thus create compatability problems. This is an important consideration when a business tries to use the Internet for communication and/or commerce. It is important to realize that barriers exist in both hardware and software systems used in Internet communication.

The fifth characteristic is that the Internet is **platform independent,** meaning that no matter what kind of computer or operating system you use to connect to the Internet, you can still communicate with other computers and operating systems. A platform is specific computer hardware or a specific combination of hardware and operating system. Unix, Windows, and Macintosh are examples of three different computer platforms.

Finally, making a presence on the Internet is no longer a task that requires a technical expert or huge financial clout. With the price of computers becoming more affordable and the availability of Web page authoring programs, anyone with a connection to a Web server can publish a home page in literally hours. One need not worry about complicated HTML (Hypertext Markup Language) codes that control the appearance of a Web page.

1.4 THE INTERNET AND E-COMMERCE

E-commerce is the new buzzword in the global economy. The heart of the global financial center, the New York Stock Exchange, has been transformed into a roller coaster because of the introduction of Internet-based companies. At its golden days, it seems that a new dot-com is coming on the scene every day. Media and television are saturated with advertisements and promotions for these dot-coms. E-commerce has now taken a more sophisticated approach and is being integrated into the strategic planning processes of many companies.

Business-to-consumer e-commerce in the hospitality and tourism industry has about 95 million online travelers in the United States alone, or about 45% of the U.S. adult population (TIA 2001). A number of researchers (Buhasz 2001; TIA 2001; Zhou and Lin 2000) have reached the conclusion that travelers are increasingly using the Internet for travel planning and reservations. The TIA (2001) reported that 66% of online travelers use the Internet to get information on destinations or to check prices and/or schedules. This figure confirms Zhou and Lin's finding that about 60% of the respondents will use the Internet for similar tasks (Zhou and Lin 2000). In terms of online buying, over 39 million people booked travel using the Internet in 2002, a 25% increase over 2001 (TIA 2003). It was reported that by the end of 2000, 59% of Canadian Internet users have gone online at least once to research travel information, and 18% have used the Internet to book some element of their travel plans (Buhasz 2001).

1.5 THE INTERNET AND COMMUNICATION

The hospitality and tourism industry is an information-rich industry. Most of its products and services are intangible, perishable, emotionally appealing, and people oriented. In addition, exposure to the services and products are typically brief. Since such products and services are intangible, consumers rely heavily on information about the product or service before they buy. Consumers need up-to-date, fast, **interactive information** that is available 24 hours a day, seven days a week. In addition, customer service assumes a much more important role than in any other industry since it is part of the travel experience. Fast, interactive, 24-hour customer service has been the ideal goal for the hospitality and tourism industry. For the first time, the Internet has made that dream come true. With the capability of the Internet, communication between service providers and customers can be done in a timely manner.

The Internet has broken both time and geographic barriers. Today, no matter where you are, you can communicate with your customers by e-mail as long as they have an access to the Internet. Changes in weather conditions, price, schedules, and programming can be communicated instantly to your customers. Previously, because of budget constraints and market limitations, small businesses in remote areas had difficulty marketing their services to potential customers. With the Internet, geographic location is no longer a problem. A small bed-and-breakfast inn in a small town, previously unknown to outsiders, can now reach potential customers by having their own Web site or having their products and services listed with a Web site.

The ability to communicate with customers 24 hours a day, seven days a week, and without the limitation of the geographic location can help travel and hospitality service providers. It builds up their customer relationships and therefore increases customer loyalty. Through data mining and other customer information collection methods, market segmentation and market customization can be done to deliver **customized information** to customers.

Today, many companies are setting up their own Internet portals to attract and allow customers to communicate with them on a regular basis. Many Internet tools, such as e-mail, e-newsletters, newsgroups, and discussion forums are being utilized to communicate to consumers.

The Internet is used not only for business-to-consumer communications but also for business-to-business and within-business operations. The creation of intranets and extranets provides new opportunities for businesses to conduct communications with each other more efficiently and more effectively. It also increases the convenience and savings for businesses to communicate with their own employees.

1.6 THE INTERNET AND E-MARKETING AND INFORMATION DISTRIBUTION

Internet marketing, also called **e-marketing,** opens up new opportunities for companies to market their services to consumers in ways that could only be dreamed of in the past. Marketing is about bringing product information and services to targeted consumers in a timely, accurate fashion. The Internet is a perfect medium for doing precisely that. More companies are realizing that they need to devote more resources to Internet marketing to capture this growing online travel market.

Companies are paying more attention to Internet marketing because of both the size of the market and the ability for market segmentation and consumer interaction. **Traditional marketing media,** such as television, radio, and newspapers, constitute one-way mass marketing. Internet marketing, on the other hand, can be done so that target markets are clearly selected and interactivity is built into the marketing message.

The technology that enables this type of target marketing is called **push** technology. Using push technology, companies send their marketing messages to individual consumers based on their predefined preferences. In this model, users do not have to search their way through what the Internet has to offer. Instead, they simply enter a variety of interests and needs into a server-side database. The server then collects all the information it feels is relevant and pushes the customized marketing information to the user's desktop. This is typically in the form of an e-mail message or portal Web site through client software that is sometimes a standard browser and sometimes a proprietary interface, such as PointCast or Yahoo News Ticker.

The intangible nature of travel and hospitality products and services dictates that information has paramount importance to both consumers and the industry. This industry has always been looking for new ways to distribute travel and marketing information to consumers and to provide comfort and convenience to travelers. Similarly, consumers are constantly seeking new sources of information to help them make decisions before purchasing travel services and to make their trips more satisfying. With the new capabilities of the Internet, consumers can now "fly" the skies, "cruise" the seas, "climb" the mountains, "sleep" on the hotel bed, "drive" the road, "hear" the roar of tigers and "explore" the cities, towns, and countries they want. If they like the products and services, they can purchase them right from the comfort of their personal computers. They can also keep in close contact with their homes, offices, and businesses while traveling. In other words, for the first time, the Internet has made it possible for intangible travel and hospitality products and services to be tangible.

The dynamic information provided on the Internet obviously is superior to the static information displayed in a traditional printed copy of a brochure. From a consumer's point of view, one can access information anytime, anywhere. The information on the Internet is richer, more varied, and time sensitive. From the service provider's point of view, information about service, price, weather conditions, programs, and schedules can be updated all the time and any time. Marketing information can be highlighted on the Web site and information catered to the target consumers. The Internet has struck a perfect match between the needs of travel and hospitality companies and the traveling public.

1.7 THE IMPACT OF THE INTERNET ON THE HOSPITALITY AND TOURISM INDUSTRY

The impact of the Internet can be said to include every aspect of the travel and hospitality business, from information distribution and marketing to travel and hospitality product and service purchases. According to projections by Forrester Research (2002), the number of Americans making online travel purchases in 2002 grew to 23.3 million households. Forrester also predicted that online leisure travel sales totaled $20.4 billion in 2002 and that hotel reservations booked online reached $3.8 billion. Zhou and Lin (2000) conducted a survey on the use of the Internet versus the printed brochure. Their findings show that the majority of respondents have access to the Internet; just over half the respondents had Internet access at home, followed by 34% at the library and 31% at the office. When asked which source of information they will depend on the most for their future trip planning, about 43% reported that they would use both printed brochures and the Internet, and 37.8%, would use only printed brochures.

However, if we add those who will use both printed brochures and the Internet and those who will use only the Internet, we come up with a figure as large as 58%. In other words, nearly 60% of people will use the Internet either as the sole or as a complementary source of travel information (see Table 1.2).

TABLE 1.2 Information Sources for Future Travel Planning		
INFORMATION SOURCE	NUMBER	PERCENTAGE
Printed brochures and the Internet	335	42.8
Printed brochures	296	37.8
Word of mouth	184	23.5
Internet	116	14.8
Travel agents	54	6.9

SOURCE: Zhou and Lin (2000).

Note in Table 1.2 that only about 7% of the people use a travel agent for travel advice and planning. In fact, the biggest impact on the travel and hospitality industry is in the area of travel planning and reservations. The International Air Transport Association (IATA; www.iata.org) conducted a survey on business travelers' use of the Internet (Levere 1999). The survey showed that business travelers worldwide are increasingly embracing the Internet to research and book their flights. Almost two-thirds of the survey's approximately 1,000 respondents from Europe, North America, and the Asia-Pacific region said that they used the Internet to find flight information—a 50% increase over the survey's results from two years ago.

On the suppliers' side, a number of the third-party travel Web sites have loomed large in travel information distribution and travel reservations. All these sites have strong financial and marketing clout from some of the largest corporations in the United States. Expedia (www.expedia.com) is owned by Microsoft, while Travelocity (www.travelocity.com) is owned by Sabre, one of the largest global distribution systems. Other third-party travel reservation sites include Priceline.com (www.priceline.com; a company that claims that consumers can name their own prices), Lowestprice.com (www.lowestprice.com); and Orbitz.com (www.orbitz.com).

Suppliers, such as hotels, airlines, rental car companies, and even cruise lines, are beginning to offer online real-time reservations. Indeed, they not only make reservations available online but also use incentives to encourage travelers to book online. For example, at one time, Northwest Airlines offered a new online booking program to small and medium-size corporations that featured incentives including free tickets and upgrades, elite frequent-flier program status, airport lounge memberships, and travel management aids. United Airlines offered a bonus of 25,000 miles to participants in its frequent-flier program who stayed at least 10 times at Regent International Hotels by December 30, 2000; each stay had to be a minimum of three nights. Travelers also had to register with Regent and pay the corporate room rate. British Airways established a Web site using London as a

destination (www.londontraveller.com) that contained in-depth information on the city from a variety of travel guidebooks as well as data on the
newest restaurants, bars, clubs, theaters, and art exhibits. Visitors to the site
could also buy airline tickets and reserve hotel rooms.

With the increased interest of travelers in online information and booking
and the aggressive marketing efforts of travel suppliers to sell tickets online,
travel agencies have been caught in the middle. Suppliers, starting with the
airlines, began to cut their commissions as early as 1997, and this has turned
out to be a deadly blow to the travel agencies.

Faced with this tremendous pressure to survive, travel agencies have used
various strategies to cope with the new reality. These strategies range from early
denial of the Internet's impact to attempts to free themselves from the control
of the traditional global distribution systems by setting up their own central
reservation systems. Travel agencies are going through a period of restructuring
and reorganization. Some of the small mom-and-pop travel agencies have
closed; some have been taken over by large travel companies, and some have
begun to take advantage of the Internet to turn it into a profit-making opportunity. In Chapter 8, we discuss these impacts and their ramifications.

1.8 THE INTERNET AND HOSPITALITY AND TOURISM RESEARCH

Research is an important function and planning in the hospitality and tourism
industry. Morrison (1996) defines marketing research as "the function which
links the consumer, customer, and public to the marketer through information." In essence, research is about collecting information about your own
business, your competitors, and your customers and making sense of the
information gathered for the purpose of making intelligent business decisions.

The Internet, as pointed out earlier, is a vast collection of information.
Some of this information is **static** information that does not change over time,
but some of it is **dynamic** ("hits," or information that can change over time such
as ticket price, number of online visitors, and weekly promotions). Both static
and dynamic information can provide valuable information for businesses if
properly collected and analyzed.

1.9 THE 21ST CENTURY AND BEYOND

The Internet, despite its wide adoption and rapid development, is still in its
infancy. The technology that has brought about the Internet is undergoing
rapid changes. Every new development in technology gives rise to new
opportunities and solutions to the hospitality and tourism industry. New

technologies, such as broadband communication, wireless application and artificial intelligence, will certainly change the landscape of conducting business in the hospitality and tourism industry.

These technologies are already making inroads into the hospitality and tourism industry. For example, Datalex (www.datalex.com), a leading provider of information technology–based solutions to the airline and travel industries, is among the first technology providers to make a live airline reservation using WAP (Wireless Application Protocol) technology on a Nokia 7110 cell phone. The reservation was made from the company's office in Dublin, Ireland, using Datalex's Internet travel reservations system, BookIt!, on a server located in Atlanta, Georgia. Datalex developed the interface using WAP, WML (Wireless Markup Language), and its Java-based BookIt! server. Datalex's technology will be provided to travel and cellular network companies to help them develop the global cell phone market, estimated to be over $1 billion by the year 2005 and to grow to $80 billion by 2010 (Datalex 2000).

In the years to come, hotel guestrooms will be wired with high-speed Internet connections at little or no charge to guests. In fact, many hotels have already done so. The Wingate Hotel provides high-speed Internet access to its business travelers free of charge. Small hotels are also making use of this technology to attract customers. The Willows Lodge in Washington State, with only 88 rooms, offers free high-speed Internet connection in every room. Even cruise lines are adding wireless Internet connection to their cabins. Using wireless technology and personal digital assistants (PDAs), consumers will be able to check in before they arrive at the airport or hotel.

E-commerce, the buzzword of today's economy, will be integrated into the activities of every travel and hospitality business. As a matter of fact, most of the dot-com start-ups represent new brands of products and services that in many cases are duplications of the established brands, but with a new medium: the Internet. Those established brands were slow to start in terms of using the Internet, but they are catching up quickly. They are spending hundreds of millions of dollars to compete with the new Internet brands and to improve their efficiency.

The new century will also witness new challenges and issues that come along with the new opportunities and competition. Adopting new technologies without dramatically increasing the cost of doing business will be a challenging task for every commercial manager. The issues of e-commerce security, privacy, and intellectual property rights are likely to loom large as the Internet becomes part and parcel of people's lives. We are living in an interesting time. The hospitality and tourism industry, like it or not, is right in the center of it. As an industry, we have survived through difficult times. How well the industry will thrive depends on how well the industry rides the waves of the new technologies in the new century.

KEY WORDS AND TERMS

Online Transactions   Interactive Information
Dot-com   Customized Information
Peer-to-Peer system   E-marketing
IP   Traditional Marketing Media
Hyperlink   Push
Open Architecture Networking   Static
Platform Independent   Dynamic

SUMMARY

The Internet has undergone tremendous growth since it was invented, especially with the advent of the World Wide Web. The Internet is changing the way consumers access travel information, plan their trips, and purchase the products and services. The hospitality and tourism industry is always among the first to adopt new technology and innovations. Thus, it is not surprising that the industry is among the top markets in the use of the Internet. More and more people are using the Internet for travel information, planning, reservations, and booking.

The impact of the Internet on the hospitality and tourism industry is far reaching, especially in the area of travel information distribution, marketing, planning, and booking. As the technology keeps changing, new innovations and solutions are being added daily to take advantage of this new medium. It is important to understand that the Internet is a global phenomenon. For hospitality and tourism companies, the Internet can be used as a means for communication, commerce, marketing, and information distribution and research.

WEB RESOURCES

- www.tia.org
- www.forrester.com
- www.garrett-comm.com
- www.glreach.com
- www.iata.org

CASE STUDY: *Asiatravelmart.com*

Asiatravelmart.com (http://asiatravelmart.com), one of Asia's leading online travel marketplaces, announces the completion of system integration with Pegasus Solutions, a leading provider of hotel industry e-commerce and transaction processing solutions (Nasdaq: PEGS). Asiatravelmart.com users can now enjoy real-time confirmation of availability to more than 44,000 hotels worldwide via the Pegasus online booking engine. This strategic relationship allows Asiatravelmart.com users to make bookings directly with each participating hotel's central reservation system (CRS), such as that of Hilton, Hyatt, Sheraton, Utell, and many more. Details such as room descriptions, rates, and availability are instantly posted online.

The integration was fully completed in a record time of two months ahead of the projected schedule. The strategic agreement was signed between the two parties in November 2000, and implementation of the Pegasus online booking engine was completed in early January 2001. According to Alex Kong, chief executive officer of Asiatravelmart.com, the fulfillment of this extensive project within a mere two months demonstrates the level of Asiatravelmart.com's technical excellence and the presence of a strong team with world-class expertise. "I am extremely proud of my great team of dedicated professionals who worked very hard in realizing the connectivity in such a short period with the Pegasus user-friendly interface. We remain committed to delivering our vision of providing the best e-travel experience to our customers. Asiatravelmart.com has reaffirmed our leading position once again with the completion of this major project, which empowers users with direct access to critical travel information in real time, anytime, online, in making informed decisions," Kong said. The connectivity also offers instant confirmation for all hotels with the unique confirmation number that the hotel's CRS generates to Asiatravelmart.com users. Users also enjoy the flexibility of making last-minute or same-day bookings and even cancellations at any time. Booking is guaranteed with proof of credit card ownership by submitting details online.

Asiatravelmart.com is Asia's number one online travel marketplace. It provides a unique platform and environment for travel buyers and sellers from around the world to trade their travel-related products and services over a secure Internet connection. Asiatravelmart.com is a one-stop travel shop for hotels, air tickets, tour packages, transfers, meals and car rentals. It offers more than 110,000 products from over 40,000 travel suppliers in more than 180 countries, providing users with the convenience of making travel reservations 24 hours a day at wholesale prices.

Asiatravelmart.com is among the first in the world to provide an electronic ticketing facility where travelers can plan or buy flight tickets at 30% to 60% lower than normal prices and print the ticket vouchers off the Web site. It is also Asia's first online travel site to offer mobile-commerce services through WAP technology. Asiatravelmart.com can be accessed at http://asiatravelmart.com.

QUESTIONS TO PONDER:

1. How is the early completion date of Asiatravelmart.com's integration an advantage?
2. What do you think is the most alluring aspect of Asiatravelmart.com? Why?
3. How is Asiatravelmart.com important to the tourism industry in Asia?
4. If you were an advertising adviser for Asiatravelmart.com, what would your suggestions be to promote the Web site? To promote business in general?

   SOURCE: Karin Wacaser, Vice President, Corporate Communications, Pegasus Solutions, Inc.

REVIEW QUESTIONS

1. Why did the Internet grow so rapidly?
2. Why is the hospitality and tourism industry a major driving force for the rapid growth of the Internet?
3. What are some of the major characteristics of online travelers?
4. Describe the characteristics of the Internet.
5. What makes hospitality and tourism e-commerce such an appealing function of the Internet?
6. Why is the Internet an excellent communication medium for the hospitality and tourism industry?
7. List some of the evidence that use of the Internet by travelers is increasing.
8. Which sector of the hospitality and tourism industry was impacted most by the Internet? Why?
9. Why is the Internet a valuable place for conducting hospitality and tourism research?
10. List some of the challenges for the hospitality and tourism industry in the 21st century.

■ REFERENCES

Buhasz, Laszlo. (2001). "Travel Net Use Overview."
www.glovetechnology.com.

Cortese, A. (1997). "A Census in Cyberspace." *BusinessWeek*, May 15, 83–84.

Datalex. (2000). www.datalex.com.

Forrester Research. (2002). www.forrester.com.

Global Reach. (2003). www.glreach.com/globtats.

Levere, Jane L. (1999). www.nytimes.com.

Morrison, Alastair M. (1996). *Hospitality and Travel Marketing*. 2nd ed.
Albany, NY: Delmar.

Travel Industry Association. (2003).

Travel Industry Association (TIA). (2003). "Online Travel Booking Jumps in
2002 Despite Plateau in Online Travel Planning." Press Release. 12/9/02.
www.tia.org.

Verity, J. W., and R. D. Hof. (1994). "The Internet: How It Will Change the
Way You Do Business." *BusinessWeek*, November 5, 80–88.

Zhou, Z. Q., and Li-Chun Lin. (2000). "The Impact of the Internet on the Use
of the Printed Brochure." Proceedings of the CHRIE's 2000 Annual
Conference, July 19–22, New Orleans.

*For additional Travel and Tourism resources, go to
www.Hospitality-Tourism.delmar.com*

2

INTERNET FUNDAMENTALS

LEARNING OBJECTIVES

After you complete your study of this chapter, you should be able to:

- Define the Internet.
- Explain the history of the Internet.
- Define HTML.
- Understand the basic communication tools for the Internet.

2.1 DEFINING THE INTERNET

The Internet is a global **network** of computers that communicate using a common language. It is a huge network that contains thousands of small networks. Therefore, we can also say that the Internet is a network of networks. For example, when you view Dr. Zhou's home page (http://faculty.niagara.edu/zhou), you are connected to the Internet. Dr. Zhou's home page resides on Niagara University's network server, which in turn is connected to the Internet. It is similar to the international telephone system—no one owns or controls the whole thing, but it is connected in a way that makes it work like one big network. It provides a physical infrastructure through which all forms of communications are made possible. It is just like a highway system on which all kinds of transportation vehicles pass through. Therefore, the Internet is sometimes referred to as an **Information Super highway.**

With the Internet, time and geographic locations are no longer relevant. As long as your computer is connected to the Internet, you can communicate with anyone in the world who has a computer that is also connected to the Internet any time of the day. It is just like using your telephone. As long as the party you try to reach has access to a phone, you can always ring up that person, no matter where the person is located.

In everyday life, the Internet has been called different names that often are interchangeable to a lay person. It has been called the Net, the Web, the Information Superhighway and the **World Wide Web.** Technically, however, these terms contain specific reference to various aspects of the Internet in different settings. In the following sections, we explain the differences.

The Internet is composed of two major parts: the infrastructure, or the **hardware,** and the **software,** or the applications and protocols. The infrastructure includes things like telephone networks, cables, routers, computers, servers, and satellites. The software consists of programs, applications, and protocols that make communication, publication, and transaction online possible. For example, you need a Web browser in order to read a Web home page. You need an e-mail client to send and receive e-mails. The Web browser and the e-mail client are software. The idea that the Internet is free is really a misconception. Someone is paying for the hardware and software even though that "someone" might not be you.

2.2 HISTORY OF THE INTERNET

In the early 1960s, during the Cold War, the Rand Corporation was entrusted to developing a strategic communications system that would continue to operate during and after a nuclear war (www.rand.org). The idea was that in the aftermath of nuclear attack, the U.S. military command would still be able to function and remain in control.

To accomplish this task, it was necessary to build a system of very loosely connected command networks—a system without a central command and without any hierarchical organization at all. Any point of the communication in the network could send and receive a message as much as any other (Figure 2.1). This is the foundation of the peer-to-peer system and the beginning of what has come to be called the Internet.

It was not until the late 1960s that the construction of such a system was funded by the Pentagon's Advanced Research Projects Agency or, **ARPA.** A communication network called ARPANET was established, and communication between the networks was made possible through a common communication language, the **Internet Protocol** or **IP.** The IP enables communications between computers such as transferring data, using each other's computers, and even programming each other's computers remotely. As ARPANET expanded with more supercomputers joining in, scientists created a feature that allowed for multiple transmissions of the

FIGURE 2.1
A simple Internet.

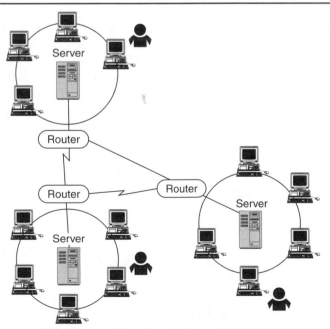

same message to several or all of the linked computers at once. These became the foundations for some of the most popular features of the Internet, namely, e-mail and group Mailing Lists.

The ability to communicate with each other electronically in the Internet soon generated interest in personal communication and collaborative research using ARPANET. Initially, only large organizations that could afford the investment and technical know-how and that saw the potential for research and better communication joined the network. These organizations typically were government agencies, universities, and research organizations.

To connect a wide variety of networks developed to meet different standards and by different vendors, ARPA developed the **transmission control protocol/Internet protocol (TCP/IP).** These protocols were used to connect incompatible computers and networks used by government agencies, the military, government suppliers, and research institutions. TCP converts data into **packets** that are sent across transmission lines to the next computer, whose TCP reconverts the packets into data it can read. TCP ensures that entire messages are delivered error-free with no loss or duplication. On the receiving side, it's also up to TCP to put the packets back in the right order. IP's task is to deliver the divided packets. To use an analogy, IP is the envelope, stamp and address of the message.

Use of the Internet spread quickly after its first demonstration to the public in October 1972 (Leiner et al. 2003). The introduction of a popular application in the same year, e-mail, generated great interest among ordinary people and prompted the rapid growth of the Internet, as described in the previous chapter. By the end of 1991, the Internet had grown to include some 5,000 networks in over three dozen countries, serving more than 700,000 host computers used by over 4,000,000 people (Internet Society 2003). In 1990, ARPANET, the first Internet network, ceased to exist (Zakon 2000).

2.3 INTERNET BASICS

THE WORLD WIDE WEB

The World Wide Web was first invented in 1989 by Tim Berners-Lee, a graduate of Oxford University in England, while he was working at CERN (http://cern.web.cern.ch/CERN), the European Particle Physics Laboratory. However, it was not until 1994 that the World Wide Web (WWW) caught the imagination of the public and gained widespread popularity. There are several reasons why WWW was an instant hit. It adds a graphical interface to what previously had been pretty much text-only capability, which, in turn, makes searching and retrieving information much easier. In addition, it makes presentation of voice, data, graphics, video possible and attractive. Its hyperlink capability enhances the potentials of the Internet.

Before the birth of the Web, communication and publication on the Internet were achieved by the use of text, or **ASCII** (American Standard Code for Information Interchange) files. There was no color, pictures, or graphics, and you used commands rather than the icons you see today in a Windows environment. You can still see some of this in the offices of travel agencies where reservations and bookings are still mostly made by issuing commands.

Just like a highway can accommodate all types of vehicles, the Internet may be used to send and receive different types of information. However, before programs were developed to make these formats accessible, graphics, sound, voice and other multimedia information could not be presented online. To use the highway analogy, before automobiles were invented, a road could be used only for bicycles and carriages.

The Web is an abstract, imaginary cyberspace that enables hypertext information. The main components of the Web are **Web servers** and **browsers.** Web servers are computers that store data in Hypertext Markup Language (HTML) format to be retrieved by the Web users as Web pages. HTML is a very capable formatting tool that allows the author of a Web page to specify colors, fonts, the inclusion of voice, video, images and photographs and to define links. Web browsers between computers on Internet, will be discussed in the next section.

THE BROWSER

A browser is the **interface** that allows you to see the graphic and text files that make up the Web and the Internet. An interface is a program that translates and presents information on your computer screen. To put it simply, an interface is a graphically rich area of the screen allowing human-machine communication.

To communicate with each other on the Internet, you need applications to help you get connected to the Internet and send and receive information. Before the World Wide Web, one of the first applications developed and made publicly available was **telnet,** a terminal emulator that would allow your computer to dial a phone number and then act as a terminal to the computer you contacted. Telnet was the interface for text-based communications between computers on the Internet. The telnet command is used to log on to another computer on the Internet. A valid user ID and password for the remote computer is required to complete the login process. For communications to take place between the user and the Web, you would need a different interface than telnet: a browser.

Although Berners-Lee created the first browser, called the World Wide Web, the first commercialized browser that was capable of reading graphic images was developed by the National Center for Supercomputing Applications and commercially released in 1993 under the name Mosaic. Many browsers have been developed since then, the leading ones being Microsoft Internet Explorer and Netscape Navigator. Most Internet Service Providers

(ISPs) provide their subscribers with the software and installation packet for one of these commercial browsers, but subscribers are free to use any compatible browser they choose.

There are two important concepts to understanding how the Web works. The first is the **universal resource locator (URL),** which is the address of a Web page located anywhere on the Web. For example, to locate the homepage of the College of Hospitality and Tourism Management at Niagara University, you will need to use URL, http://www.niagara.edu/hospitality/. The second concept is the hypertext transfer protocol **(HTTP),** a method of accesses to the Internet. HTTP is the protocol used to transport WWW information between a computer and the WWW server being accessed.

Hypertext and HTML

One of the reasons the Web is so popular is its ability to utilize a very old activity: cross-referencing. A footnote in a book is an example of a **hypertext.** Hypertext on the Web, however, means that the item designated as a hyper-link, when clicked, will send the user to another location. This location could be somewhere else on the same page, on another page within the same Web site, or on someone else's Web site.

Not all hyperlinks are words. They can be image maps in which the links are embedded in various parts of the graphics. Hypertext may join two entirely different kinds of entities. Instead of sending you to another Web site, a hyperlink may send you to an **FTP** (File Transfer Protocol) site or to a newsgroup. It may activate an e-mail form for you to fill out and send to a Webmaster. It could offer a download of a graphic file, run a QuickTime movie, or link you to an **IRC** (Internet relay chat room), allowing you to conduct live conversations with real people in an imaginary world.

HTML (Hypertext Markup Language) is a collection of **platform-independent** styles indicated by markup tags that define the various components of a Web document (NCSA 2001). It is platform independent in that it offers a language style that all types of computers can understand and thus breaks communication barriers between computers. When Berners-Lee invented the Web, he also invented HTML. HTML documents are plain-text (ASCII) files that can be created using any text editor, such as Emacs on Unix machines, SimpleText on a Macintosh, or Notepad on a Windows machine. You can also use word-processing software, such as Microsoft Word or WordPerfect, if you remember to save your document as "text only with line breaks."

Simply put, HTML is a hypertext document format used on the Web. In an HTML document, different codes and symbols are used to indicate different text styles and appearance when viewed by a browser. For example, "tags" are embedded in the text. A tag consists of a "<", a symbol "directive" (case insensitive), zero or more parameters, and a ">" symbol. Matched pairs

| **TABLE 2.1** |
| Common Tags Used in HTML |

Every HTML document should contain certain standard HTML tags. Each document
consists of head and body text. The head contains the title, and the body contains
the text, which is made up of paragraphs, lists, and other elements. Required
elements are shown in this sample bare-bones document:

    <html>
    <head>
    <TITLE>A Simple HTML Example</TITLE>
    </head>
    <body>
    <H1>HTML is Easy To Learn</H1>
    <P>Welcome to the world of HTML.
    This is the first paragraph. While short it is still a paragraph!</P>
    <P>And this is the second paragraph.</P>
    </body>
    </html>

The required elements are the <html>, <head>, <title>, and <body> tags
(and their corresponding end tags).

of directives, like "<TITLE>" and "</TITLE>," are used to delimit text
that is to appear in a special place or style. The World Wide Web Consortium,
(W3C) is the international standards body for HTML. Table 2.1 explains
some of the common tags used in HTML.

A simple, convenient way to see what an HTML file looks like is go to
your browser. For example, in Microsoft Internet Explorer, go to View and
then click on Source. You will see the HTML text file that you cannot see in
a normal browser window. Today, with so many HTML authoring programs
on the market, you no longer need to learn how to write codes and tags.
Programs such as Microsoft FrontPage provides you with many functions
that in the past only HTML programmers could dream of. These programs
provide what is called **WYSIWYG** "what you see is what you get" interface;
that is, whatever you type and see on your computer screen is what you will
see and get when displayed on a browser. The following is a list of the major
Web authoring programs on the market:

❑ Claris Home Page
❑ Corel Web Designer
❑ Microsoft Frontpage
❑ Hotdog Pro
❑ Hotmetal Pro
❑ Internet Creator

- ❏ Micromedia Backstage Designer
- ❏ Netobjects Fusion
- ❏ Pagemill
- ❏ Visual Page

There are other ways to write an HTML document. If you do not own one of the commercial HTML authoring programs, you can either use a word-processing program such as Microsoft Word or WordPerfect, or a Web browser, such as Microsoft Internet Explorer or Netscape Navigator, to write simple HTML documents.

E-MAIL

E-mail consists of the electronic transmission of digital messages over the Internet. The messages can be letters, notes, or documents—or in some cases, files, images and software—sent to any other user on the Internet. Every e-mail address is composed of three elements:

- ❏ A screen name
- ❏ A domain
- ❏ An extension

The most common extensions are "com," for "commercial"; "edu," for "education"; "org," for "nonprofit organization"; "mil," for "military"; and "gov," for "government". Suppose your e-mail address is Johndoe@ niagara. edu. "Johndoe" is your screen name; "niagara" is the domain, referring to Niagara University; and "edu" is its extension. The domain and the extension are commonly referred to as the domain name. Countries other than the United States assign similar domain names but often add a country code. For example, a typical Chinese Internet address would look like this: peace @ sina.com.cn. Cn indicates China.

MAILING LIST

A **Mailing List,** sometimes referred to as e-mail discussion groups, is a list of e-mail addresses that is used to send messages to many people at once. These are usually subscribers to the list who are expected to share a common interest in the contents of the message. E-mail discussion groups are often associated with academic institutions as well as with scholars and experts in a specific field of interest. A Mailing List is different from a traditional mailing list, which is simply a collection of names and addresses used for mailing purposes that are managed by a software program. Three of the most popular Mailing Lists are Listserv, Majordomo and Listproc. All these programs have similar functions and operations. You can find many Mailing Lists at www.liszt.com.

TABLE 2.2	
A Mailing List and Its Basic Elements	
LIST NAME	ADVENTURE (RENO)
Purpose	An adventure forum for passionate and adventurous people: sports, travel, global escapes.
List type	Unmoderated discussion
Subscription	Does not require owner approval
Archive	Readable by anyone
Created	Mar 05, 1999
Owner	reno marioni
To join	Subscribe here, or send an e-mail to adventure-subscribe@topica.com
To post	Send mail to adventure@topica.com
Stats	62 subscribers/<1 messages per week

Perhaps the most widely used Mailing List programs is Listserv. This software program allows you to create, manage, and control electronic Mailing Lists on your corporate network or on the Internet (see www.lsoft.com). These common-interest groups form what we have come to call **virtual communities**; they are virtual since they exist only in cyberspace. These are different from real-world communities in that they have no country or neighborhood boundaries and you are not required to reveal your true identity. Therefore, you can usually join and leave the list as you see fit without feeling guilty. Table 2.2 shows a sample Mailing List and its basic elements.

A **list owner,** or sometimes several owners for large lists, manages a Mailing List. The list owner is responsible for the operation of the list and serves as a kind of moderator or referee. The list owner establishes the list's goals and objectives and sets up rules and policies for the subscribers. By subscribing to the list, the subscriber is expected to abide by the list's rules and policies. The list owner is also responsible for all administrative matters and for answering questions from the subscribers.

Mailing Lists are highly interactive and can be either moderated or unmoderated. When you send a message to a Mailing List, the list server will distribute it immediately to all the subscribers in an unmoderated situation. In this situation, every message that is sent to the list will be redistributed to every subscriber. In a moderated situation, the list owner decides which message received gets to be sent out to the subscribers. Since moderating a list is almost a full-time job, most Mailing Lists operate in an unmoderated mode.

Mailing Lists can become an annoyance to the subscriber if too many messages get sent to the list each day. Being a subscriber means that your e-mail inbox can be flooded with hundreds of e-mail messages each day. Fortunately, most list programs provide *digest* subscriptions for those

TABLE 2.3	
The INFOTEC-TRAVEL Mailing List	
Mailing List Name	INFOTEC-TRAVEL
Description	Information Technology in Travel and Tourism Worldwide
To subscribe	Send a message to infotec-travel-subscribe@ yahoogroups.com with only "subscribe infotec-travel your name" in the message body.
To post a message	Send the message to infotec-travel@yahoogroups.com
To unsubscribe	Send a message to infotec-travel-unsubscribe@ yahoogroups.com
For more information	www.infotec-travel.com
List owner e-mail	infotec-travel-owner@yahoogroups.com

subscribers who do not want to receive so many messages every day. A digest is simply a larger file with everything that was sent to the list in a particular day or week and condensed into a low-volume list. These digests are typically not edited and contain the same information as a normal subscription, but put together in a single message so that the list subscribers who choose the digest form will not be flooded with many individual messages.

Mailing Lists can be regarded as a virtual encyclopedia that is always up to date on the topic you are interested in. Today, there are nearly 10,000 public Mailing Lists, covering virtually any imaginable topic (see www.lsoft.com). No matter what your interests are, chances are that you will be able to find a list that meets your need.

To show you how a Mailing List works, a real Mailing List is presented in Table 2.3, the INFOTEC-TRAVEL Mailing List owned by Maucus Mendicott (www.infotec-travel.com). You can subscribe to the list by sending a message to infotec-travel-subscribe@yahoogroups.com with only "subscribe infotec-travel" and your name after it in the message body. To send a message to all the people currently subscribed to the list, just send mail to infotec-travel@yahoogroups.com. This is called "sending mail to the List" because you send mail to a single address, and the list makes copies for all the people who have subscribed. The address infotec-travel@yahoogroups.com is also called the "list address." You should never try to send any Mailing List command, such as "unsubscribe," to that address, as it will be distributed to all the people who have subscribed to the list.

USENET, NEWSGROUPS, AND DISCUSSION FORUMS

Usenet is a distributed bulletin board system (BBS). As its name suggests, it is really a users' network. A bulletin board is a computer and associated software that provide an electronic message database where people can log in, post, and/or read messages, just like you can use a pin to post a message on a bulletin board. Usenet existed before the World Wide Web was born. In the beginning, not all Usenet hosts were on the Internet. It was originally implemented in 1979–1980 by Steve Bellovin, Jim Ellis, Tom Truscott, and Steve Daniel at Duke University and supported mainly by Unix machines (www.foldoc.org 2003). It has grown now to be perhaps the largest decentralized information database on the Internet.

Usenet is usually maintained and used by government agencies, universities, high schools, businesses of all sizes and home computers of all descriptions. In 1993, it hosted over 1,200 newsgroups and an average of 40 megabytes (the equivalent of several thousand paper pages) of technical articles, news, discussion, chatter and flamage every day. By the end of 1999, the number of newsgroups had grown to over 37,000 (see www.foldoc.org 2003).

Newsgroups are more broadly based than Mailing Lists. There are thousands of such groups, covering thousands of topics that can be found on any server maintaining a master list known as Usenet. The topics include virtually everything, and the discussions range from silly to highly serious to paranoid delusional. Another difference between the newsgroup and the Mailing List is that with a Mailing List, you send and receive e-mail messages, while with a newsgroup, you have to log in to the site to post a message for others to read or to read messages posted by others.

Before the advent of the Web, you needed a newsreader program to participate in a newsgroup. In 1995, a Web gateway company, Deja.com, began to offer a user-friendly Web interface to newsgroups. As a result, you do not need a newsreader to sign in, post or read the news. Deja.com was acquired in February, 2001 by Google Inc. (www.google.com), renaming www.deja.com to http://groups.google.com.

A newsgroup is one of Usenet's huge collection of topic groups. For this reason, newsgroups are sometimes referred to as **discussion forums.** Just like Listserv, Usenet groups can be unmoderated or moderated. In an unmoderated mode, anyone can post with permission, while in a moderated mode, your submissions are automatically directed to a moderator, who edits or filters and then posts the results.

Usenet uses a traditional indexing and cataloging system. The top level of the discussion is called a **category,** such as "alt." The next level will be indexed with a period, such as "alt.travel," The next level will contain messages divided into even more specific topics, such as "alt.travel.Canada," "alt.travel.marketplace," "alt.travel.road-trip," and "alt.travel.uk." Ultimately, you can create small index, such as "alt.travel.uk.marketplace."

JAVA AND JAVASCRIPT

Java is a simple object-oriented, distributed and general-purpose programming language developed by Sun Microsystems (www.sun.com). It was named after the Indonesian island of Java Island for its reputation of natural stimulants. When Java was first developed by Sun, it was hailed as a revolution in computer programming. Java is similar to C++, a Microsoft programming language, but is much simpler and as powerful. Java supports the creation of virus-free, tamper-free systems with authentication based on **public-key encryption,** an online security system for transferring messages. According to Sun, Java offers some major benefits over Microsoft C++:

❑ **Get started quickly:** Although the Java programming language is a powerful object-oriented language, it is easy to learn, especially for programmers already familiar with C or C++.

❑ **Write less code:** Comparisons of program metrics—class counts, method counts, and so on—suggest that a program written in the Java programming language can be four times smaller than the same program in C++.

❑ **Write better code:** The Java programming language encourages good coding practices, and its garbage collection helps you avoid memory leaks. Its object orientation, JavaBeans component architecture, and wide-ranging, easily extendible API let you reuse other people's tested code and introduce fewer bugs.

❑ **Develop programs more quickly:** Your development time with Java may be twice as fast as writing the same program in C++ . Why? You write fewer lines of code, and Java is a simpler programming language.

❑ **Avoid platform dependencies with 100% Pure Java:** You can keep your program portable by avoiding the use of libraries written in other languages. The 100% Pure Java™ Product Certification Program has a repository of historical process manuals, white papers, brochures, and similar materials online.

❑ **Write once, run anywhere:** Because 100% Pure Java programs are compiled into machine-independent byte codes, they run consistently on any Java platform.

❑ **Distribute software more easily:** You can upgrade applets easily from a central server. Applets take advantage of the feature of allowing new classes to be loaded "on the fly," without recompiling the entire program.

The most common Java programs are applications and applets. **Applications** are stand-alone programs, such as the HotJava browser from Sun Microsystems that can execute programs written in the Java programming language. **Applets** are similar to applications but do not run stand-alone. Instead, applets adhere to a set of conventions that let them run within a Java-compatible browser, such as Microsoft Internet Explorer versions 5 and higher or Netscape Communicator versions 4.7 and higher. If you are using a browser that can view applets, you should see small windows (Java applets or programs) popping up right in front of you. That is because an applet can be embedded in an HTML document, and when you open that document, the applet will execute.

JavaScript is only vaguely related to Java and was developed by Netscape. It is a simple cross-platform Web scripting language. JavaScript can be thought of as an extension to HTML, allowing authors to incorporate some functionality into their Web pages, and thus is intimately tied to the World Wide Web. It currently runs in only three environments – as a server-side scripting language, as an embedded language in HTML and as an embedded language run in browsers. Commercial Web sites make frequent use of Java and other similar technologies to give visitors access to a wide variety of functions online such as stock tickers, shopping carts, and other enablers of e-commerce.

JavaScript is even simpler than Java, though it runs slower than Java. Its simplicity makes it easier to learn and program. Initially, only Netscape products supported JavaScript. Now Microsoft also supports it but calls it JScript. This inconsistency makes it difficult to write JavaScript that behaves the same in both Netscape Navigator and Microsoft Internet Explorer.

2.4 CONCLUSION

The Internet has been compared to a superhighway, and not without good reason. Highways can be built with different materials and with different widths and shapes as well as different road signs and directions. Similarly, the decentralized Internet allows for the imagination and creation of its users to build and expand it with all kinds of equipment and infrastructures that suit the needs of the organizations. Just like a superhighway that can accommodate all types of vehicles, the Internet welcomes all types of information distribution and communication tools to be used to transfer data and information. The only barrier to this flow of information is the carrying capacity of the Internet: the bandwidth. We discuss bandwidth in the next chapter.

KEY WORDS AND TERMS

Network	Packets
Information Superhighway	ASCII
World Wide Web	Web Servers
Hardware	Web Browsers
Software	Interface
ARPA	Telnet
Internet Protocol (IP)	URL
TCP/IP	HTTP

Hypertext	Virtual Communities
FTP	List Owner
IRC	Usenet
HTML	Discussion Forum
Platform Independent	Public-Key Encryption
WYSIWYG	Applications
E-mail	Applets
Mailing List	

SUMMARY

The need to create a military communication system in the early 1960s that would continue to operate during and after a nuclear war led to the development of what has come to be called the Internet. The Internet is composed of two major parts: the infrastructure, or the hardware, and the software, or the applications. There are many communication tools to help people communicate with each other. These tools include, but are not limited to, browsers, e-mail, newsgroups, Usenet, mailing lists, HTML, Java, and JavaScript.

WEB RESOURCES

- http://e-comm.webopedia.com
- http://ecommerce.internet.com
- http://cyberatlas.internet.com
- www.netvalley.com/intval.html
- www.livinginternet.com
- www.isoc.org/internet-history
- www.foldoc.org

CASE STUDY: *Commissions in the Hotel Industry: Agents for Change?*

Concurrent with the increased use of the Internet, travel agencies may go the way of the buggy whip and the carbide lantern. The Internet is now a major channel for the travel industry to reach potential customers. It gives consumers more options to book their travel, and it provides airlines, car rental firms and hotels the ability to reach these same consumers directly, therefore bypassing third-party agencies.

Like all industries, the travel industry constantly examines the relative cost/benefit of the various distribution channels available to make contact with customers. Because of this comparative analysis, most airlines, and a growing number of car rental firms, have determined that travel agents do not represent a relatively cost-effective channel for booking business, given the cost of commissions paid. Therefore, these segments of the industry are beginning to eliminate or severely reduce the commissions they pay to travel agents.

American hotels have yet to implement the industrywide changes to travel agent commission policies that we have seen in the airline and car rental sectors of the travel industry. Historically, hotels have been less dependent on travel agents for their guests as compared to airlines and car rental agencies.

Given the current industry downturn, hotel owners and operators are looking at all their expenses. Seeing what the airlines and car rental firms have done, hotel managers are now examining their policies toward travel agent commissions. For a hotel or company to properly analyze the cost/benefit of travel agent commissions, the following data are needed:

- Commissions paid
- Volume of revenue/profit derived through travel agents
- Potential lost revenue/profit
- Lost revenue/profit that could be captured through an alternative channel
- Cost of operating an internal distribution channel
- Cost of alternative distribution channels

In an effort to provide some context to the magnitude of travel agent commissions as an expense to the hotel industry, we extracted data from our *Trends in the Hotel Industry* database. An analysis of travel agent commissions was performed on 696 "same-store" hotels for which we have consecutive years of data from 1995 through 2001. The sample consisted of 420 full-service hotels and 276 limited-service properties. Please note that hotels report only room revenue and travel agent commission data for our *Trends* survey. Therefore, the other data listed is not available to complete a full analysis.

SMALL YET DECLINING

From 1995 through 2000, travel agent commissions for the entire study sample averaged 2.0% of room revenue. This same ratio varied from 1.1% for the limited-service hotels to 2.3% for the full-service properties. The year-to-year increases in commissions paid tracked closely to the annual increases in room revenue.

While the commission-to-revenue ratio has not changed much from 1995 through 2000, we see a shift in this strong relationship during 2001. As expected, the drop in room revenue experienced in 2001 caused a decline in the amount of commission paid to travel agents. On average, the typical hotel in our sample paid $472.32 per available room (PAR), or 2.0% of room revenue, in travel agent commissions during 2001. This is down from the $532.82 PAR, or 2.1% of room revenue, paid in 2000.

Of note is the disparity between the magnitude of the decrease in commissions paid compared to the degree of decline in room revenue. In 2001, our sample of hotels suffered a 10.9% decline in room revenue from the prior year. This compares to the 11.4% decline in travel agent commissions paid. That suggests two factors at work. Either the volume of revenue booked through travel agents declined to a greater degree in 2001, and/or hotels have already begun to adjust their commission policies.

The decline in commissions paid was greater at full-service hotels than at limited-service hotels. From 2000 to 2001, our sample of full-service hotels experienced a 12.5% decline in room revenue. Concurrently, these same properties paid 14.3% less in travel agent commissions during the year. For the limited-service sample, room revenue declined 5.5% in 2001, while travel agent commissions dropped 13.6%.

ALTERNATIVE CHANNELS

As an expense that consistently equaled less than 2% of total revenue during the 1990s, travel agent commissions were not given much attention. After all, revenues and profits were improving at record levels. During the current industry recession, U.S. hotel managers are examining all expenses. However, any changes in a hotel's policy toward travel agent commissions has to be examined for its impact, not just as an expense reduction but also for a potential loss in revenue.

Given recent history, there appears to be good reason to believe that the falloff in revenue for most hotels would not be that great from either an elimination or a decrease in travel agent commissions. Of course, the relative revenue and cost impact for a resort property in a remote destination may be different than that of a roadside motel, so each individual property's situation should be thoroughly examined.

Looking at the airline industry for guidance, it appears that people who continue to need the services of a travel agent for airline reservations have just absorbed the service fees charged by the agents. As an alternative to travel agents, people are already getting comfortable booking their air travel directly through the airlines' sites or through services like Expedia.com or Travelocity.com.

If travelers can gain a comfort level and an understanding of how to book air travel on their own, then they certainly can achieve that same skill for the process of reserving a hotel room. A November 5, 2001, Lehman Brothers study reported that the Internet already accounts for 4% of Hilton's reservation volume and 3% of Marriott's. For Hilton, the increased use of the Internet by hotel guests was just one factor that contributed to a 38% reduction in costs per reservation from 1992 to 2001.

We believe that hotel companies should begin to examine their policies toward travel agent commissions. If hotel companies can efficiently and effectively operate their own Web sites, they can not only reduce the commissions paid to travel agents but also save money in their reservations department and earn back some of the "spread" captured by other third-party booking channels.

QUESTIONS TO PONDER:

1. What is the major motivation for the travel industry to reduce the use of the travel agents?
2. Why is the hotel industry failing to reduce the dependence on travel agents?
3. What data are needed to conduct a cost/benefit analysis? Does it make sense to you? Why?
4. Why do any changes in a hotel's policy toward travel agent commissions need to be examined for their impact not just as an expense reduction but also for a potential loss in revenue?

    SOURCE: This case study was provided by Robert Mandelbaum, director of research information services for the Hospitality Research Group of PKF Consulting.

REVIEW QUESTIONS

1. Define the Internet.
2. What is the Internet composed of?
3. What was the idea behind building the Internet?
4. Who funded the first Internet network project?
5. What is the name of the first communication network funded by ARPA?
6. What common language was employed to enable communications between computers?
7. Who showed early interest in the ARPANET? Why?

8. When was the e-mail application first introduced?
9. Define the World Wide Web.
10. What is the difference between the Internet and World Wide Web?
11. Who founded the Web?
12. Describe the functions of a browser.
13. Describe the major functions of the HTML language.
14. What are the basic elements of an e-mail address?
15. Compare the differences between a Mailing List and a traditional mailing list.
16. What is Usenet's cataloging system?
17. What is the difference between a newsgroup and a Mailing List?
18. What is the difference between Java and JavaScript?

REFERENCES

Berners-Lee, Tim. (2003). www.w3.org/People/Berners-Lee/FAQ.html#What.

Internet Society. (2003). www.isoc.org/internet/history/cerf.html.

Leiner, Barry M., Vinton G. Cerf, David D. Clark, Robert E. Kahn, Leonard Kleinrock, Daniel C. Lynch, Jon Postel, Larry G. Roberts, and Stephen Wolff. (2003). *A Brief History of the Internet.* www.isoc.org/internet/history/brief.html#Origins.

NCSA. (2001). www.ncsa.uiuc.edu/General/Internet/WWW/HTMLPrimer.html.

Zakon, Robert Hobbes (2000). *Hobbes' Internet Timeline v5.2.* www.zakon.org/robert/internet/timeline.

For additional Travel and Tourism resources, go to www.Hospitality-Tourism.delmar.com

3

CONNECTING TO THE WORLD

LEARNING OBJECTIVES

After you complete your study of this chapter, you should be able to:

- Understand the basic Internet connection.
- Explain the difference among the various ways of connecting to the Internet.
- Understand the relation between speed and bandwidth.
- Explain the difference between wired and wireless communications.

3.1 ESTABLISH A STANDARD CONNECTION

You have learned that the Internet is a network of networks, consisting of millions of computers connected to each other. In order to access the rich information on the Internet, you will need to connect your computer to this network of networks, the Internet. There are many ways to get connected to the Internet, depending on who you are and what your purpose of using the Internet is. A standard connection (Figure 3.1 and 3.2), probably the most common type of connection at the time of this writing, is to use the existing telephone line. To connect to the Internet this way, you will need the following:

- ❏ A computer
- ❏ A modem
- ❏ An Internet Service Provider
- ❏ A browser

FIGURE 3.1
Three common transmission techniques.

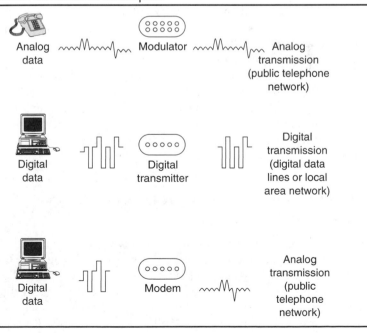

MODEM

The word 'modem' is taken from two words: **modulator** and **demodulator.**
A modem is an electronic device for converting between digital data from
a computer or an audio signal suitable for transmission over telephone lines.
Information that a computer can store and manipulate is composed of
bits, which are encoded as the digits 0 and 1 hence the term **digital.** The transmission of information from one independent computer to another requires
a way to convert the computer's digital signals to the analog (aural, nondigi-
tal) signals of the telephone. The modem is such a device to make the conversion possible.

For instance, you are going to send a message to your friend Bob. You
type it in your computer, which produces digital data. When you send it, your
modem transforms (modulates) that digital data into an audible (aural) signal
that can be transmitted over the phone line. The signal reaches Bob's modem,
which then changes the audible signal back (or demodulates it) into its digital
data form that Bob's computer can display and he can read. The speed of data
transmission is measured in bits per second (bps), or in kilobits per second
(kbps). One kilobit equals 1,000 bits. Modems come in different speed
capacities, which are measured in bauds (named after the French engineer
J. M. E. Baudot [1845–1903], or in bps/kbps. A 2400-baud modem is the same
as a 2400-bps (bauds per second) modem.

In the early days of modem technology, modems were used primarily
(if not exclusively) for fax transmissions. Faxes do not require much speed, so
1200- and 2400-bps modems were quite common; 9600- bps modems were
considered race cars. Simple text files, such as e-mail, can function at 2400 bps
and does quite well on 9600 bps. However, using a 9600-bps modem to
browse the Web will test your patience, even for "text-only" sites. The pro-
liferation on the Internet of graphics, large downloadable files of all kinds and
multimedia has made any modem slower than 14.4 kbps (or 14,400 baud/bps)
completely impractical. Today, the most common speeds for Internet users
are 28,800, 36,000 or 56,000 baud/bps. A modem may either be internal, connected to the computer's bus, or external (stand-alone), connected to one of
the computer's serial ports.

INTERNET SERVICE PROVIDERS AND ONLINE
SERVICE PROVIDERS

Now that you know what a modem is and how it works, you will still need a
gateway to get connected to the Internet. The gateway you need is called an
ISP (Internet Service Provider) and OSP (Online Service Provider). Figure 3.2
shows how this type of connection works. In the early days of the Internet
and the Web, there were only a few of these gateways, such as America
Online, CompuServe, and Prodigy. Today, there are 9,600 ISPs worldwide

FIGURE 3.2
A standard connection to the Internet.

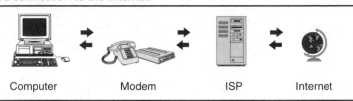

| Computer | Modem | ISP | Internet |

(from http://thelist.internet.com). However, there are only a few large ISP and OSP companies that dominate the market. The following is a list of some of the most popular ISPs and OSPs in the United States:

- ❑ America Online (AOL) (www.aol.com)
- ❑ Microsoft Network (www.msn.com)
- ❑ AT&T Worldnet (www.att.net)
- ❑ EarthLink Network (www.earthlink.com)
- ❑ Netzero (www.netzero.net)
- ❑ Palm.net Service (www.palm.net)
- ❑ MCI WorldCom (http://mci.worldcom.com)

By now, you might wonder what the difference is between ISPs and OSPs. If you are customers of an ISP such as MCI Worldcom.net, once you are connected, you are connected directly via the ISP's network to the Internet. Your ISP has no control over what you can access on the Internet. In other words, whatever is available on the Internet is also accessible to you, if your computer, programs, and connection speed are powerful enough to handle the information. In essence, you are part of the ISP's network, which in turn is connected to the Internet. If you are a customer of an OSP such as AOL, you are connected only to a service that is offered through AOL's network; you are not connected directly to the Internet. What you see and get from AOL is information that has been selected and filtered by AOL.

Originally, AOL prevented its customers from directly surfing the Internet. Later, it changed its policy and gave its customers the option to get full access to the Internet.

Selecting a right ISP/OSP can be tricky. The most important issue when choosing an ISP is to find one with a local phone number. Long-distance phone charges can cost more than the ISP itself. Other issues to pay attention to are modem connection speed, features, pricing, and reliability. Table 3.1 explains these terms. There are free ISPs you can subscribe to, but these typically ask that you allow them to display a banner ad on your computer screen in exchange for the free service. In the golden days of the dot-com boom, there were many free ISPs, but now only a couple exist. For a complete list of the current free ISPs and comments, go to www.epinions.com.

TABLE 3.1
Issues in Selecting an ISP

ISSUES	EXPLANATIONS
Connection speed	ISPs offer different modem connection speeds, ranging from 28.8 to 56. Pick one with higher speed even if your modem is capable of only 28.8 baud.
Features	Features offered by an ISP may include the following: an e-mail account to send and receive e-mail, access to Internet newsgroups and a personal Web page, and a hosting service (you can own our own domain name Web site instead of the ISP's domain name). Within these features, the extent of service may vary widely. For instance, storage for Web page files can range from a few megabytes to up to 100 megabytes.
Pricing	An ISP may offer different pricing plans. Pricing often is determined by the number of hours you use the service and the features you select to be included in the plan. Typical pricing plans include either hourly or unlimited access.
Reliability	An ISP is a gateway between your computer and the Internet. If an ISP's connection to your computer or to the Internet has frequent problems, you will be affected; that is, you will not receive reliable service.
Local phone access number	To avoid long-distance charges, make sure the ISP you select has local phone access. Otherwise, you will be charged at a long-distance phone rate on top of what you have to pay monthly for the ISP's service.

3.2 ALTERNATIVE CONNECTIONS

While the previously discussed method is by far the most common way to access the Internet, there are better and faster ways to do so. In fact, these other ways to connect are rapidly replacing the old way, the main reason being that they are much faster and more capable of handling the data transmission. However, in most cases, they come with a price. Because of their data-carrying capacity, these alternative ways to connect are also commonly referred to as **broadband communications channels.**

The major alternative connection methods include the following:

❑ ISDN (Integrated Services Digital Network)
❑ Cable modem
❑ DSL (Digital Subscriber Line)
❑ Wireless

The broadband industry showed strong growth in 2002, with over 17 million households subscribing to a high-speed Internet service in North America. The broadband market research firm Kinetic Strategies (2002) estimates that 11.3 million U.S. and Canadian households subscribe to cable modems and 5.9 million use DSL.

The Kinetic Strategies study showed that cable operators represent about 70% of the residential broadband Internet market. Cable modems and DSLs are the two leading methods of high-speed Internet access, though wireless and satellite options also exist. For years, broadband services were used largely by so-called early adopters, or customers who were eager to trade off the headaches of a new technology in favor of being on the cutting edge. But as the high-speed Internet market approaches 17 million customers, it appears to be taking hold among mainstream consumers as well.

The cable modem industry is a very competitive market. There are many players. Some of the largest ones in the U.S. include Time Warner, Comcast, AT&T, Charter Cox, Helphia, Cablevision, Mediacom and Insight. In Canada major players include Rogers, Shaw, Videotron and Cogeco.

ISDN

ISDN is a system of digital phone connections allowing a single wire or optical fiber to carry voice, digital network services, and video. ISDN was intended to eventually replace **POTS** (plain old telephone system). In the 1960s, the phone company began replacing analog voice-switching systems within internal networks with digital voice switching. The all-analog phone system (POTS) would have severely limited modem capabilities. By changing the network technology to a digital one, the phone companies made possible the use of 28.8-kbps modems. ISDN cards are similar to modems but five times faster. They require special telephone lines that cost a little (or a lot, depending on the phone company) more than normal phone lines.

An important concept in the discussion of these different kinds of connections is **bandwidth,** which is the amount of data that can be sent through a given communications circuit per second. The more bandwidth, the faster data can be sent and received through the same communication channel. Using our highway analogy, POTS is like a country path, allowing only small wagons and bicycles to pass. If there are many vehicles traveling at the same time, tie-ups may happen, slowing the speed of travel to a crawl.

The ISDN connection, on the other hand, is an interstate highway with several lanes. It not only can accommodate big trucks and other types of vehicles but also allows them to travel at the same time and at a faster speed. The Web is full of graphics, videos, and other multimedia data that are similar to large trucks and buses and therefore require a lot of bandwidth. However, just as it is not uncommon to see traffic jams on our highway system, the use

TABLE 3.2	
Advantages of ISDN	
Speed	The modem converts digital information into an analog signal. There is an upper limit to the amount of information that an analog telephone line can hold. Currently, the maximum speed is 56 kbps. ISDN allows multiple digital channels to be operated simultaneously through the same phone wiring used for analog lines. It uses a digital signal instead of an analog signal to transmit across the line.
Multiple devices	Previously, it was necessary to have a phone line for each device you wanted to use simultaneously. For example, one line each was required for a telephone, fax, computer, bridge/router, and live video conference system.
	ISDN allows many different digital data sources to be combined and to have the information routed to the proper destination. Technically, ISDN refers to a specific set of digital services provided through a single, standard interface. Without ISDN, distinct interfaces are required instead.
Signaling	Instead of the phone company sending a ring voltage signal to ring the bell of your phone, it sends a digital packet on a separate channel. A V.34 modem typically takes 30 to 60 seconds to establish a connection; an ISDN call usually takes less than 2 seconds. The signaling also indicates who is calling, what type of call it is (data or voice), and what number was dialed. Available ISDN phone equipment is then capable of making intelligent decisions on how to direct the call.

of ISDN does not guarantee that data will travel as fast as we want it to. The speed of the transmission depends on many other factors in addition to the amount of the data we are handling at a particular point in time. Because of its broad capacity in carrying data, ISDN is also referred to as a broadband communication channel. Table 3.2 summarizes the advantages of an ISDN connection over a traditional modem connection.

CABLE MODEM

If you subscribe to cable television, you might have noticed that the cables used to connect your television are much thicker than the telephone lines. These cables can deliver much more data, such as video and graphics, to homes and businesses at the same time and at a faster speed. Speed is the most important factor in surfing the Internet. Traditional dial-up modems provide online access through the public telephone network at up to 56,000 bits per second (kbps). A cable modem, on the other hand, provides high-speed

Internet access through a cable television network at more than 1 million bits per second (mbps). Cable modems are typically external devices placed next to the computer.

Many cable companies and ISPs boast that cable modems are as much as 100 times faster than a dial-up modem connection running at an ultrafast speed of 5 million bits per second (mbps). In theory, their claim is valid. However, actual transfer rates may be much lower, depending on the number of other simultaneous users on the same cable. A more realistic speed is about 1 mbps, or about 20 times faster than a typical 56,000-bps dial-up connection. Nevertheless, that is quite a leap in performance. You may notice that Web pages that can take minutes to load with a traditional dial-up connection will load instantly with a cable modem. If you frequently download or upload large files, such as video and audio clips or software, a cable modem will save valuable time.

To set up a cable modem connection (and assuming that your home or business is already wired with cable—if you subscribe to cable television, you are wired), you need to install a network (Ethernet) card for the computer, perform some software configuration and install an external cable modem that you simply plug into the network card. However, unlike the traditional dial-up modem, there is no phone number to dial. As soon as you turn on the computer, you are connected. Simply click on the browser, and you are on the Internet. No more waiting, no more busy signals.

Cable modem connections typically are handled by local cable companies whose responsibilities are different from those of cable modem service providers—cable ISPs (Table 3.3). One of the largest cable ISPs is Road Runner (www.rr.com), which was created by Time Warner Cable and MediaOne, and which AT&T recently purchased.

TABLE 3.3	
Responsibilities of Cable Companies and Cable ISPs	
COMPANY	RESPONSIBILITIES
Local cable companies	Installing the cable modem and managing the quality of service over the local cable network. At the cable company's main network office, called the "head end," you are connected to the cable ISP's national backbone. This, in turn, is plugged into the Internet. The ISP provides the Internet connectivity, while the cable company provides basic technical support.
Cable ISPs	Providing Internet services, such as one or several e-mail accounts and free or paid Web hosting, as well as a lineup of national and local content tailored to high-speed connection.

Two other cable ISPs—High Speed Access Corp. (www.hsacorp.net) and ISP Channel (www.ispchannel.com) serves the U.S. and Canadian broadband households respectively. Some cable companies, such as Adelphia (www.adelphia.com) in the United States and Videotron (www.videotron.com) in Canada, offer their own cable modem service. Cable modem subscribers are typically charged for service on their cable bill, rather than paying the ISP directly.

DSL

DSL belongs to a variety of digital telecommunication protocols designed to allow high-speed digital broadband data communication over the existing copper telephone lines between end users and telephone companies. With a conventional modem, the POTS telephone network treats the data as voice signals. The advantage is that there is no investment required from the telephone company, but the disadvantage is that the bandwidth available for the communication is the same as that available for voice conversations (usually 64 kbps or lower).

DSL technology supplies the necessary bandwidth for high-speed access to the Internet. The DSL modem maintains the digital link from home or business to a DSL network and can deliver much faster speed than conventional dial-up modems for data transmission needs. This modem plugs into the existing local area network (LAN) or can be attached to a home PC using a special cable.

DSL service typically costs more to provide than cable modem. Cable service costs less than DSL because it is a shared facility. A coaxial cable traveling through a neighborhood from house to house can provide high-speed service to thousands of customers, and a single piece of equipment at the cable company's office can patch those thousands of customers onto the Internet. DSL, on the other hand, requires a separate pair of wires for each subscriber. The phone company needs to install a special DSL modem for each phone line at its central office. Thus, high-speed Internet service delivered over cable should be less expensive than the same service delivered over a DSL link.

There are many varieties of DSL technology, commonly referred to as xDSL. SDSL (Symmetric Digital Subscriber Line) is by far the best available method of connection. This technology provides the same bandwidth in both directions—when you are uploading data and when you are downloading data. That means that whether you are uploading or downloading information, you have the same high-quality performance. SDSL provides transmission speeds within a T1/E1 range of up to 1.5 mbps at a maximum range of 12,000 to 18,000 feet from a central office over a single-pair copper wire. For most small- and medium-size businesses, this technology is ideal for fast interactive customer communications. Table 3.4 provides a brief description of other varieties of DSL.

	TABLE 3.4	
	Other Varieties of Digital Subscriber Lines	
LINE TYPE	DESCRIPTION	
ADSL (Asymmetric Digital Subscriber Line)	This technology reports a downstream speed, but its upstream speed is a fraction of the downstream. It is used primarily in residential applications, and many providers do not guarantee its bandwidth levels.	
RADSL (Rate-Adaptive Digital Subscriber Line)	This technology automatically adjusts the access speed based on the condition of the line.	
IDSL (ISDN Digital Subscriber Line)	This technology is symmetrical (similar to SDSL) but operates at slower speeds and longer distances.	
HDSL (High-Data-Rate Digital Subscriber Line)	This technology is symmetrical but is deployed mainly for PBX over a T1 line.	
VDSL (Very-High-Rate Digital Subscriber Line)	This is a high-speed technology but has a very limited range.	

WIRELESS INTERNET CONNECTION

The term **wireless** refers to a computer network that has no physical connection (either copper cable or fiber optics) between sender and receiver but instead is connected by radio and other wireless technologies. **Wireless Internet** connection describes a system of connecting to the Internet using such a network scheme. Broadly defined, a wireless Web, as it is more commonly called, refers to any method of accessing the Internet without using a physical connection, such as a phone line. Wireless networks are becoming popular among large corporations and educational institutions for their **mobility** and **adaptability**. It is mobile because members of the network can use their electronic devices, typically laptop computers, wherever they go as long as it is within the range of the wireless coverage. Adaptability refers to its ability to adapt a large range of wireless devices, including modems that hook to laptops, **PDAs** (personal digital assistants), wireless networks, satellite access and cellular phones. Wireless Internet access has become part of a broader wireless network that is the backbone of wireless communications. Wireless communications are enabled by packet radio, spread spectrum, cellular technology, satellites and microwave towers. They can be used for voice, data, video and images. Sometimes wireless networks can interconnect with regular computer networks.

One increasingly popular use of the wireless Internet connection is to use small cellular-enabled devices, such as PDAs and cellular phones, to access the Internet. Demand for the popular features of wireless Internet access is increasing. Some of the most popular features include easy-to-use and secure mobile e-mail, calendars, maps, stock news and quotes, weather, and management of contacts. Other advanced features are being developed. For instance, in Europe, Ericsson Microsoft Mobile Venture has established a global partnership with LINQ, a provider of wireless and wire-line corporate portals, to provide advanced team collaboration services, such as document sharing, the ability to locate colleagues on the move, and chat, all available from a mobile phone (from www.telecomclik.com).

Wireless Internet access is a worldwide phenomenon. This is made possible by a world wide wireless communications standard called *Wireless Applications Protocol,* or *WAP* for short. It was developed by the WAP Forum, a consortium of device manufacturers, service providers, content providers, and application developers. One of the problems with cell phones is that they can not handle HTML. Because of this, Web pages written in HTML can not be read by WAP phones, and therefore special Web pages have to be created to meet the needs of the cell phone users. What the WAP Forum was trying to do was to bring all proprietary standards by various device manufacturers and service providers to be able to talk to each other, so that digital content can be delivered to consumers through the air regardless of standards used.

As a result, WAP supports a special language called **WML,** or wireless markup language. Without WAP, consumers would be wedded to the wireless service provider that supported their phone. Wireless service providers also would have to deliver unique and appropriately formatted content to each different type of digital phone, and content providers would have to customize their content for each service provider's network.

Indeed, the United States lags far behind in terms of the technology applied and the number of users. Some of the technologies that are available in Europe and Asia are in their infancy in the United States. In Europe, consumers are already moving to broadband wireless cellular networks to access their wireless data via their cell phones. In Asia, many citizens have access to a technology called **W-CDMA,** or **I-Mode,** which allows them to view 256 color graphics and HTML on their phones.

I-mode is the key competitor of WAP, a communications protocol and an application environment that works with various wireless networks. In fact, in some countries, I-mode is the dominant wireless Internet system. In Japan, for instance, I-mode enjoys a 62% market share in 2001 and has 40 million users in 2002 (Krishnamurthy, 2003). What makes I-mode such a popular wireless system is its creative business model. It focuses on four areas: entertainment, news, tickets and living. Table 3.5 shows the features offered by I-mode wireless system.

There are many differences between I-Mode and WAP. First, WAP was invented in Europe and is the primarily dominant wireless standard in Europe. Secondly, WAP-based services in Europe focuses on business applications such as financial services, business news and airline ticketing, whereas

TABLE 3.5
What you can do with I-mode

Play videogames

Reserve airline and concert tickets

Check train schedules and download city maps

Create photo albums and access them online

Read news and check weather reports

Find restaurants

Online banking (check balance and transfer funds, etc.)

Download wallpaper images and cell phone ring-tone melodies

TABLE 3.6	
Differences between WAP and I-mode	
WAP-BASED SERVICES	**I-MODE SERVICES**
Dominant in Europe	Dominant in Japan and spreading to Asia
Focuses on business applications (banking, financial services and airline ticketing)	Focuses on entertainment, fun, ticket and everyday living
Use only text and no image	Multimedia environment that includes images, animated images and color
Market primarily to business users	Market primarily to ordinary consumers
Uses interface (display) that shows only four lines of text in black and white without images	Uses interface (display) with full color and with large screen for animated full-color gif images and ten lines of text or more
Charges consumers by connection time	Charges consumers by packet of download information. If you don't download, you won't get charged except for the basic monthly access fee
Uses circuit switching; have to dial up to connect each time for access to the network	Uses packet switching; connection stays on all the time, saving dialup time

I-mode focuses on entertainment, fun and living. Thirdly, I-mode provides a multimedia environment that includes images, animated images and color, where as the European WAP-based services use only text and no images. There are many other differences, in addition to the above mentioned. Table 3.6 presents all of the differences between WAP and I-mode.

In the United States, there are two main programming languages that make up the wireless Web: **WML** (Wireless Markup Language) and **HDML** (Handheld Device Markup Language). WML is the HTML of wireless devices. HDML is a markup language similar to HTML that runs on a **microbrowser** that is designed for handheld devices, such as cell phones. Traditionally, this microbrowser could view sites only in HDML, but newer phones can interpret both languages. HDML uses its own gateway (software on the server) to provide access to the wireless Web.

WML is a more advanced protocol than HDML since it is based around **XML** (Extensible Markup Language). This new language is what newer browsers and gateways are now supporting. Handheld devices that use their own method of accessing wireless data have browsers that will view WML as well. However, a problem with these wireless devices is that the screens are very small, and therefore they are difficult to read and type on. Another problem is that information on the wireless Web is limited as compared to the vast ocean of data on the Internet.

Despite the initial wide adoption of WAP standard, it is being rapidly replaced by other newer standards. In addition to I-mode, another new standard is the **3G** being developed by the **International Telecommunications Union** (ITU), an intergovernmental organization responsible for adopting international treaties, regulations and standards governing telecommunications. The 3G is an ITU specification for the third generation of mobile communications technology. The two generations are analog cellular and digital PCS. The 3G claims to be able to increase bandwidth, up to 384 kbps when a device is stationary or moving at pedestrian speed, 128 kbps in a car, and 2 mbps in fixed applications. The 3G is designed to work with current wireless systems such as **Global System for Mobile Communications (GSM),** one of the leading digital cellular systems, and **Code-Division Multiple Access (CDMA),** a digital cellular technology that uses a different transmission technique than GSM. Both GSM and CDMA are dominant and competing systems in Asia.

3.3 NETWORKING: LAN AND WAN

As mentioned earlier, the Internet is a network of networks. Two of the most widely used network structures are **LAN** (local area network) and **WAN** (wide area network). The computers you use on a college campus most likely are connected to a LAN associated with the college. A LAN is a high speed data communication network that connects computers and other terminals within a geographically limited area, typically within adjacent buildings or complexes. The high-speed can be achieved because a LAN is typically wired by cables which allow for more data traffic than traditional telephone line imports. A LAN may connect as few as two or three computers in the home or home office or as many as thousands of users in an FDDI (Fiber-Distributed Data Interface) LAN. LANs also allow you to share resources, such as printers and fax machines, in small-business applications.

LANs are extremely popular for business and organizations not only because they provide high-speed communications, but also because they offer many other benefits. First, LANs allow you to share resources such as printers, document scanners and large hard disks in a business. The savings from this sharing can increase dramatically as the number of people in the network increases. Secondly, LANs make information sharing in a department or business much faster, easier and more convenient since all the computers are interconnected and files can either be stored in the server or individual computers. Thirdly, software can be shared in two ways. One way is to use the groupware designed for a group of people to work together in a network environment. The other way is by taking advantage of software vendor's group licensing practice. This practice allows an organization to buy a single copy of a piece of software designated to be shared by the users of a LAN. It usually costs much less to buy this type of vendor license than to purchase individual copies for every computer you own in the organization. Fourthly, response to service requests is faster and better since there are fewer users to service and the LAN management understands the needs of the local users better than a centralized remote management.

A LAN requires a server that typically keeps a suite of application programs. Users can choose to run those programs from the server or download them to their local computer hard disk and run them from their own computers. Users can share files with others at the LAN server; read and write access is maintained by a LAN administrator. When a LAN is connected to the Internet, you can access the Internet directly from the computer that is connected to the LAN without having to dial an access phone number.

A LAN server may also be used as a Web server so that other people from outside can access Web information located in the server. For example, my Web site (www.niagara.edu/zhou) is located in the Niagara University LAN server, which also serves as a Web server. When you access my home page, you are really accessing Niagara University's LAN server. However, safeguards need to be taken to secure internal applications and data from outside access.

One safeguard is to install a **firewall** on a separate network gateway server. A firewall is a set of related software programs that protect the resources of a LAN or a private network from users from other networks (Figure 3.3). For example, a company that owns a LAN or an Intranet (discussed in Chapter 4), can set up a firewall that prevents outsiders from accessing its private data resources and controls what outside resources its employees or users have access to.

There are four main LAN systems: **Ethernet**, Token Ring, Arcnet systems, and FDDI. Ethernet is the oldest of LAN-technologies (Figure 3.4). It was developed in 1980 by Xerox in cooperation with Digital Equipment Corporation and Intel. Ethernet cables are classified as **XbaseY**, where "X" is

FIGURE 3.3
Location of a firewall, which guards against unauthorized access to a LAN or Intranet.

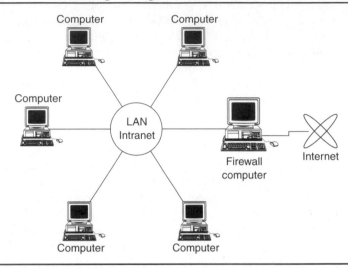

FIGURE 3.4
A bus–typology Ethernet LAN.

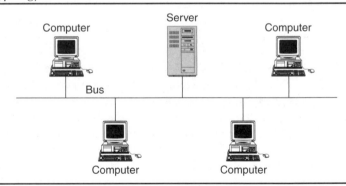

the data rate in mbps, "base" means "baseband" as opposed to "radio frequency," and "Y" is the category of cabling. For instance, a 10base5 Ethernet
cable is one that is capable of carrying data at a speed of 10 mbps, using baseband transmission for a maximum of 500 meters. However, the most common
type of Ethernet is 10baseT, which yields 10 mbps over twisted pair wire and
normally for a distance of about 100 meters. Today, 100baseT ("T" for
"twisted-pair cable"), also called "fast Ethernet," is gaining popularity. With
ever-increasing demand for high speed and more bandwidth, vendors are
developing Gigabit Ethernet, also called 1000BaseT.

FIGURE 3.5
A token ring LAN.

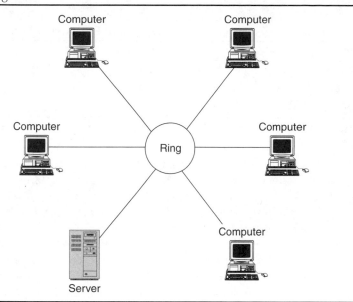

Token Ring was developed by IBM and is second to Ethernet in terms of popularity (Figure 3.5). It operates at speeds ranging from 4 mbps to 16 mbps.

FDDI technology was developed by ANSI (American National Standards Institute) in 1990. Due to its wider bandwidth, FDDI is used for LANs that require a very high speed or have a large number of users. FDDI LANs are based on a ring typology. FDDI greatly expands the speed and operating distance's of LANs. Arcnet was developed by Datapoint Corporation, in 1977. It is a baseband, token ring architecture, and can transmit data at speeds ranging from 2.5 mbps to 20 mbps on coaxial cable. Although it costs less because of easy installation, it is not a universal standard, and this is not as popular as Ethernet and Token Ring LANs.

Ethernet cable delivers the fastest speed in communication, even though some of its counterparts claim to match its speed. For example, downloading a Yahoo Messenger file via Ethernet to the local computer hard drive takes only 12 seconds, while it takes about 2 minutes for a DSL or cable modem to complete the download (Table 3.7). In addition, Ethernet usually is more reliable and delivers more constant speed.

Companies and organizations have begun to recognize and are increasingly adopting a new type of LAN: wireless LAN. In wireless LAN, cables do not physically connect computers. Instead, they are connected by radio frequencies.

TABLE 3.7
Comparison of Estimated Downloading Time for Yahoo Messenger with Different Internet Connections

CONNECTIONS	ESTIMATED DOWNLOAD TIME
28.8-kb modem	11 minutes
56-kb modem	6 minutes
DSL/cable (128 –kb)	2 minutes
T1/LAN (1572 –kb)	12 seconds

NOTE: Yahoo Messenger's download size is 2.46 mb.

In a typical wireless LAN configuration, a transmitter/receiver, called an access point, connects to a wired LAN using standard cabling as shown in Figure 3.6. Usually, an antenna is mounted in a high point so as to provide coverage for the desired area. The access point acts like a hub, receiving, buffering, and transmitting data between the wireless workstations and the wired network. A single access point can cover up to several hundred feet and can support up to about 50 users. In a large facility, multiple access points can be installed to provide coverage for all desired area so that users can move freely without disruption to their LAN communication. This capacity has been commonly referred to as **roaming** as the term has been used in a cellular telephone system.

In a wireless LAN, users access the network with wireless LAN adapters. These adapters are installed as PC cards in the computers. The wireless LAN adapters serve as the interface between the computer and the radio signal

FIGURE 3.6
A wireless LAN with two access points.

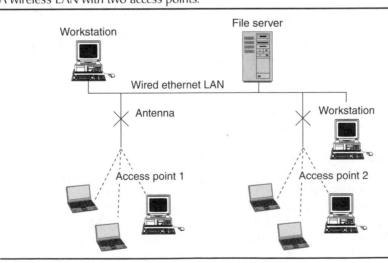

through an antenna. Both computers, their software and their users are not aware of the fact that the connection to the LAN is wireless rather than through a standard cable.

With more people using laptops instead of desktop computers, mobility and connectivity have become a big issue with traditional cabled LAN. However, the reliability of wireless LAN is still in question, and until this and other issues can be resolved, the spread of wireless LAN use will be slow.

A WAN is similar to LAN in that it is also a network that connects computers to each other for sharing resources and speedy communication. However, it differs from LAN in that it covers greater geographic distances than LAN. WAN is typically owned and managed by large corporations with branches and offices across a large geographic area.

3.4 CONCLUSION

As Internet technologies rapidly evolve, new ways of connecting to the Internet may be found and old ways modified and improved. For the foreseeable future, we will see all the connecting methods discussed in this chapter continue to be used in different sectors of the population. The hospitality and tourism industry will aggressively pursue the use of broadband communications. However, Internet communication is a two-way street, and the technologies adopted by consumers will affect the decisions of the business world when implementing Internet information technology strategies.

There are many issues to be resolved before any means of connecting to the Internet becomes widely adopted. These issues include reliability of connection, speed, ease of access, security, and privacy, not to mention cost. Understanding these issues will help the hospitality and tourism industry make better decisions when considering the adoption of new technologies.

KEY WORDS AND TERMS

Broadband Communications Channels	Microbrowser
POTs	XML
Bandwidth	3.G
Wireless Internet	GSM
Mobility	CDMA
Adaptability	LAN
PDAs	WAN
WML	Firewall
I-Mode	Ethernet
HDML	XbaseY

SUMMARY

To establish a standard Internet connection, you need a modem, an Internet Service Provider, and a browser. This type of connection is by far the most popular since it uses the existing telephone system and cost is minimized

Internet Service Providers are gateways to the Internet. They also provide a variety of services, including e-mail and personal Web site hosting. There are many other ways to connect to the Internet besides the standard modem dial-up. These broadband communications channels are faster and better but are more expensive than the standard connection. Some of the most important developments in broadband communications include ISDN, DSL, cable modem and wireless.

WEB RESOURCES

- www.cable-modem.net
- www.epinions.com
- whatis.techtarget.com

CASE STUDY: *American Airlines*

American Airlines employs about 99,000 people, and the newly acquired TWA brought an additional 17, 625 people with it when it merged with American. With corporate headquarters in Fort Worth, Texas, American is one of the largest airline companies in the industry and is still growing.

American has been one of the travel industry leaders in the use of the Internet. Today, American is largely bypassing the travel agents, relying heavily on its Web site (www.aa.com) and a partnership Web site, Orbitz.com (www.orbitz.com), for reservations.

Before the Internet became a popular way to book flights, American was dependent on travel agencies and their central reservation system, called Sabre. Travel agencies were given a commission that encouraged them to book clients with American, and American posted information on the Central Reservation System (CRS). Marketing was done on television, on posters in travel agencies, on billboards, and so on. Television commercials were the best way to encourage people to fly on American's planes.

The Internet came into popularity in the early 1990s, at which point the airlines started to cut travel agent commissions. Soon the Web became the preferred way for customers to book and plan flights. American threw its energy into the Web and the American Web site continues to be a major draw for marketing and promotion. American introduced its site in 1995—adding online reservations capability in 1996—to enhance communication with its customers and to offer an online vehicle for travel planning and AAdvantage account management.

By 1996, American was capable of handling online reservations. In 1998, American completely redesigned its Web site so that it could suit specific kinds of customers. Since then, more than 7.8 million people have logged on to the American site. The site averages about 683,000 hits per day and more than 18.8 million visits monthly. The site ties into American's extensive AAdvantage frequent-flier database to instantly display personalized information and messages according to customers' preferred airports, destinations, and interests.

American's site was built in three tiers: the presentation layer; middleware, or the services and images generated on screen; and the back end, which is the database the server uses to retrieve information. The sites content is divided into parts devoted to travel planning, AAdvantage, NetSAAver and special offers (available only online), programs and services, and general information about American. Visitors can get all the information they need, thus encouraging them to book flights with American.

You can personalize American's Web site by logging in, after which specified, pertinent information will appear, making it even easier to navigate and find the necessary information. The database works with the telephone center of AAdvantage, so information is updated immediately. The reservations system works with the GDS Sabre reservation system, so all flights and destinations are available. Special fares may be available through booking online only—another marketing strategy that encourages people to use the site.

American has received recognition for its outstanding job in designing and marketing its Web site. In November 2001, American received the WebAward from the Web Marketing Association for excellence. For two years, from 2000 to 2001, American was ranked among the Top Business 50 as one of the top 50 businesses that successfully incorporated the Internet and related technology into its operations. It was also named one of Yahoo's most popular travel sites because of its marketing ability with Yahoo links. As early as 1999, American received four awards (Gold, Gold, Silver, and Bronze) for outstanding achievement in interactive advertising from the Web Marketing Association.

The cost of utilizing the Internet is now a critical issue for American. After the terrorist attacks of September 11, 2001, the company found itself in dire financial trouble, and reevaluation of the company's budget has become necessary. The changing nature of reallocating resources makes it impossible to predict the amount of revenue that will need to be spent on Internet marketing.

American is one of the top travel sites on the Internet. In the future, the Internet will become even more useful as a tool for the airline industries.

QUESTIONS TO PONDER:

1. What were the major elements in the design of the American Airlines Web site?
2. What do you think are the major reasons that the American's Web site is a success?
3. What do you think will be some of the challenges for American in its continued success with the Internet?
4. Do you think the designers of the American Web site took consumers' Internet connection speed into consideration? Support your argument with evidence. You can visit the American site to investigate this issue further.

REVIEW QUESTIONS

1. How do you set up a standard connection?
2. How does a modem work?
3. How is a modem rated in terms of speed?
4. What is an ISP?
5. What is the difference between an ISP and an OSP?
6. What are some alternative connection methods?
7. Describe the difference between DSL and cable modem.
8. What are the benefits of wireless connections?
9. How do you set up a cable modem connection?
10. What is WML?
11. What is the function of a firewall?
12. What is the difference between a LAN and a WAN?

REFERENCES

Kinetic Strategies. (2002). www.kineticstrategies.com.

Krishnamurthy, Sandeep. (2003). *E-Commerce Management*. Canada, Thompson/South-Western.

For additional Travel and Tourism resources, go to www.Hospitality-Tourism.delmar.com

4

E-COMMERCE FUNDAMENTALS

LEARNING OBJECTIVES

After you complete your study of this chapter, you should be able to:

- Define what e-commerce is.
- Understand the different types of e-commerce.
- Know the process of setting up an e-commerce business.
- Be able to tell the difference among different types of online payment systems and the issues involved.

4.1 THE INTERNET AND E-COMMERCE

One of the hottest words in business today is **e-commerce**—and rightly so. E-commerce revenues were estimated to reach $1 trillion in 2001 (Shim et al. 2000). The importance of e-commerce to business has never been so obvious. As discussed in Chapter 1, those people who are using the Web typically are well educated and financially well off. In addition, they are not just surfing. It is estimated that about 40% of these Web users are also online buyers (Shim et al. 2000). For businesses that encounter fierce competition, the need to move fast in conducting their affairs has never been greater. E-commerce allows businesses to be more effective and efficient in responding to customers' needs and wants as well as in conducting transactions with suppliers and within the company itself. E-commerce has changed the way business is being conducted.

4.2 E-COMMERCE DEFINED

Despite the fact that e-commerce is one of the most commonly used terms in the age of the Internet age, the word may mean different things to different people. To some, e-commerce simply means putting up a Web site to provide product and service information along with an e-mail address allowing customers to orders. To others, e-commerce means creating a Web site to sell online directly to consumers with a credit card. To still others, e-commerce involves (1) a Web site where customers can find information, and place an order, (2) an order fulfillment center that tracks and ships orders, and (3) a customer service mechanism by which questions and feedback about products and services and returns can be handled.

So what is e-commerce? E-commerce is the compound of two words: **electronic** and **commerce**. *Webster's Dictionary* (2000) defines e-commerce as "the conducting of business communication and transactions over networks and through computer technology." One of the common definitions of e-commerce is that it is the buying and selling of goods and services on the Internet (Shim et al. 2000). However, e-commerce is more than the act of buying and selling online. It encompasses all activities associated with buying and selling, such as financial transactions, business data exchange, and communicating with customers and suppliers.

For the purposes of this book, we will define **e-commerce** simply as a system of conducting business activities using the Internet and other information technologies.

Specifically, e-commerce refers to using computer networks (the Internet; intranets; and extranets) to conduct business. This includes buying and selling online, electronic funds transfer, business communications and other activities associated with the buying and selling of goods and services online. By this definition, e-commerce includes all inter and intracompany functions, such as marketing, finance, manufacturing, selling, and negotiating.

By defining e-commerce as a system of conducting business activities using the Internet and other information technologies, we hope to broaden our conceptualization and operationalization of the term. It reflects our belief that technology is an integral part of conducting business and that the Internet acts only as an agent of change in impacting the way the hospitality and tourism business is conducted.

By this definition, e-commerce is not a separate entity of a company but rather an integral part of a company's business operation. In our view, the use of the Internet and information technology (in this case, e-commerce) is an important part of meeting the needs and wants of consumers while making a profit for the company. A special case of e-commerce consists of the dot-com companies, whose entire operations use the Internet platform and other information technologies. The meltdown of the dot-com companies believed to represent the cutting-edge technologies illustrates the importance of our belief, namely, that technology alone will not succeed unless it becomes an integral part of business operational strategies. To put it simply, e-commerce, just like any other business, requires planning, marketing, customer service, and other traditional business functions. The main difference from the traditional business model is that the channel of communication has changed, and the concepts of time, space, and distance have been completely altered.

4.3 COMPONENTS OF E-COMMERCE

There are three major components to our definition of e-commerce. First, e-commerce requires a systematic approach in conducting business. Just like traditional brick-and-mortar types of business, e-commerce has to deal with all aspects of business, such as research and planning, operation and selling, marketing, budgeting, customer service, and human resource management. The difference here is that most of these activities are done through the Internet and other electronic means.

Second, e-commerce is a special type of business, but it is still a business. Just as there are many kinds of businesses, there are many kinds of e-commerce businesses. E-commerce can be done between businesses (business to business; or **B2B**) or between businesses and consumers (business to consumer; or B2C). E-commerce can also be classified by the products or services a business sells or provides. Some e-commerce businesses sell tangible products, such as computers and clothes. Others offer intangible products and services, such as providing information and reservations. Most hospitality and travel industry e-commerce is a mix of these two (if tickets can be considered a tangible product).

Finally, e-commerce is conducting business by using technologies. For a company to be successful in e-commerce, it must understand these technologies and make the best use of what are available to the business. The question here is not what technologies you are using, but how you use technologies to accomplish your business goals.

4.4 CLASSIFICATION OF E-COMMERCE

E-commerce can be classified in two ways—businesses that base their entire operation online are **online-only businesses** and businesses that operate both online and in a physical space are **bricks-and-clicks businesses** (Figure 4.1). Online-only businesses such as Travelocity.com, expedia.com and bedandbreakfast.com have an online presence only while bricks-and-clicks businesses such as Nwa.com, Marriott.com and Southwest.com businesses are existing traditional bricks-and-mortar companies but with an online e-commerce presence.

Online-only businesses can be further divided into several categories. These are **direct sellers, intermediaries, fee-free-and-ad-based businesses,** and **fee-based businesses**. Direct sellers operate by selling products and services directly to the consumers without a middleman. Most of the hospitality and tourism companies are engaged in direct selling by selling tickets and

FIGURE 4.1
E-commerce classification.

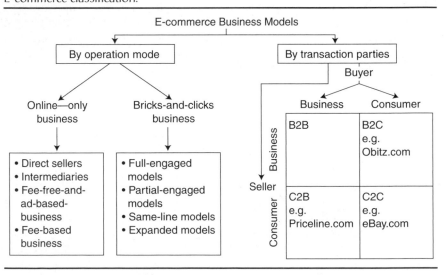

reservations online. The Internet is supposed to bring death to middlemen or intermediaries, creating a process called **disintermediation.** On one hand, it does bring about great impact on the traditional intermediaries such as travel agencies. On the other hand, it helps to create a new generation of online intermediaries, a process called **re-intermediation.** The Internet does not really eliminate intermediaries; it simply helps to replace the old ones with new ones.

The fee-free-and-ad-based online businesses build their business model on user traffic. The premises are that advertisers care for traffic and by providing services that attract a large number of users to the site, the business will be able to sell ads to the advertisers. Very few hospitality and tourism business build their e-commerce on this model. However, outside hospitality and tourism, there are many companies making money with this model, companies such as Yahoo.com. Sina.com and CNN.com.

A subset of the fee-free-and-ad-based e-commerce is **virtual-community-based model.** The type of e-commerce provides free communication services to the users to build virtual communities in which users can chat in the chat-rooms, share information in discussion forums, newsgroups and Mailing Lists, and publish information by building their own Web sites. A good example is the Yahoo Geocities where users have a variety of communication tools at their disposal. Virtual communities are a great way to build online brand and loyalty. Many hospitality and tourism companies are beginning to incorporate this feature into their e-commerce business. By keeping a large number of loyal users, the virtual-community-based business makes money by selling to advertisers.

Fee-based online businesses support their operation by charging fees for accessing contents and information or for using special services provided in their Web site. Currently, few hospitality and tourism companies make use of this model, but there are many companies in the information and media business that rely on this model. For instance, *Wall Street Journal* (wsj.com) and *New York Times* (nytimes.com) charge fees for accessing their proprietary news and information online.

Bricks-and-clicks businesses can be generally divided into four groups—**full-engaged models, partially-engaged models, same-line business** and **expanded models.** Full engaged businesses make their complete line of products or services available online to sell directly to the consumers. To these businesses, online selling adds another channel of retailing to their existing brick-and-mortar business and therefore broadens its market reach. Most of the airlines today are full-engaged businesses, selling their ticket inventories and providing e-service online. Southwest and Northwest airlines are two good examples.

Partially-engaged businesses limit their e-commerce to part of their business either to avoid conflict of distribution channels or because not all of its products or services are suitable for e-commerce. Same-line businesses can be either full-engaged or partially-engaged businesses, but they sell the same line of products or services online. Expanded models see e-commerce as an opportunity to expand its line of business to target consumers previously out of reach or to include partner products or services that could not be marketed and sold without incurring large cost. For example, on Northwest.com Web site, customers can make online hotel reservations through Northwest partners hotels.com and hotwire.com.

E-commerce can also be classified according to transaction parties, that is, buyers and sellers. This classification yields many different e-commerce models—**B2B, B2C, C2C,** and **C2B.** B2B is probably the most promising application of e-commerce. It is estimated that 90% of e-commerce is between businesses. In its simplest definition, B2B e-commerce is any business process between two companies that uses Web-based network technology. It can include functions that provide the exchange of information, facilitate business transactions and completely integrate the shared business processes for a company. For this reason, this type of B2B e-commerce is also called **e-marketplace** or **B2B exchanges.** Some of the functions executed by these e-marketplaces and B2B exchanges encompass a variety of functions, such as digital invoicing, inventory management, electronic payment, and auctioning a finished product. This Web-based e-commerce is gradually replacing older electronic data inter-change, **EDI, or paper-based systems** for the simple reason that it is faster, cheaper, and easier to modify and expand according to changing market dynamics.

The basic idea behind the e-marketplace or B2B exchanges is efficiency and convenience. It replaces the old method of procurement, which, for example, may have involved looking through dozens of parts catalogs the size of a Chicago telephone book, making several phone calls, filling out forms and ultimately faxing out an offer. It is a labor-intensive business and it creates many jobs, for better or worse. From management's perspective, however, it was costly and inefficient. The e-marketplace puts all those catalogs online, adds a search feature and some order processing functionality, and makes finding and comparing similar products from multiple suppliers easier. Theoretically, the concept of the e-marketplace is a great invention.

One of the issues in B2B e-commerce is the issue of security and reliability. To a great degree, hospitality and tourism companies are little more than the sum of their business processes. Consequently the value of the information that travels across the process network can be extremely high. Digitized B2B processes need to be absolutely secure and thoroughly reliable. B2B solutions might use **VPN** (virtual private network) technologies to exploit the Internet as a cost-effective international carrier, in which case the company will have the additional responsibility of thoroughly researching the legal implications of trading across the relevant geographical boundaries. A VPN is a private data network that makes use of the public telecommunication infrastructure, maintaining privacy through the use of a tunneling protocol and security procedures. The idea of VPN is to give the company the same capabilities at much lower costs by using a shared public infrastructure rather than a private one. Companies today are looking at using a VPN for both extranets and intranets.

B2B exchanges are, in fact, service centers dedicated to a particular market, providing all the players in that market with the opportunity to digitally communicate with each other. Exchanges can deliver market-specific information by providing access to industry directories, product databases, discussion forums, articles and industry-specific bulletin boards. They can also act as a matchmaker between multiple buyers and suppliers through the use of auctions and reverse auctions. A well-executed system should also be able to conduct transactions between members that wish to buy and sell.

It is believed that the private e-commerce network centers will form the cornerstone of the multi-trillion-dollar e-commerce market. Various business models can be found in practice. One of the models is the e-marketplace discussed previously where buyers and suppliers come together to manage their inventories. For instance, the hotel sales and distribution companies First Internet Travel, Inc. (http://reservations.1800usahotels.com), and Tourist Bureau Marketing, Inc. (www.allresnet.com), formed TIMA in May 2002 in an effort to help form a long-term relationship between hotels and wholesale room marketers based on mutual control and benefit.

The TIMA system bridged the gap between suppliers who wish to sell room nights and price-conscious consumers who formerly spent hours monitoring multiple sites to find the best rate for their stay. The TIMA system broadens the suppliers' reach, benefiting them with increased distribution while benefiting the consumer with wider access to Web-only and special room rates.

Through the system, hotels and their wholesale partners can manage inventory that would otherwise go unsold. Another company, IntraPorta (www.intraporta.com), set up a transparent e-marketplace for individually oriented travelers and travel providers such as tour operators, accommodation providers, and custom vacation providers, the Worldwide Electronic Travel Market. Independent travelers from all over the world can send their own travel requests by e-mail to all travel companies that are members of this virtual e-marketplace. Travel providers can freely utilize the travel requests as travel referrals. They make selections among these and send quotes based on the traveler's requirements. No commissions will be charged on bookings.

It is important for a business to understand that e-commerce is not just buying and selling. Rather, e-commerce should be considered part of the corporation's overall business strategy. The Internet-based B2B exchanges have increased the interconnectedness among suppliers, customers, and even competitors. If a business is to survive and prosper in the e-marketplace, it must understand and optimize the relationships among its different components and participants. One company that understands the importance of this principle is Marriott. Marriott realizes that for its business to go smoothly in the fast-paced e-marketplace, it must place a special focus on aligning its e-commerce and **IT** (information technology) strategies with its business goals. Marriott realized that erasing boundaries between the IT and business sides is a crucial step in making the company the most admired player in the hotel business.

That e-commerce should be part of a company's business strategy can be shown by the way two competitors, Marriott and Hyatt, work together to achieve efficiency and effectiveness in e-procurement. In 2000, Marriott International Inc. and Hyatt Corp. announced that they were working together to launch a company that will serve as an e-procurement network. This network will enable both companies to combine their buying power and have suppliers bid for business rather than work separately to buy towels, toilet paper, and mints for their various properties. It is estimated that the two chains need to supply items for more than 2,000 hotels and resorts worldwide and that it is worth more than $5 billion of supplies annually.

B2C e-commerce gets the most publicity in the media, even though it occupies only about 10% of the total e-commerce marketplace compared to B2B. The reason is simple. Consumers are excited about the new freedom and choices they find in the e-commerce marketplace, namely, the hundreds of virtual retail stores on the Web. Businesses are also excited about the new channel they found, which enables them to market and sell their products and services directly to consumers. The process of a simple e-commerce operation looks like the following:

❏ Establish a Web presence
❏ Provide information (online catalog and product information)
❏ Get the customers (marketing)
❏ Fill the order (secure payment methods and fast shipping service)
❏ Provide customer support and service (communications through both the Web and traditional means)

For consumers, taking advantage of e-commerce means that they will do the following:

❏ Identify their needs and wants
❏ Search for information (a source or sources) to fulfill their needs and wants
❏ Evaluate the sources and the goods or services provided by the sources
❏ Select a source for possible purchase
❏ Buy the goods or services
❏ Use the goods and services and evaluate the experience

Understanding the consumer's e-commerce process is very important for businesses. They should realize that, like the old-fashioned retail business, consumers are still attracted to e-commerce by their pleasant experience from finding information, buying the goods and services, waiting for the purchased goods and services to be shipped and delivered and evaluating postpurchase customer service and the quality of the goods and service.

C2C businesses involve transactions between or among two or more individuals. This type of e-commerce makes money by providing an e-marketplace for online sellers and buyers, both of whom being consumers themselves. Online auction sites represent this group of businesses. Ebay.com and Yahoo! Auctions (http://auctions.shopping.yahoo.com/) are probably two of the most well known auction e-commerce. Hospitality and tourism businesses have not been particularly interested in this type of e-commerce model since there is no money to be made.

C2B e-commerce businesses refer to the model that relies on consumers for initiating interactions and transactions. There are two ways to accomplish this task. One is to collect ideas and opinions from the consumers and make them available to the public to help the public to make purchase decisions. The e-commerce businesses make money by selling advertisements and by collecting commissions on products and services sold through the site. The best example is epinions.com, which serves as a source for unbiased advice, personalized recommendations, and comparative shopping, so that people can make informed buying decisions.

The other way is the so-called **reversed auctions** in which the e-commerce business allows the consumer to submit binding bits for a product or service. **Priceline.com** is probably the best known e-commerce business in hospitality and tourism. The success of Priceline.com has prompted other online travel agencies to include the service. Travelocity.com, for instance, began to offer reversed auction to consumers in 2002.

4.5 ESTABLISHING WEB PRESENCE

The following are required in establishing an e-commerce presence on the Web:

- ❏ Apply for a domain name or use a third party's domain name
- ❏ Find a server to host the domain
- ❏ Create Web pages and load them to the server
- ❏ Set up payment methods to receive payment over the Internet

APPLYING FOR A DOMAIN NAME

People call their Web site a "home page." A Web site or home page is really a home in cyberspace. Like a home that needs a postal address, a Web site needs a cyberaddress, too. A domain name is a convenient way of recognizing one's home in cyberspace and locating information on the Internet. To own a domain name is to own a home page, just as you may own your home instead of renting.

A **domain name** is a logical name for the host computer. The IP address is a 32-bit integer. You need this address in order to send a message to its destination. It is too complicated to use numbers, so people prefer to give machines easy and logical names: host names, or domain names. An advantage of using logical names is that you can keep the domain name even if you change your computers or location. For instance, once you register for a domain name, such as acupuncture2000.com, you can move the name to any servers to host it and people can still identify and locate you using the same name.

The Domain Name System (DNS) is a distributed database used by **TCP/IP** (Transmission Control Protocol/Internet Protocol) applications to map between hostnames and IP addresses and to provide e-mail routing information. The DNS provides the protocol that allows clients and servers to communicate with each other.   TCP/IP is the basic communication language or protocol of the Internet. When you are set up with access to the Internet, your computer is provided with a copy of the TCP/IP program, as is every other computer that you may send messages to or get information from.

ICANN, (Internet Corporation for Assigned Names and Numbers) (www.icann.org), is a not-for-profit organization that handles IP address space allocation, protocol parameter assignment, domain name system management, and root server system management functions. Currently, there are ten generic **Top-Level Domains** (TLDs) authorized by ICANN (Table 4.1).

The existing TLDs are having difficulty keeping up with the exponential growth of the Internet. According to Name Intelligence, Inc. (www.whois.sc 2003), the total number of domains registered worldwide reached over 30

TABLE 4.1 The Ten Top-Level Domains in Use in 2002	
DOMAIN NAME	MEANING
.com	Commerical organizations
.edu	Educational institutions
.gov	Government institutions
.mil	Military groups
.net	Major network support centers
.org	Organizations other than those listed here
.int	International organizations
.biz	Businesses
.info	Unrestricted use
.name	For registration by individuals

TABLE 4.2		
Seven New Top-Level Domains Adopted in 2002 by ICANN		
DOMAIN NAME	PURPOSE	STATUS IN 2002
.aero	Air transport industry	Operational
.biz	Businesses	Operational and accepting live registration
.coop	Cooperatives	Operational
.info	Unrestricted use	Operational and accepting live registration
.museum	Museums	Operational
.name	For registration by individuals	Operational and accepting live registration
.pro	For accountants, lawyers, physicians, and other professionals	Under negotiation

SOURCE: InterNIC (www.internic.net), January, 2003.

million, of which more than 22 million were registered with the domain name .com (dot com). Each day, more than 39 thousand domain names were being bought and registered in 2002. To ease the problem, in November 2000, the ICANN board selected seven new TLDs for negotiation of agreements (Table 4.2). Most of these TLDs were ready for registration in 2002. The hospitality and tourism industry's proposal for a TLD named TRAVEL was not among the seven adopted by ICANN.

To register a domain name, you need to go to an ICANN-accredited registrar. There are hundreds of such registrars worldwide (Table 4.3). Typically, you need to pay a fee for registering a domain name. Some of these registrars may waive the fees if you buy into their hosting service packages. Some of the most popular registrars include Network Solutions, Inc. Registrar (www. networksolutions.com), Go Daddy Software, Inc. (www.godaddy.com), and Internet Domain Registrars (www.registrars.com).

Alternatively, you can "rent" a cyberhome on other people's domains. For example, the author's home page resides in Niagara University's domain name, Niagara.edu. Therefore, the author's home page address is www. niagaraedu/zhou. However, having your own domain name has many benefits that renting does not have. The following are the benefits of registering your own domain name:

❏ **Credibility on the Web:** When you own a home, you are considered more credit worthy than when renting a home. When you own a domain name, you have demonstrated to Internet consumers that you are serious about your business, and thus you will earn more credibility with them.

| **TABLE 4.3** |
| A Selected List of Companies Accredited as Registrars |

- 123 Registration, Inc. (www.123registration.com) (United States)
- Capital Networks Pty Ltd. (Australia)
- Domaininfo AB, aka domaininfo.com (Sweden)
- DomainPeople, Inc. (Canada)
- DomainRegistry.com, Inc. (United States)
- Go Daddy Software, Inc. (United States)
- Internet Domain Registrars, d/b/a Registrars.com and IDR (Canada and United States)
- Key-Systems GmbH, d/b/a domaindiscount24.com (Germany)
- Melbourne IT Limited, d/b/a Internet Names WorldWide (Australia)
- Mr. DomReg.com, Inc. (Canada)
- Namebay (Monaco)
- Network Solutions, Inc. Registrar (United States)
- NORDNET (France)
- Register.com, Inc. (United States)
- Xin Net Corp. (China)

SOURCE: ICANN (www.icann.org). For a complete list, see ICANN's Web site.

❏ **More power in marketing:** Every e-mail message and marketing information you send out to consumers carries your domain name. When people visit your Web site, they also see your domain name, which typically is the same as your business name. This improves your site's visibility on the Web.

❏ **Better control:** You decide where you want your domain to be located; you can move your domain to any hosting service in any location in the world, depending on your needs and financial ability. You can, for instance, change your host service to a better-valued host. The important thing is that none of your visitors' bookmarks will need to change, nor will the move break any links to your site. This is impossible without a domain name.

❏ **Professionalism and security:** It is just as if you own a home, your bank credit rating would be higher and most people would associate owning a home with having a stable, decent job. Having a domain name gives your visitors a sense that you are a professional and helps them feel more secure about dealing with your business.

❏ **Branding opportunity:** A domain name, especially an easy-to-remember one, creates a lasting memory and thus improves your branding opportunity. A memorable domain name is a brand itself, such as Yahoo.com.

FINDING AN INTERNET SERVICE PROVIDER OR WEB HOST FOR YOUR DOMAIN

Once you register your domain name, you need to find a server to park or host it. Many domain name registrars are also domain name hosts. Your Web site is a series of Web pages (HTML files) that reside on a server that is connected to the Internet. Your customers need to connect their computers to the server in order to be able to view your files. For fast, smooth viewing of your files, both the server that hosts your files and the Internet connections that your visitors use to connect to the server need to be fast and powerful enough. A poor-quality server and a slow Internet connection will prevent you from communicating quickly with your visitors and may even drive visitors away from the site.

There are two ways you can host your Web site. The first is to purchase your own server, set it up, and manage your own site. This is an expensive way to host a Web site. Most large corporations like to control their own e-commerce process and are more likely to choose this route. The second way is to find an Internet Service Provider (ISP) or Web hosting company without having to invest in the server hardware and software as well as other management responsibilities. Many small- and medium-size e-commerce businesses prefer to go this route. These ISPs typically offer hosting packages that contain different levels of services. These range from simply providing server space for Web site files to sophisticated e-commerce solutions, such as creating and managing the site, handling customer support, and collecting payment online.

There are hundreds of ISPs and Web server hosts to choose from. In addition, there are a variety of hosting packages and options that you can pick to suit your e-commerce needs and financial means. For this reason, you need to choose your ISP carefully so that you avoid the risk of either spending too much money for what you do not need or spending too little money without achieving your e-commerce objectives. Table 4.4 presents some guidelines for shopping for an ISP or Web hosting company.

CREATING WEB PAGES AND LOADING THEM TO THE SERVER

The next step is to create your Web pages. Depending on the package you purchase from your ISP, you might need to create your own Web files and then load them up to the server. If this is the case, your ISP will provide instructions on how to do it. Other packages may provide you with complete e-commerce solutions. These packages typically are expensive. In this case, the Web host company will create the Web files for you based on the information you provide.

Regardless of whether you create your own Web files or your host company provides them, there are several things you need to be aware of to

TABLE 4.4	
Guidelines for Choosing a Web Hosting Company	
ISSUES	EXPLANATION
Allocated Server Storage Space	You need to store your Web site files on the server for visitors to view them. A small e-commerce business needs as little as 400 mb of server storage space, while a full-scale e-commerce site may need at least 9 gb (gigabytes) of space. Most ISPs offer the option of upgrading as your business grows.
Shared hosting or dedicated server	A busy server will slow down the access speed of a Web site by consumers. A small, less busy e-commerce site can opt for a shared server, while a large, busy site might have to arrange for a dedicated server. A dedicated server works faster and provides more power in management. Look for an ISP that provides both options for flexibility.
E-mail accounts	All ISPs will give you at least one e-mail account. For a small business, this might suffice. For a large business, several e-mail accounts might be needed for difference services and purposes. Most ISPs will give you options. Check if more than one e-mail account is included in the package.
Service and technical support	Service and technical support can be very expensive if not included in the package. Make sure you understand the terms of the package. Choose an ISP 24/7 customer service with no additional fees or with minimum fees.
Online Security	Online financial transactions, such as credit card payments and customer information, require a secure server. Make sure that your ISP's server is secure and that the transaction process is SSL (Secure Socket Layer) encrypted.

avoid costly mistakes. Table 4.5 summarizes what you need to pay attention to when creating your Web site. After creating your Web files, it is time to upload them to your host server. Typically, when you sign up for an ISP or Web server, you are given instructions as to how to upload files to the server. You need a software program called **FTP** (File Transfer Protocol). An FTP program enables a user on one computer to transfer files to and from another computer over the Internet or a TCP/IP network. There are many popular FTP programs on the market.

Some FTP programs are offered free of charge and can be downloaded from the Internet. Others are referred to as shareware, or programs that you can evaluate first and pay later on a volunteer basis (for more information on shareware, go to http://sharewarecnet.com). Still others are full-fledged

TABLE 4.5
Things to Consider in Creating a Web Site

THINGS TO CONSIDER	EXPLANATION
Purpose of your Web site	Before you even begin building your Web site, think about what you really want to do with it. What kind of business will you conduct on the site?
Determine who your customers are	Without knowing who your customers are, you will not be able to pick the right style and online communication strategies. For instance, if your customers are teenagers, you might want to pick a style that is lively and full of bright colors.
Avoid excessive use of graphics and animations	A Web site dotted with graphics and animations can be attractive. However, these take up a lot of room and can considerably slow down the surfing speed of visitors, who typically are impatient. Yahoo's success represents one simple rule: Focus on information and usability rather than site appearance.
Put yourself in the visitor's shoes when designing a Web site	When designing your Web site, project yourself as an online visitor and anticipate your visitor's online experience. Ask yourself these questions: How user friendly is the site? Can my visitors find the information they want? If they cannot, will they be able to contact me instantly for further assistance?
How to make visitors repeat visitors	To encourage repeat customers, give the visitor a good first-time surfing experience and a reason to come back. Elements of success include user friendliness, rich and updated information, fast access, quick response time, interactivity, security, and 24/7 customer service.

commercial programs. One of the most popular FTP programs is WS_FTP Pro, which you can download from www.ipswitch.com/Products/WS_FTP. This powerful, user-friendly file transfer application allows you to transfer Web files between your local PC and your Web server.

Unlike another file transfer protocol, HTTP, FTP is not limited to the type and the size of the files you can transfer. HTTP is used by your browser, such as Internet Explorer, to transfer HTML files from Web servers to graphically display them on your monitor. However, HTTP is not designed to transfer large files. You might not need an FTP program to upload HTML files to the Web server if your ISP provides you with direct online Web site building tools. In that case, you will be working directly on their server, and when you save your files, you save directly to their server. Some ISPs provide their own FTP programs, in which case you need not acquire an FTP program of your own.

You may not need your own FTP program if you use a commercial Web authoring program, such as Microsoft FrontPage. An FTP program is built into the program, so you can save, load, retrieve, and download your Web files directly to as well as from the ISP's server.

SETTING UP PAYMENT METHODS TO RECEIVE PAYMENT OVER THE INTERNET

One of the most important processes in e-commerce is the payment arrangement. Without some kind of trusted and user-friendly **payment system,** e-commerce will be almost impossible. Because of some widely publicized horror stories about credit card numbers being stolen over the Internet and hackers stealing financial information from Web servers, consumers are deeply concerned about using their credit cards and other financial information over the Internet. These concerns focus on three areas. First, consumers are concerned about the secure transmission of credit card and financial information from their computers over the Internet to the online merchant's Web site. Second, they are concerned about the safety of the information stored in the merchant's server. Finally, they are concerned about who has access to the information they provide over the Internet since they cannot see the faces of the people who are sitting on the other end of the connection.

It is not consumers alone who are concerned about the security of the payment system. Merchants are concerned about the verification of the identities of the involved parties. They want to know that the person is the person he says he is. Failing to identify the real person who is the owner of the credit card can cost the merchant dearly if they cannot collect the payment.

There are many solutions now in use to help solve these problems (Table 4.6). **SSL** (Secure Sockets Layer) is a protocol used to transmit private documents over the Internet. SSL employs a private key to encrypt data transferred over the SSL connection. Both Netscape Navigator and Internet Explorer support SSL, and many Web sites use the protocol to ensure a secure online financial transaction environment. Encryption refers to a mechanism that allows the translation of data into a secret code. In **asymmetric encryption,** also called **public-key encryption,** the sender encrypts the data with a public key, which requires a corresponding private key. The receiver uses the paired private key to decrypt the data and read it.

In **symmetric encryption,** both the sender and the receiver use the same key for secure communication. Two additional developments in making online financial transactions secure and accurate are the **digital signature** and the **digital certificate.** A digital signature is simply a digital code attached to the date being sent over the Internet to uniquely identify the sender. Like a written signature, a digital signature provides proof that the individual sending the message really is who he or she claims to be. A digital certificate serves the same purpose to identify the sender. However, it is issued by a **Certificate Authority** (CA). A

TABLE 4.6
Security Solutions in an E-commerce Payment System

ISSUES	SOLUTIONS	WHAT IT DOES
Security	SSL, SHTTP	SSL creates a secure connection between your local computer and the Web server, over which any amount of data can be sent securely. SHTTP is used to transmit individual messages securely over the Internet. These two security systems complement each other for a secure transmission of data over the Internet.
Privacy and Identity	SET, digital signature, digital certificate	SET (Secure Electronic Transaction) is a new standard that enables secure credit card transactions on the Internet. It was quickly endorsed by almost all major players in the e-commerce marketplace, including Microsoft, Netscape, Visa, and Mastercard. One of the major breakthroughs in SET is that it allows merchants to verify that buyers are who they claim to be. In the meantime, SET protects buyers since the buyer's credit card information is transferred directly to the credit card issuers for verification and billing, rather than to the merchants, who by this mechanism are not able to view the buyer's credit card information. Digital signature and digital certificate are two additional mechanisms to ensure that senders are who they claim to be.

CA is a third party that issues digital certificates for authentication and authorization for secure interactions over the network. A CA also provides all the services required to issue, store, manage and revoke certificates for a business or organization. One of the most popular CA companies is VeriSign (www.verisign.com), which claims that over 90% of secure Web sites worldwide use VeriSign Secure Server IDs to authenticate themselves and to enable SSL encryption to protect sensitive data and transactions (www.verisign.com). With VeriSign's Site Trust Services, your e-commerce business can have the VeriSign check-mark logo displayed on your Web site. This tells your visitors that your site is a trusted and secure e-commerce business and that your customers can feel safe to send their private and other financial information via their Web browsers to you.

There are two popular means for online payment: traditional credit cards and e-money. E-money is a secure online payment mechanism that uses public-key encryption. We know that public-key encryption keys come in pairs. The sender owns a private key that pairs with a public-key known to everyone. For example, the sender (say, a customer) uses his private keys to encrypt (for security) and sign (for identification) blocks of digital data that represent money orders. The receiver (say, a bank) uses the customer's public key to verify the money orders and identification.

There are many other types of payment systems for different types of e-commerce. Systems like **eCash, PayPal, BillPoint, Smart Cards** and **PowerWallet** are being used by various e-commerce companies for online financial transactions. As e-commerce matures, existing online payment systems will become even more secure and easy to use. New payment systems will be introduced to build trust and security for all parties involved in e-commerce. However, for a payment system to gain popularity, it must meet some basic conditions. These conditions include but are not limited to security, reliability, privacy, convenience, user friendliness, universality (widely accepted worldwide), and being cost free (to users). By all these standards, the existing credit card payment system appears to have a bright future for being the main payment system for B2C e-commerce.

4.6 CONCLUSION

E-commerce, as defined in this book, is a system of conducting business using the Internet. Defining e-commerce in this way highlights the integration of technology and business. Specifically, the Internet is used as a platform for conducting business. However, e-commerce is still a business, so it must abide by the same rules as traditional commerce. To be successful in e-commerce, we still need to learn how to plan, research, meet customers' needs and wants, market services and products to our customers and take care of the bottom line: making money.

The Internet has leveled the playing field for all types of business. Technology has changed our concepts of time, space and distance. Understanding these new rules is the key to implementing e-commerce solutions in hospitality and tourism companies. This chapter will provide some background in understanding these rules.

KEY WORDS AND TERMS

E-Commerce	Domain Name
B2B E-Commerce	Domain Name System
EDI	TCP/IP
E-Marketplace	ICANN
B2B Exchanges	Top-Level Domains
VPN	FTP
B2C E-Commerce	Payment System

SSL   Certificate Authority
Asymmetric Encryption   eCash
Public-key Encryption   PayPal
Symmetric Encryption   BillPoint
Digital Signature   Smart Cards
Digital Certificate   PowerWallet

SUMMARY

E-commerce is a system of conducting business using the Internet. This definition emphasizes the integration of technology into the business process. As a result, to be successful in e-commerce, hospitality and tourism companies need to understand not only traditional business principles but also the constantly changing technology.

There are five basic e-commerce activities: B2B, B2C, research, e-marketing, and intermediaries. Each activity involves similar as well as different functions in different parts of e-commerce. For example, setting up an e-commerce business requires four steps: providing information, getting the customers, filling the order, and providing customer support and service.

Establishing an e-commerce presence on the Web, requires four steps as well: applying for your own domain name or using a third party's domain name, finding a server to host your domain, creating your Web pages and loading them to the Web server, and setting up payment methods to receive payments over the Internet.

WEB RESOURCES

- www.networksolutions.com
- http://cism.bus.utexas.edu
- ww.worldwide-travelmarket.com
- www.ga2online.com

CASE STUDY: *Sandals All-Inclusive Resorts*

The use of the Internet has increased not only among consumers but also among businesses for marketing purposes. Companies have been affected differently by the new technology. Some have revolutionized the way they market their products or services, while others have made a few changes in their techniques just to cope with changing times.

Sandals Resorts is an example of a company that has welcomed the innovative Web as a source of marketing yet continues to adhere to more conventional media. The all-inclusive company was developed in 1981 by Gordon Stewart in Montego Bay, Jamaica. The goal was to be the Ritz-Carlton of all-inclusives, a goal the company believes it has reached with one of its newly renovated properties.

The Internet has affected Sandals' marketing efforts in a positive way, especially in using the Internet specifically for marketing purposes. Both the marketing and the advertising department focus on the Web site. The company has set up an extensive site for agents and consumers providing in-depth information. The company's staff tend to the site and oversee its profitability. The site is set up in a way that will appeal to its target market: couples on vacation or their honeymoon. On the site, viewers can find information on the various resorts, dining, diving, watersports, and so on. Viewers can also find information about package deals, specials (such as weddings and honeymoons), passport requirements, temperature, checkout time, tipping, evening dress code, and availability of guest rooms.

Sandals has targeted markets in many countries, including England, France, Germany, Spain and Japan. Its Web site can be displayed in several different languages. Sandals has cooperative agreements with several tour operators and their Web sites. Travel agents can learn from Sandals site about Sandals-certified specialist program workshops as well as new products and promotions. Travel agencies can also place a link on their Web sites to the Sandals site. Sandals sees Internet marketing simply as a means to advertise.

In addition to using the Internet, Sandals still does mass faxing to travel agencies and tour operators and runs ads in newspapers and magazines. However, the company has spent a huge amount of money on printed brochures and videos, outlets for which are traditional travel agency offices. With Internet technology, Sandals may now be able to drastically reduce costs in the marketing department and increase sales. For the time being, however, they are behind the times in relation to other companies who have embraced Internet technology.

QUESTIONS TO PONDER:

1. Sandals Resort uses a combination of new and old methods to attract its customers and has been successful. Would you suggest that Sandals incorporate more information technology into its business strategy or stick with its current system?

2. If you were the owner of the company, how would you reallocate financial resources to traditional marketing and Internet marketing? What is the basis for your reallocation?

3. Do you believe that Sandals will be better off outsourcing its Internet marketing to a professional Internet marketing organization or consulting company?

REVIEW QUESTIONS

1. What are the different definitions of the term **e-commerce**?
2. Explain the difference between the author's definition of e-commerce with other definitions.
3. What are the major activities of e-commerce? Briefly describe them.
4. What basic steps need to be taken to create a presence on the Internet?
5. Why is it important for a business to have its own domain name?
6. What should you look for when choosing an ISP or OSP to host a Web site?
7. What are the major factors to consider in designing and creating a Web site?
8. What is a Certification Authority?
9. Describe the security systems currently being used for payment systems.
10. List some of the payment systems mentioned in this chapter.
11. According to the author, what major criteria must be met before an online payment system can become dominant?

REFERENCES

Shim, Jae K., Joel G. Siegel, and Roberta M. Siegel Shim. (2000). *The International Handbook of Electronic Commerce*. Glenlake Publishing Company.

www.Internic.net

www.whois.sc

For additional Travel and Tourism resources, go to www.Hospitality-Tourism.delmar.com

5

A NEW MEDIUM OF COMMUNICATION

LEARNING OBJECTIVES

After you complete your study of this chapter, you should be able to:

- Understand why the Internet is a new medium of communication.
- Know the different Internet communication platforms.
- Understand what Intranets can do to enhance communication inside a business.
- Explain the difference between Intranets and Extranets.
- Know the various kinds of Internet communication tools.

5.1 INTRODUCTION

Since the beginning of humankind, people have tried every means possible to improve communication—first as a means of survival and later to increase understanding, the effectiveness of socialization, and the accumulation of knowledge. Three major barriers to communication have been time, space, and speed. We want to be able to access information and communicate any time we want, wherever we happen to be, and instantly to the parties we wish to contact. The invention of the telephone and fax was the beginning of this human quest for freedom of communication. However, the "Holy Grail" of the communication paradise did not happen until the birth of the Internet.

5.2 THE INTERNET: A NEW MEDIUM OF COMMUNICATION

As we discussed in the previous chapters, the Internet has broken the major barriers to communication. It has changed not only the way we communicate but, more important, the way we think about communication. The Internet has created what we call **virtual communities** or **e-communities** in which your neighbors may be living anywhere in the world and you may never know their true identity. The Internet is a global, faceless, virtual community within which reside millions of virtual subcommunities.

Today, businesses of all stripes and scopes are rushing to take advantage of this new medium of communication. For instance, International e-Commerce, Inc. (IeC), a Houston-based interactive television company, provides a new NetForAll Hotel Solution. IeC and its business partners provide hotels with a complete Internet and entertainment solution for its guests and conferences. IeC has integrated its advanced interactive television services with core hotel services to deliver broadband Internet to each hotel room—interactive television, e-commerce, e-mail and videos on demand—as well as hotel services such as room service, housekeeping and checkout all through the guest's television. IeC and its business partners rewire hotels to create a complete internal network that will provide broadband access to every guest room and meeting room. Almost all major airlines have installed or are considering installing Internet connections to their fleets. Kiosks can be found in all major airports that enable travelers to access their e-mail accounts.

▌ 5.3 DIFFERENT INTERNET COMMUNICATIONS PLATFORMS

Applications of Internet communication include internal communication inside a business (Intranets), B2B online and through VPN (virtual private network), and B2C online. Table 5.1 shows the differences among three different communications platforms. Table 5.2 provides an overview of these classifications.

No matter what types of applications and platforms you use, the purpose of Internet communication for business can be summarized as follows:

❏ Sales and marketing
❏ Human resources management (online manuals, forms and directories, and recruitment and application)
❏ Manufacturing and operations
❏ Customer service and support
❏ Finance and accounting
❏ Customer service
❏ Customer relationship management (CRM)
❏ Public relations and information distribution
❏ Employee knowledge sharing and dissemination
❏ Employer–employee communication

TABLE 5.1 Comparasion Chart of the Internet, Intranet, and Extranet		
	INTERNET	INTRANET	EXTRANET
Right of access	Public; accessible to anyone	Private; access right determined by the owner	Private; controlled access to the public
Types of users	Everyone	Employees, staff, and other authorized users of a company	A company's internal and external customers and business partners
Data and information	Decentralized, unorganized, and fragmented	Proprietary, specialized, and organized	Targeted information designed to be shared among the users

	TABLE 5.2 Classification of Internet Communications
CLASSIFICATION	EXAMPLES OF APPLICATIONS
Intranet (communication within the business)	**Putting forms on the Intranet:** Paper forms, reports, documents, company phonebook, the human resources literature on benefits, new pay scale information and organization chart, FAQs, and online polls and surveys. **Web-based discussion forum.** **Live chat:** Chat rooms that provide instant interactive communication.
Extranet and Internet (B2B communication— B2B online and/or through VPN)	**Information sharing:** Share product catalogs exclusively with wholesalers or those in the trade; share news of common interest exclusively with partner companies. **Collaboration:** Joint development efforts; jointly develop and use training programs. **Customer service:** Allow customers to access selected business information as well as their own account information; allow customers real-time business transaction; provide instant customer service. **B2B transactions:** Real-time business transactions over the Web—the core of the e-commerce.
Internet and Extranet: (B2C online C2B and C2C)	**Communication:** E-mail, e-newsletters, discussion forums, newsgroups, mailing lists, and instant chat. **E-commerce:** Online access of customer information, online payment, marketing goods and services, selling directly to the consumers.

5.4 INTRANET: ENABLING COMMUNICATIONS INSIDE A BUSINESS

An **Intranet** is basically an Internet within the business corporation. Some business organizations set up Web servers on their own internal networks so that employees have access to the organization's Web documents. Technically, an Intranet is a local area network that may not be connected to the Internet but that has some similar functions. An Intranet becomes an **Extranet** when it allows selected customers, suppliers, and mobile workers to access the company's private data and applications available on its servers (Figure 5.1). This is in contrast to, and usually in addition to, the company's public Web site, which is accessible to everyone.

FIGURE 5.1
Differences between Intranet and Extranet.

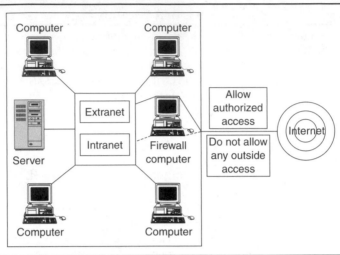

In an Intranet environment, you feel as if you are working on the Web. Intranets use hypertext, colors and graphics and all those functions you would expect from the Web. What you see on your screen is exactly what others will see on their screen. This eliminates problems related to the use of different computer programs and platforms, which often creates communication errors. Intranets have several advantages over traditional network communications for a business.

First, as mentioned previously, Intranets provide a common communication platform for the exchange and sharing of private corporate information. Second, they give the business the opportunity to take advantage of all the functions that the Web is capable of, such as e-mail, discussion forums, chat, mailing lists, calendars and scheduling, searching, and expert systems, to name a few. Third, information can be provided in a multimedia format that increases the Intranet's communication power and effectiveness. Finally, Intranets provide the convenience of being a communication channel for e-commerce by connecting to the Internet, thus making it an Extranet, which can be used to better serve customers, be they corporate or individual.

An increasingly popular application for Intranets is the sharing of expert information inside the company. Over the years, most businesses have accumulated valuable data about their customers, products, processes, and competitors. However, few of them are taking advantage of this free but valuable information. Applications can be developed to facilitate the sharing of these data for the people who need this information for decision-making purposes. One of the companies that does this is AskMe Enterprise (www.askmecorp.com).

AskMe Enterprise has developed an application on the basis of the following assumptions:

❑ Employees often do not know who can help them solve their business problems.

❑ Employees with expertise often answer the same questions repeatedly.

❑ The exchange of workplace knowledge takes place via e-mail, phone calls or meetings. Most of the resulting knowledge stays undocumented and therefore is unusable by others.

By using AskMe Enterprise's application, a company is expected to have the following business benefits:

❑ Share best practices across the organization
❑ Replace reinvention with innovation
❑ Respond faster to key business issues
❑ Make better decisions
❑ Significantly increase productivity
❑ Improve the depth and breadth of business skills

5.5 EXTRANET: B2B AND B2C COMMUNICATIONS

An **Extranet** is a private network that not only connects to the Internet but also uses the same special set of rules (protocol) for communication. It can be considered part of a company's Intranet that is extended to users outside the company. While the Internet is public and no one really owns it, an Extranet is privately owned and managed. With the Internet, you have no control over either its contents or its access. With an Extranet, both contents and access must be controlled and managed. In fact, security is an overriding issue in the development of an Extranet.

The purpose of an Extranet is to securely share part of a business's information or operations with suppliers, vendors, partners, customers, or other businesses. It tries to capture the capability of the Internet and to use it to do business with other companies and to sell products to customers. Like the Intranet, an Extranet reaps the benefits of all functions available to the Internet. Some of these benefits include HTML, Hypertext Transfer Protocol (HTTP), Simple Mail Transfer Protocol (SMTP) and other Internet technologies.

An Extranet requires security and privacy. In recent years, reports of security problems have abounded in the news media. On September 11, 2000, hackers struck Western Union EEF Network, copying the credit and debit card information of 15,700 customers. In the same month, ABN MRMO bank accounts were targeted by hackers who diverted the funds into their account after bypassing the bank's security defenses. Earlier, on August 29, 2000, a British Internet bank, Egg, lost tens of thousands of dollars in credit card fraud. And if we think this happens only to large corporations, think again. A travel agency based in New York was scammed of more than $30,000 in credit card fraud. It all happened despite the fact that all these Extranets employ firewall server management. Other security measures have been added recently, such as the issuance and use of digital certificates or similar means of user authentication, encryption of messages and the use of VPNs that tunnel through the public network.

A **firewall** is a set of related programs, located at a network gateway server, that protects the resources of a private network from users on other networks. An enterprise with an Intranet that allows its workers access to the wider Internet installs a firewall to prevent outsiders from accessing its private data resources and to control what outside resources its own users have access to. A firewall is often installed in a specially designated computer, separate from the rest of the network so that no incoming request can get directly at private network resources.

As discussed in Chapter 4, a digital certificate is an electronic "credit card" that establishes your credentials when doing business or other transactions on the Web. It is issued by a **Certification Authority** (CA). It contains your name, a serial number, expiration dates, a copy of the certificate holder's public key (used for encryption messages and digital signature) and the digital signature of the certificate-issuing authority so that a recipient can verify that the certificate is real. Digital certificates can be kept in registries so that authentication users can look up other users' public keys.

5.6 INTERNET COMMUNICATIONS TOOLS

Customer service is at the core of any business success. Internet technology can help a company accomplish the following:

- ❏ Reduce call center loads and e-mail backlogs
- ❏ Empower customers to find their own answers and share information across the organization
- ❏ Reduce service response time
- ❏ Cut employee training time and costs
- ❏ Create ongoing customer dialogue
- ❏ Improve customer satisfaction and loyalty

Many companies specialize in this type of e-service. RightNow Technologies (www.rightnow.com) is one of these companies. It provides Web site customer service solutions as well as Intranet communication support. Traditionally, customer service is performed from call centers, phone banks, or customer service representative offices. With RightNow's customer service solutions, customer service is handled online, reducing the high cost of human intervention while improving the speed and quality of response. These customers consist of external customers that purchase a company's goods and services and internal customers, that is, employees of that organization. The following tools are used by the company for customer service:

- ❏ E-mail
- ❏ E-newsletters
- ❏ Mailing Lists
- ❏ E-mail mailing lists
- ❏ Discussion forums and FAQs
- ❏ Live online chat
- ❏ Webcasting

E-MAIL

E-mail likely is the most frequently used tool for electronic communication in the Internet. It is estimated that two billion e-mail messages travel through the Internet every day. One of the best things about e-mail is that you can access it anywhere you go, as long as you can gain access to a computer with an Internet connection.

Another advantage of e-mail is that it allows you to personalize your message to your customers. The **personalization** can apply to either a group or an individual. To personalize your message to a group, you can create an e-mail mailing list (do not confuse this with the Mailing List discussed later in this chapter). There are many e-mail programs on the market that you can install on your computer for your e-mail needs.

Table 5.3 summarizes some of the most popular desktop e-mail programs on the market. These programs are unique in that they allow you to pull information from your customer's database to incorporate into your e-mail messages, achieving the goal of personalization.

Other e-mail programs are mostly Web based. Some of the most popular ones include America Online (www.aol.com), Netzero (www.netzero.com), Mail.com (www.mail.com), Yahoo (www.yahoo.com), and Hotmail (www. hotmail.com). Still other programs are proprietary and part of **PMS** (Property Management Systems). For example, AlphaNet (www.alphaNet. net) introduced an e-mail client, InnMail, with a unique e-mail-to-fax capability. Guests staying in InnFax-equipped rooms are able to receive both a private fax number and a private e-mail address. E-mail messages sent to this private address will automatically print on the InnFax machine. In the summer of

TABLE 5.3	
A Selected List of Desktop E-Mail Programs	
PROGRAMS	FEATURES
Microsoft Office 2000 www.microsoft.com/office	A complete suite that includes Access, PowerPoint, Excel, Word, and the Outlook e-mail program. These can incorporate documents or files from those applications to create customized e-mail.
ArialSoft Enterprise, 5.0 www.arialsoftware.com	A very powerful program offering scheduling, HTML e-mail, and other higher-end features. Its users include Dell, 3Com, Citibank, and AMD.
MailWorkz Broadc@st HTML www.mailworkz.com	Broadc@st HTML boasts that it is the most effective program to send and manage bulk e-mail campaigns.
Gammadyne Mailer www.gammadyne.com	An incredibly powerful e-mail automation utility. Features include multitasking, direct delivery, list serving, autoresponding, autoforwarding, command-line support, exclusion lists, unlimited mailing list size, message preview, personalized attachments and duplicate elimination.

2001, Doubletree Hotels and Suites entered into an agreement with AlphaNet, making it the exclusive provider of in-room fax services for its properties. The first four Doubletree Hotels to install InnFax included those in New York, Boston, Pasadena, and Glenview.

It is estimated that by 2001, Internet access will be provided in approximately 100,000 guest rooms in the United States. According to Jupiter Communications (www.jmm.com), by 2002, 4 million guest rooms will include some kind of Internet access. Guest room connectivity varies by type and includes modem, wireless, Ethernet, DSL, in-room PC, or television-based Internet access. In fact, one of the hottest areas in hospitality and tourism technology is in-room Internet service, with e-mail access being demanded most by customers. In a hotel room, cable television, phone and fax are no longer enough. Travelers, both leisure and business, are demanding that their hotel rooms be equipped with Internet access so that they can at least check their e-mails. Some hotels even provide network printers for guests to print out their e-mail documents. For instance, at the luxurious Royal Sonesta Hotel in New Orleans, guests simply plug in their laptop to the wall jack and start their Internet browser or e-mail package. There is no laptop reconfiguration necessary, and the transition is seamless.

Hospitality and tourism companies are increasingly aggressive in adopting new technologies, although this is not always the case. Starbucks Corp., for example, offers high-speed wireless LAN access to its customers in over 1,000 of its world wide outlets. (www.starbucks.com 2003). Starbucks hopes that access to the technology will drive traffic into its coffee shops during off-peak postbreakfast hours. With increasing demand from its customers, Starbucks, after studying several technologies, decided to adopt wireless LAN, which is more suitable for people on the go.

E-mail is also being used widely to serve the needs of Starbucks' internal customers: the employees. The company can use its Intranet for e-mail programs to increase employee productivity, as was outlined in Table 5.1. Most of the e-mail programs today are powerful enough to handle other messaging functions, such as scheduling and document sharing.

E-Newsletters

An e-newsletter is a powerful way to bring your company's latest news about products and services to your customers. With an e-newsletter, you can send targeted HTML and text e-mail information to your customers. Microsoft's Listbuilder (www.listbuilder.com) enables a company to place a subscriber profile page on its Web site so that the customer can opt to sign in as a subscriber. Once subscribed, the customer will receive customized e-newsletters on scheduled dates.

One of the biggest advantages of the e-newsletter over other types of electronic communications is that the readers have voluntarily consented to receive them based on their particular areas of interest. It helps ensure that the content of the e-newsletter is of interest to the reader and that it is more likely to be read. A second advantage is that newsletters are sent on a predetermined schedule, providing a high degree of consistency in terms of content and format. In the next chapter, we discuss in more detail how companies are using e-newsletters for marketing purposes.

Mailing Lists

In Chapter 2, we discussed in great detail what a Mailing List is. A Mailing List is a list of e-mail addresses that is used to send certain messages or announcements to many people at once. These are usually subscribers of the list and are expected to share a common interest in the contents of the message. As you may recall, a Mailing List is different from a traditional mailing list, which is simply a collection of names and addresses used for mailing purposes.

A Mailing List is a popular way to communicate and share information with customers and business partners. Since a Mailing List contains e-mail addresses of the people who typically share the same interests and who subscribe voluntarily to the list, companies have a great way to create a virtual community—to reach them with upcoming sales, promotions, and hot deals as well as customer relations announcements and updates. It is important to know that a Mailing List allows all subscribers to send e-mail messages to the list. In other words, not only can the company that owns the Mailing List send marketing and other types of information to the subscribers of the list,

Example 1: To subscribe, send any message to Join-Johndoe@whatever.com. To unsubscribe, forward this message to leave-Johndoe@whatever.com.

Example 2: To unsubscribe, send a message to leave-Johndoe@whatever.com with only "unsubscribe leave-Johndoe" (without quotes) in the message body. We will not sell, rent, or disclose your e-mail address to third parties. Any exception to this policy will be made only with your permission.

but every subscriber can also send messages to the list to express his or her views. For this reason, it is advisable to have a managed Mailing List, as discussed in Chapter 2.

To acquire such a Mailing List, you should consider placing a subscription option in your Web site and ask your visitors to sign up. To keep subscribers on the Mailing List, you should send only valuable information and tips that you know your subscribers will want. You should also include a concise privacy statement to ensure that protecting collected personal information is a top priority. The privacy statement should tell subscribers that you will not sell their name or any personal information to any other source.

Your Mailing List should allow users to be removed, and you need to faithfully carry out your promise. In each message you send out, you should include a brief explanation of how the recipient signed up for your Mailing List and provide quick and easy instructions on how to unsubscribe. You should never send out e-mail to someone who has not requested to be on your list. Table 5.4 provides a few examples of how these statements should look. Mailing Lists are often used for marketing purposes. In the next chapter, we discuss its use in marketing.

E-Mail Mailing Lists

An e-mail mailing list is like a traditional mailing list that is used to send messages and information to everyone on the list at the same time. The difference is that, instead of postal mailing addresses, the mailing list contains e-mail addresses. This is a one-way communication tool. Typically, people who are on a mailing list share some common interest or characteristics. For this reason, companies can use an e-mail mailing list to target a desirable group or groups of consumers.

There are many ways you can acquire an e-mail mailing list. One way is to place a sign-up option on your Web site for your customers or visitors. This is a good strategy, as it offers some incentive for visitors to sign up. Another way is to ask for e-mail addresses when you send out traditional communication materials, such as flyers, newsletters or catalogs. They can be instructed either to go to your Web site to sign up or to send an e-mail message directly to an e-mail address you provide them. This is usually used to collect e-mail addresses of both existing and prospective customers.

Finally, you can buy e-mail mailing lists from vendors who collect such lists by various means. It is important that you check the credibility of vendors before you buy the list. Furthermore, you need to make sure that the particular mailing list you are interested in contains only e-mail addresses that have been collected with the consent of the people who sign up for the list. Without such permission, you may end up sending out "spamming" e-mail without the permission of the targeted people. If you do so, you may be in violation of the law.

DISCUSSION FORUMS AND FAQS

Discussion forums are a convenient way to collect your customers' opinions, input, concerns and comments in one central place. This input is shared by all your online visitors, who can respond to such input whenever they want. Like a Mailing List, discussion forums often are grouped by common interests, so you, can build virtual communities around them. Therefore, these people are more likely to come back and become loyal customers.

FAQs (frequently asked questions) are a great way of communicating with customers. A FAQs section placed on your Web site can be viewed 24/7, saving a lot of time and labor. The answers to the questions should be simple and easy to understand. Most of all, the questions must be ones that customers are concerned with. You can create these questions based on our own expectations or selected from questions submitted to you by customers. Marriott's Web site (www.marriott.com) has a nicely constructed section of FAQs.

LIVE ONLINE CHAT

Live online chat has become an increasingly popular means of instant communication with customers and online visitors. It is fast and convenient. Instead of picking up a phone to call, visitors can click on the chat room and talk live with a customer service representative online. Without this ability, most visitors who use their home phone line to connect to the Internet will have to log off the Internet to use the phone. This tends to drive away customers who have instant questions about your products or services. Live chat can be provided around the clock, only during business hours, or on a regular schedule. Live chat can be expensive to a business if it has to hire additional staff to oversee the chat room.

WEBCASTING

A sophisticated form of live chat is the **Webcasting** or **Web conference,** in which you can view streaming videos and interact with the conference attendants live on the Web. **Streaming video** is a means of communication that allows you to play sound or video in real time as it is downloaded from the Internet. The difference between streaming and downloaded media lies in the fact that downloaded media are sent to the online visitor's local computer as a readable file to play later, while streaming media play the data as they are being transferred to the local computer. Streaming media start playing almost as soon as the online visitor selects them. Downloaded media must arrive in a complete and uncorrupted form on a local hard drive.

A **plug-in** is required to play streaming video. A plug-in decompresses and plays the data as they are transferred to the local computer over the Web. Streaming audio or video avoids the delay entailed in downloading an entire file and then playing it with a helper application. Streaming, however, requires a fast connection and a computer powerful enough to execute the decompression algorithm in real time. The Internet Explorer browser uses Microsoft Windows Media Player as a plug-in, eliminating the need to use other plug-ins.

However, there are streaming videos with special formats that require corresponding plug-ins in order to play. Some of these special plug-ins include Apple's **QuickTime** (www.apple.com/quicktime/download) and RealPlayer's **RealPlayer** (www.real.com). QuickTime is Apple's streaming video plug-in for handling video, sound, animation, graphics, text, music and even 360-degree virtual reality scenes.

5.7 CONCLUSION

The Internet has changed not only the way we think about communication but also how we communicate. It has given us a new set of communication tools that, if used properly, can dramatically increase the efficiency and effectiveness of communication. Successful e-commerce requires a good communication strategy to attract, keep, retain, and service the customers. Since hospitality and tourism services and products are information dependent, Internet communication becomes even more important to the hospitality and tourism companies than to any other industries.

In the age of the Internet, the rules of communication have changed, too. Issues of security, reliability, and privacy become big concerns to both business and consumers. On the one hand, the Internet has made communication much easier, more convenient, and faster, but on the other, it has created opportunities for abuses in communication. Spams not only are unwelcome by consumers but are also against the law. Only when a business respects the law and consumers' rights can Internet communication be efficient and effective.

KEY WORDS AND TERMS

Virtual Communities/E-Communities	Discussion forums
Intranet	FAQs
Extranet	Webcasting/Web Conference
Firewall	Streaming Video
Certification Authority	Plug-in
Personalization	QuickTime
PMS	RealPlayer

SUMMARY

The Internet is quickly being adopted as one of the most important media of communication. It breaks down the three major barriers of communication: time, space, and speed. Communication using Internet technology can be in different platforms. There are three communication platforms: The Internet is open to the public, Intranets are private and used for internal company communications, and Extranets are an extension of Intranets to the Internet for B2B and B2C communications.

There are many tools that you can use to communicate over the Internet. These include but are not limited to e-mail, e-newsletters, mailing lists, e-mail mailing lists, discussion forums, FAQs, live online chat, and Webcasting with streaming audio and video.

WEB RESOURCES

www.eCRMguide.com

www.emaildoctor.info

www.internetday.com

http://catalog.com/vivian/mailing-list-providers.html

www.realnetworks.com

CASE STUDY: *Dr. Pepper/Seven Up, Inc.*

Dr. Pepper/Seven Up, Inc. (DPSU), is about great brands and great people. The people at DPSU rely heavily on their corporate Intranet site, FizzBiz, to stay informed and aware of their business, their company and their brands. Communication of information through technology has always been the primary focus of FizzBiz, but as the site evolves, other possibilities are presenting themselves. So, sit back with a can of your favorite DPSU soft drink and see what can be done with a successful corporate Intranet site—you will see that the possibilities are as extensive as the DPSU brand portfolio.

In 1995, when Cadbury Schweppes acquired DPSU, things began to change rapidly for the company and its employees. At that time, the company communicated with its employees through *Kaleidescope,* a monthly newsletter. The news in the publication was often out of date by the time employees read it. More urgent matters had to be communicated via voice-mail messages to each employee's telephone extension or through e-mail. Like any mailing list with 1,200 users, high volumes of messages resulted in clutter and chaos. According to Philippa Dworkin, vice president of corporate communications, "Our employee communications system was archaic—nearly nonexistent. Our people needed to better understand where we were as a company and where we were going."

In 1997, DPSU began to look for a solution to their communication problems. Dworkin and the former president and chief executive officer, Todd Stitzer, set a goal of "creating a workforce with a greater understanding of our overall business and the role that they play in the company's success." After researching the use of Intranet systems at other large corporations, the Corporate Communications Department believed that an Intranet at DPSU would achieve the goal. Dworkin felt that "an Intranet offered us the ability to talk with our employees instantly, rapidly garner feedback from them, and even operate like a wire service, but with the pictures and graphics that make a newsletter easy to read."

There was another reason to start an Intranet site at DPSU: bottler reimbursements. Before FizzBiz, field sales employees had to fax reimbursement requests for bottlers' shared marketing and media expenses. A paper trail ensued before the information was put into the computer system at DPSU by way of data entry. The Intranet site would allow field sales employees to input the marketing requests directly into the marketing funds system. After some intensive cost benefit research, DPSU found that developing the marketing funds Intranet application would offset the costs for developing the entire Intranet site. DPSU also calculated that they would save $80,000 annually on printing costs alone, as FizzBiz would significantly reduce the amount of corporate printed material.

When FizzBiz launched on September 9, 1998, the site was basic. DPSU's corporate Intranet site included an electronic version of *Kaleidoscope* and the ever-important marketing funds reimbursement application. There were also organizational charts, media releases, job postings, compensation and benefits information, industry information, cafeteria menus and company phone numbers.

Frequent improvements, a replacement of the firm used for Web development, and even a relaunch of the site made FizzBiz the successful Intranet site it is today. In 1999, an industry news section was added to the home page. Other improvements included an online employee suggestion box, having ACNielson Topline Reports available for download and adding new sales tools for Fountain Foodservice field salespeople. In 2000, DPSU added "FizzBiz Forums," which allowed employees to post messages in different forums, such as Personal Announcements and Buy/Sell/Trade.

Many of the improvements aided employee productivity. For example, the Fountain Foodservice page on the site allows salespeople to get everything they need to be more effective and efficient in the field. Everything from syndicated data to PowerPoint presentations to sell sheets and order forms are available with the click of the mouse. Users throughout the company save time and phone calls by using the site for travel reservation assistance, the employee directory and computer-based training capabilities. Departments are able to add and customize their own pages, thus increasing work productivity.

All the additions and improvements took FizzBiz from the basic Intranet site that it was at first launch to the fresh and interactive one that it is now. For example, employees now use FizzBiz to register electronically for the national sales meeting and other corporate meetings or incentives. Besides some of the sections and applications previously mentioned, the home page for FizzBiz also features a search engine, a listing of the latest DPSU memos, a "What's New to FizzBiz" section, a "What's Up at DPSU" section, a company calendar and organizational announcements. Employees are able to access the Internet from FizzBiz, making access to both the Intranet and the Internet unlimited at DPSU. FizzBiz is not used for B2B communication or e-commerce, but DPSU does run a separate Extranet for their bottlers that accomplishes some of these applications.

The Corporate Communications Department is delighted with the success of FizzBiz. John Parkin, employee communications manager, says, "It has allowed DPSU to communicate more information than ever before and open up communication avenues that we had never even considered before." While FizzBiz is functioning quite well as an interactive Intranet site, DPSU sees more possibilities on the horizon by moving the site into the collaborative stage of Intranets. Here, each department will be able to create "sub" work areas where employees can work together on projects in a sort of "virtual office." Other planned improvements include an online company store and a personalized version of the home page for each employee. The personalized FizzBiz home page would include areas for each person's e-mail, a personalized calendar of events, and information tailored to what each individual employee is interested in. Parkin says, "My long-term utopian vision is that people can come to work in the morning, log into FizzBiz, and stay within it all day. Basically, the site becomes their permanent work area."

DPSU's steadfast determination to make FizzBiz the success it is today suggests that the future possibilities for what the site can do will most likely become a reality in the near future. Between now and then, however, the site will always serve to illustrate what can be done with a successful corporate Intranet site.

QUESTIONS TO PONDER:

1. What kinds of benefits has DPSU received from implementing an Intranet?
2. What was the situation for internal communication before the introduction of an Intranet?
3. How has the productivity of the employees improved by using an Intranet?
4. Why do employees of DPSU embrace an Intranet?
5. Do you think that DPSU put too much trust into their employees in terms of giving them free hands to use the Intranet? What kind of problems do you think this can create?

SOURCE: Dr. Pepper/Seven Up, Inc.

REVIEW QUESTIONS

1. What does International eCommerce, Inc., provide for hotel communications?
2. Describe the differences between the Internet, Intranets, and Extranets.
3. How can a business use the Internet for communication?
4. How can a business use an Intranet for communication?
5. How can a business use an Extranet for communication?
6. Why does an Extranet require tough security and privacy measures?
7. What is the difference between a mailing list and an e-mail mailing list?
8. What is the difference between e-mail and an e-newsletter?
9. Describe the benefits of using permission marketing.
10. What is the difference between downloading a file and streaming video?
11. What is Webcasting?

REFERENCES

www.starbucks.com, 2003.

For additional Travel and Tourism resources, go to www.Hospitality-Tourism.delmar.com

6

E-MARKETING AND INFORMATION DISTRIBUTION

LEARNING OBJECTIVES

After you complete your study of this chapter, you should be able to:

- Know how to use e-mail for marketing communications.
- Understand the difference between e-mail and e-newsletters when used for marketing purposes.
- Know how to use Usenet and mailing lists for marketing.
- Use chat rooms for marketing.
- Build a successful Web site to increase customer loyalty.
- Know how to conduct advertising, promotion, and public relations on the Internet.
- Understand how to combine traditional marketing with e-marketing to increase the effectiveness of a marketing campaign.
- Understand push and pull marketing, partnership marketing, and Webcasting.

6.1 INTRODUCTION

Marketing is a continuous process of matching products and services to the needs and wants of consumers by planning, research, implementation, control, and evaluation in order to achieve the goals and objectives of an organization. The classic "four Ps" of marketing are product, place, price, and promotion. are used to account for the unique nature of the industry. The four Ps are partnership, people, packaging, and programming. The Internet has created a new medium of communication with which the eight Ps take on new meanings and should be executed with different strategies.

Internet marketing, or e-marketing, like its traditional counterpart, requires a solid marketing plan with strategies based on both research and common sense. In addition, e-marketing is not an isolated activity for the traditional marketing process. For a hospitality and tourism company, e-marketing should be placed in the context of **total marketing communication** (TMC). TMC proposes that all marketing activities for a company should be complementary to each other and their total sum of effect should be consistent with the company's preset marketing goals and objectives. With this view, traditional means of marketing and e-marketing, though different, should be utilized to serve a common and unified marketing objective for a company.

E-marketing, however, differs in many ways from traditional marketing in that it operates in a total new environment in terms of time, speed, market segmentation, data-collecting means, information distribution and brand-building. The Internet has made some marketing activities much easier while rending others more difficult to carry out. For example, it makes tracking advertising online much easier, but makes retaining customers much more difficult with the ever-increasing power of online consumers, who, with a click of the mouse, can leave your site at a fraction of a second and may never come back again. E-marketing offers both new opportunities and challenges at the same time.

6.2 E-MARKETING PLAN

E-marketing, as pointed out previously, should be part of an e-commerce business' total marketing communication plan. Once its relationship with the traditional marketing activities, if any, is set, the next step is to design a marketing plan with a clear marketing objective. Launching a marketing campaign without an objective is like driving your car for vacation without knowing which destination you are going to. In e-marketing planning, you still have to ask the following traditional marketing questions.

- ❏ Where are you now (your product/service; your market positioning)?
- ❏ Where are you going to be (marketing objectives, market positioning)?
- ❏ How are you going to get there (marketing strategies; marketing mix, budgeting)?
- ❏ How do you make sure you get there (implementation)?
- ❏ How do you know you get there (measurement; evaluation)?

Just like traditional marketing, large and small e-commerce businesses use different marketing strategies. Generally speaking, large e-commerce businesses such as Travelocity.com have the financial clout to go for a large segment of the population with aggressive marketing campaign for attracting and retaining customers. Small and new e-commerce businesses have to find niches to succeed. Bedandbreakfast.com saw an unfilled niche in providing information and services in the bed-and-breakfast online market. Instead of trying to be a site for all types of lodging, it focuses on the bed-and-breakfast. The company wants the consumers to remember the site and use it when they think of bed-and-breakfast. It is obvious that bedandbreakfast.com knows its market position and employs right marketing strategies to achieve its goals.

In e-commerce, it is important that you have a marketing plan before you build a Web site, as a well-thought-out plan plays a key role in determining the type, layout, and style of the site to be built. For small business, the marketing plan should define the **unique selling proposition** (USP). The USP defines what makes your business unique from every other competitor in a particular field and sorts out the precise niche that your e-commerce seeks to fill. For instance, the Bedandbreakfast.com's USP could be as follows: "The Bed and Breakfast is committed to being your one source for every kind of bed-and-breakfast inns in the world. We not only provide quality information and reservation service but also provide related services to enhance your travel experience."

6.3 INTERNET MARKETING TOOLS

E-MAIL MARKETING

E-mail marketing can be an inexpensive but effective way of bringing marketing information to a target audience. According to a report issued by Forrester Research (Schwartz 2000), mailing out a catalog can cost $1 per customer, while a personalized e-mail costs about 5 cents. In addition, e-mail messages have been found to be more effective than the more expensive banner advertisement. It was reported that the **click-through** rate by consumers reading banner advertisements was only less than 1% but the response to e-mail messages was at about 10%. It is not surprising that e-mail has become one of the most popular means of marketing for business. It is estimated that by 2004, American business marketers will send almost 210 billion e-mail messages (Schwartz 2000).

For consumers, e-mail has become one of the most common ways of communication in the age of the Internet. Indeed, in the United States, the number of e-mail users will have jumped from an estimated 20 million in 1996 to predicted 105 million by 2002. In 1996, it was estimated that there were 500 million e-mail messages being sent per day, and that number will increase to 1.5 billion per day in 2002 (Deitel et al. 2001). Today, we can be almost certain that as long as one can use the Internet, one most likely will own an e-mail account. By asking your customers to provide you with their e-mail addresses, you can compile an e-mail list for various purposes, including marketing.

E-mail marketing offers several advantages that other types of online media can only dream of. First, an e-mail message can be personalized and the content customized. **Personization** and **customerization** are two of the most important benefits of using e-mail marking. Both increase the effectiveness of the marketing message. Second, e-mail can deliver timely marketing information to target consumers. In today's rapidly changing world, nothing beats timely information. Third, e-mail messages stays in the inbox of consumers until read or deleted. It is harder to ignore an e-mail message than an online banner ad. Finally, the effectiveness of an e-mail message can be measured more precisely and instantly.

Mechanisms can be built into an e-mail message so that when the message is opened and read, it will send back a message to that effect, telling marketers instantly how many targeted consumers opened the e-mail. If the e-mail contains Web links and the consumer clicks on the link, that can also be documented. It is not exaggerating to say that e-mail probably is the most measurable marketing medium ever. Finally, e-mail marketing has the shortest response time than any other medium. Typically, consumers take action when they are exposed to the message, either deleting or ignoring it or opening and reading it. Either way, e-mail marketers will know how effective their marketing campaign is.

The success of an e-mail marketing campaign depends largely on the following factors:

❏ Correctly identifying the target audience
❏ Personalizing the e-mail
❏ Customizing the message
❏ Delivering only the content that the consumer needs and wants
❏ Building consumer trust by providing assurance of privacy and the option to stop receiving the e-mail

Like traditional marketing, identification of target consumers is an important step in designing an Internet marketing plan. To a large extent, mass marketing has died in the age of Internet marketing. Internet marketing is all about choosing the right market segmentation, finding the strategy and delivering a **customized marketing message** to the target market. Identifying a right target audience requires research, which is discussed in detail in Chapter 9.

An important step in segmenting the online consumers is to understand their online behaviors. According to Krishnamurthy (2003), online consumers can be classified into six segments: **Simpliers, Surfers, Bargainers, Connectors, Routiners**, and **Sportsters**. Simpliers, as the name suggests, respond positively to anything that is easy, convenient, ready-made, and hassle-free. They do not like things that are impulsive, interfering, and unsolicited. Accordingly, sophisticated Web site designs, popup banners ads, lengthy buying process, spam e-mails are turn-offs for this group of people.

Surfers spend more time than any other groups of online consumers. They are online for various reasons and therefore they are the least loyal consumers. They tend to move from site to site, checking out sites and features and looking for new online experience. To attract this group of consumers and retain them can be a daunting task. The best way to appeal to them is to make your site as interesting, informative, and innovative as possible, so that each visit to your site is a new experience.

Bargainers come online for great deals. Although they are not the majority online, most of them have purchased something at least once online. In another words, they will buy if prices are good and of value. They are the true bargain hunters. Most of the auction e-commerce businesses are very attractive to this group of consumers. Online travel agencies such as orbitz.com and expedia.com make use of pricing strategies to attract them.

Connectors use the Internet to connect to the outside world. Their main interest is using the Internet for communication. They like to use e-mails, frequent chat rooms, and visit online greeting card sites. They are mostly new to the Internet. They can be cultivated by providing friendly communication service and earning their trust. They can be potential customers when they become more mature in their Internet experience.

Routiners are those who come online for news and financial information. Hospitality and tourism e-commerce sites can add travel-related news to ticket/reservation-only features to attract this group of people. Routiners can be very loyal customers since their interest is in reliable news and information rather than surfing experience. It is harder, however, to make them pay for the service.

Sportsters use the Internet for sports and entertainment. These consumers respond very negatively to sites that are boring. A boring site can be due to two reasons: unattractive layout and design or lack of interesting contents. For hospitality and tourism Web sites, making the site visit an interesting experience can increase the loyalty from these consumers.

The next step is to find ways to reach them. You can collect target audience information by yourself or by resorting to a third party for customers information and e-mail addresses. There are many ways to collect the e-mail addresses of customers or online visitors. In the previous chapter, we discussed this issue. Here we recap some of the major methods. First, you can either use the e-mail addresses you have already collected through your customer database or mail out a letter to ask for e-mail addresses. Another way is to ask your visitors to sign in or register on your Web site in exchange for discounts or free e-mail information about products or services they are interested in.

There are companies who specialize in so-called **opt-in e-mail marketing.** These companies maintain a large database of visitors' e-mail addresses with the permission of those visitors to use their e-mail addresses for marketing purposes. You can contact these firms for lists of e-mail addresses. Two of these companies are Yesmail.com (www.yesmail.com) and Postmasterdirect.com (www.postmasterdirect.com). Typically, each address costs between 10 and 40 cents, and the company can send out the e-mail message for you if you prefer (Fine 2001).

Once you have obtained the customer's e-mail list by market segmentation, you can personalize your message by using the customer's name. This is similar to how a front-desk receptionist greets guests by their first names, creating a sense of individual attention and respect. Consumers are more likely to take a look at the content of the e-mail when they see their names in the greetings.

The next step is to customize the content, which means to deliver only the information that would be of interest to consumers. This is important not only because it is more effective and more likely to generate a **response rate,** or the percentage of responses generated from the target market, but also because you can avoid being accused of **spamming,** or sending mass e-mails to people who have not indicated an interest in receiving e-mail from you.

There are many companies that specialize in e-mail marketing. The two previously mentioned companies that offer mailing lists, Yesmail.com and Postmasterdirect.com, also provide e-mail services. Another company, LifeMinders (www.lifeminders.com), sends highly personalized e-mail messages in more than 20 categories to its member base. These targeted messages are based on detailed member profiles that are obtained during the permission-based registration process. When you visit LifeMinders Web site, you are invited to register your interest with the company in exchange for free information by e-mail.

Yesmail provides e-mail marketing solutions for customer retention and acquisition. Yesmail's proprietary e-mail marketing technology, YesConnect™, allows marketers to select audiences, acquire counts, develop messages, schedule delivery, and track results in real time. This technology enables a marketer to pinpoint the audience most responsive to your e-mail campaign and messages. It helps create and test a message, schedule delivery of a campaign, and track campaign results. In addition, it can track beyond click-through by identifying audience segments that clicked through on the advertised offer but did not follow through. Later, you can increase your **return of investment** (ROI) by remarketing to these nonconverters, giving them a second chance to consider and act on the advertised offer.

One issue in e-mail marketing that concerns both customers and marketers is spamming. Spamming can cause several problems for a business. First, spamming can cause hard feelings against a business from the targeted receivers since they feel their privacy is being violated. Second, spammed messages will not be effective since they most likely are not tailored to the needs and wants of the targeted receivers. Finally, spamming will most likely be outlawed in the future, as the federal government is considering introducing legislation, such as the Unsolicited Electronic Mail Act, to protect legitimate e-mail communication and consumer privacy.

E-mail marketing is no longer limited to plain text messages. Today, there are many innovative ways to deliver customized e-mail marketing messages. For instance, instead of plain text, e-mail messages can be delivered and viewed in **HTML format,** making it possible to present marketing information in color and graphics. In fact, an HTML e-mail message looks and feels like a Web document that comes with all the features of the Web, such as hyperlinks, color, sound, and graphics. E-mail messages can also come with streaming audio and video to provide a multimedia presentation.

Some Internet companies, such as MediaRing.com (www.mediaring. com), provide their customers with the capability to send e-mail with streaming audio to increase the personal touch of the e-mail message. Shockwave. com (www.shockwave.com), on the other hand, sends e-mail messages to its customers with streaming video. Another company, Mindarrow.com (www.mindarrow.com), uses a program called MindArrow RadicalMail™, which has the capability to seamlessly combine streaming video, audio, Macromedia® Flash™, or e-commerce within any e-mail message or to stream video from banner ads or your Web site with no plug-ins.

However, it is important to realize that customers may use different e-mail clients (that is, programs) to read their e-mail. Unfortunately, not all e-mail clients can handle information-rich messages such as streaming audio and video or HTML-formatted e-mail. It is critical that marketers make sure that the targeted customers can read these messages before utilizing these new innovations.

An effective way to collect your targeted customers' e-mail addresses for marketing purposes and avoid being accused of spamming is to ask the consumers who visit your site to register their e-mail address and then ask if they would give permission to use their addresses to send information regarding certain products or services they have expressed interest in. This practice results in the opt-in e-mail marketing discussed previously. Many companies even offer incentives to entice their customers to read e-mail. For example, Hilton offers its Hilton Honors members an incentive program called e-Rewards. It is a sponsored program that pays members to read e-mail. Among the sponsors are Blockbuster Inc., Delta Airlines, Hertz, and United Airlines.

When using opt-in e-mail marketing, it is imperative to provide the receiver with an option to opt out. For long-term customer relationships, building trust in your company should outweigh any short-term gain in forcing exposure to your marketing messages. In addition, even if you have the permission to send marketing e-mail messages, you should make sure that you do not overwhelm your customers with excessive e-mail messages or unsolicited contents.

E-NEWSLETTER MARKETING

An e-newsletter is a special kind of e-mail published and sent to the target audience on a regular basis. It has the convenience of e-mail as well as the power of a newsletter in which customized information and marketing message can be presented in an attractive way. Most e-newsletters today are sent to targeted consumers on a permission basis and often are part of the customer service that is built into a company's Web site. A common approach is to ask the site's visitors to sign up for an e-mail newsletter, which can be published daily, weekly, or monthly. There are many free e-newsletter publishers, including Yahoo! Groups (www.yahoogroups.com) and Topica (www.topica.com).

Strategies are needed to make the best use of an e-newsletter. First, an e-newsletter give readers a reason to return to the company's Web site to get more information. The e-newsletter should be interesting and valuable when introducing a new product or offering special sales and offers. An e-newsletter should be well designed and brief. If you want your readers to get more details, you can provide a link to your Web site for further information. You need to grasp the attention of readers with just a few lines. Remember that most of your readers might have dozens of e-mails to read every day. They will not want to spend all their time reading your long e-newsletter. You should also remember that just because people give you permission to send them e-newsletters does not mean that they will continue to give that permission. You should always provide a means for them to opt out in every e-newsletter sent to them. It shows that you respect their rights and privacy. Table 6.1 shows an example of an opt-in e-newsletter from Northwest Airlines.

There are companies specialized in helping you develop a business e-newsletter. One of these is iMakeNews (www.imakenews.com). This is an **application service provider** (ASP) that focuses exclusively on the full cycle of creating and distributing e-newsletters. An ASP is an information technology company that offers a complete access solution over the Internet to applications and related services that would otherwise have to be located in an individual's or organization's computer. For example, MakeNews provides its own proprietary software that allows individuals to create and distribute e-newsletters right on the Web. Alternatively, you can still find a free e-newsletter service if

TABLE 6.1
Northwest Airlines' Opt-in E-Newsletter

Dear Northwest Airlines WorldPerks Member:

Fuel up your WorldPerks Account with up to 15,000 WorldPerks Bonus Miles. When you sign up for Sprint® Nickel Nights℠ residential long distance, Sprint will deposit 5,000 WorldPerks Bonus Miles in your account after your first, sixth, and twelfth month invoices.

You will earn 5 miles for every dollar you spend each month with Sprint (exclusive of taxes and credits), and 7 miles if you are an Elite member. Visit http://csg.sprint.com/offsite/nwa_0201_e-mail/nickelnights_jump.html to sign up!

This is a post-only mailing. Please do not respond to this message unless you wish to unsubscribe. To unsubscribe, please reply to us and type "unsubscribe" in the subject line or visit NWA Promotional E-mail Registration at http://www.nwa.com/deals/unreg.html. For a response to any other correspondence, please send an e-mail to TTNWA@nwa.com.

you are willing to do a little bit more of the work. YourMailinglistProvider (www.yourmailinglistprovider.com) provides a free, easy-to-use mailing list to set up an e-newsletter for a site. After you sign up for an account, you will be given a piece of HTML code that you can copy and paste into one of your Web pages source code. The HTML code will show up on your site as an invitation for visitors to subscribe to your e-newsletter.

USENET AND MAILING LIST MARKETING

As discussed in Chapter 2, Usenet is a distributed bulletin board system (BBS) where people can log in and post and read messages, just like you can use a pin to post a message on a bulletin board. Unlike e-mail and e-newsletters, in Usenet you do not receive messages delivered to your e-mail box. Instead, you go to the BBS system, many of which are now Web based. A company can post information about its products and services if the information posted fits the interest of the discussion group. There are thousands of interest groups, as Usenet is probably the largest decentralized information database on the Internet.

Ethical issues might arise as to whether you can or should use Usenet newsgroups for commercial purposes. In addition, readers might find it objectionable if they discover that you are trying to market products or services to them in a noncommercial environment. There are ways in which you can overcome these problems. First, a company should be honest about its purpose and be truthful about its products and services. Second, a company should post only information that is relevant to the interest group. If postings are for educational and informational purposes or are intended to clear up a misconception about a company's product, readers likely will be more accepting of the message. Finally, there are no regulations that prohibit a company from creating its own newsgroups for the customers of the product or service who are interested in updated news and information. A company can set up a newsgroup specifically for such interested people to share information and exchange views. In newsgroup marketing, marketers are taking some risks since people who are not happy with the product or service may use this forum to express and spread their dissatisfaction and bring an unfavorable impression on the business.

Mailing Lists, as discussed in Chapter 2, are a subscriber-based two-way e-mail system for message sharing and communication. It is highly interactive and instant. When a subscriber sends a message to a Mailing List, the list will distribute it immediately to all the other subscribers of the Mailing List. In a way, a Mailing List and Usenet have something in common: Both are based on the concept that people with the same interests will want to share information with each other. Therefore, each Mailing List typically is formed by a group of people with the same interests.

Like Usenet marketing, Mailing List marketing has the same potential risks that Usenet does. However, if the product or service matches the interests of the subscribed readers and a company is honest about the benefits and quality of the marketed product or service, these messages might still find welcoming readers. Promotional messages can be welcomed as well if they honestly represent the truth.

There are commercial Mailing List programs on the market that you can use to create your own Mailing List for those customers who want to share information and receive offers and promotions. The three most popular Mailing List programs are the following:

❑ Listserv (www.lsoft.com)
❑ Majordomo (www.greatcircle.com/majordomo)
❑ ListProc (www.cren.net/listproc)

The popularity of the Listserv program can be seen from Table 6.2.

TABLE 6.2 Listserv Statistics	
Number of public lists	52,542
Number of local lists	127,173
Total number of lists	179,715
Total membership (public + local)	89,803,305
Total messages delivered a day	34,259,500

SOURCE: Listserv (www.lsoft.com), 2003.

CHATROOM MARKETING

A chatroom is a real-time interactive Internet communication tool. Like newsgroups in Usenet, a chatroom is often the gathering place for people with a common interest, although not as commonly defined as the former. Marketers in the hospitality and tourism industry can identify chatrooms to see what travelers are talking about and may choose to participate in the chat to provide information about their products or services that are of interest to the chatters. Since people regard chatters as ordinary people like themselves, the information provided will be much more trustworthy. However, cautions need to be taken so as not to provide false or harmful information, which is very unethical and, if discovered, will ruin a company's reputation.

THE WEB SITE AS MARKETING TOOL

A well-designed Web site is probably the most powerful marketing tool on the Internet. A Web site tries to attract people by pulling them in with the promise of content, while e-mail pushes its message into a previous visitor's mailbox. A Web site, if it is a dot-com e-commerce business, is an online storefront. It is a branch of a company (an office) if the company is a brick-and-mortar business. The quality of a Web site directly reflects the quality and image of the business it represents. Just like a retail store that wants to make repeat customers by satisfying customers' needs and wants, a Web site must be able to not only draw people to visit it but also make them come back again and again.

Just like Internet marketing requires a marketing plan, designing a Web site needs a **Web site construction plan** (WCP). A WCP defines the objectives and goals of a business and identifies the elements of a Web site. The plan should include three parts: before designing a Web site and during and after construction of the site. Before designing a Web site, ask these questions:

- ❏ What is the nature of business (product and service)?
- ❏ What is the purpose of the Web site? Information? Customer service? Selling and buying?
- ❏ Who are the existing customers, and who are likely to be the customers?
- ❏ What are the characteristics of the existing and potential customers? Young? Old? Male? Female? Active? Educated? Well off?
- ❏ Where are these customers (locally, regionally, nationally, or internationally)?

During the construction of a Web site, ask these questions:

- ❏ Can our Web site's visitors find the information they want?
- ❏ How easy can they find the needed information?

- ❏ How fast can they access the information?
- ❏ What mailing lists or newsgroups do they use? Or should we start one for them?
- ❏ How can we present the information in an attractive and interesting way? How do we define attractiveness and interestingness in the eyes of my visitors?
- ❏ What can we do to make them stay longer in my Web site?
- ❏ Are we able to answer questions right away should they have questions about our services and products? What can we do to make this type of communication possible? Can we afford to do that? If not, what can we do to satisfy our customers' communication needs?
- ❏ What will turn our Web site visitors "on" and "off"?
- ❏ What do we have in our Web site to give visitors a reason to come back again and again?
- ❏ What can we do to make these visitors always use our Web site as a starting point to look for information they want?
- ❏ Does our Web site enable us to find out who these visitors are?
- ❏ How can we build trust with our visitors? Privacy policy or statement? Security measures?
- ❏ What marketing tools can we use in the Web site?

After setting up a Web site, ask these questions:

- ❏ Can visitors find our Web site?
- ❏ Where and how can visitors find our Web site?
- ❏ How can we increase the probability that visitors can find our Web site?
- ❏ What are the means available for us to market our Web site? Registering in search engines? Banner ads? Affiliate programs? Customer communication? Traditional media?

The first important step in Web site marketing is to register the site with the main Web search engines (Wilson 2001a). Most search engines work by looking for titles and **Meta tags** in an HTML Web document. A Meta tag is an HTML tag that contains information about a Web page. It contains a description of the Web page, key words, and the page's title. The quickest way to find out how your competitors write their Meta tags is to go to their site and use the browser's source code feature to check it out. Another way to do a search on the product or service that you want to provide through your Web site and then see whose site comes up as the top ranking. You can then examine their Meta tags and learn from them.

According to Wilson (2001b), the following tips will increase the chances of a Web site being found by search engines:

1. **Write a page title.** Write a descriptive five- to eight-word title for each Web page since search engines search each Web page for matching titles. Use words that will catch the attention of visitors. Place the title at the top of the page between the <HEADER></HEADER> tags. It will look like this: <TITLE>the Internet as an Agent of Change—E-commerce and Information Technology in the Hospitality and Tourism Industry</TITLE>.

2. **List key words.** Online visitors use key words to look for information in search engines. Therefore, prepare a list of the most important key words that you think a typical visitor will use to search for information similar to what you provide in your Web site. This list should contain about 20 words. Place those words at the top of the page between the <HEADER></HEADER> tags. It will look like this: <META NAME = "KEYWORDS" CONTENT = "Internet, e-commerce, internet marketing, online marketing, e-mail marketing, hospitality and tourism, tourism, information technology, INTERNET MARKETING, Internet marketing, ... ">. Do not use the same key word more than three times since that is considered to be key-word spamming by search engines. Also consider using both lower- and uppercase forms of your most important words since some search engines are case sensitive.

3. **Write a page description.** Search engines usually take the first couple of sentences from a Web page to use as a description of that page. Therefore, it is advisable to write the most important descriptive key words in the first couple of sentences. These descriptive sentences should not exceed 250 characters, including spaces. Place those words at the top of the page between the <HEADER></HEADER> tags in a Meta tag. It will look like this: <META NAME = "DESCRIPTION" CONTENT = "Understanding the e-commerce rules and tools, mastering the Internet marketing techniques and examine the impact of the Internet">.

4. **Submit the Web page to search engines.** After completing the Web site design, it is time to submit the Web pages to important search engines and directories. You can go either to individual search engines to register your Web pages or to a submission service, as Submit-It (http://submitit.linkexchange.com) or All4one Submission Machine (www.all4one.com/all4submit).

5. **Submit the page to other directories.** There are specialized Web site search engines and directories. It is a good policy to try to list the Web site in the search engines or directories that specialize in your area of business. For example, if you are in the bed-and-breakfast business, you can go to www.bedandbreakfast.com to submit the Web site. This site claims to have listings of 27,000 bed-and-breakfast inns around the world.

The second important consideration in Web site marketing is the ease with which your online visitors can access your site. The issue here is download speed. In designing your Web site, you should consider what type of Internet connections your existing and potential customers have in their homes and offices. If you build a fancy site with a lot of charts, colors, and graphics all on the same page, your visitors might have to wait for a long time for the page to display on their screens, especially if they use a standard modem connection, as discussed in Chapter 3. Research has shown that most visitors will leave a Web site even before its fully downloaded; Internet users are notoriously impatient (refer to Chapter 3 for connection considerations).

The third strategy for Web site marketing is to make it a Web portal for existing and potential customers. A **portal** is a gateway or entrance to a room or space. A **Web portal** is a Web site that offers a broad range of services, resources, and links for various interests or for a specified area of interest (Table 6.3). In this definition, most online service providers are portals since they offer a gateway to the Internet and provide a rich array of Internet tools, such as e-mail, newsgroups, discussion forums, and other resources. Most search engines have evolved into Web portals to increase their appeal to a larger audience.

Some of the largest travel Web sites are portals with diverse functions in a focused area of interest: travel. Sites such as Expedia.com (www.expedia.com) and Travelocity.com (www.travelocity.com) attempt to provide everything on their sites related to travel and trip planning. They do not attempt to serve other needs unless they are travel related.

Similarly, small businesses can make their Web sites focus on one area of interest for a specific type of customer. In other words, they can create a Web portal for a niche market. For instance, a travel agent specializing in ecotourism can create a Web portal that provides services and sources for the needs of those visitors who are interested in ecotourism. For example, some of the things to be included in the Web portal are the following:

❏ Planning of trips to and reservations for ecotourism destinations
❏ Maps and descriptions of the destinations

TABLE 6.3
Disney Brings Mickey Mouse to China via the Internet

BEIJING, Aug 27 (Reuters)—Entertainment and media giant The Walt Disney Co. launched a Chinese Web portal on the weekend in its first foray into a major foreign Internet market after online disappointments at home.

Actors dressed as the universally adored Mickey Mouse and his fictional companion, Minnie Mouse, joined Disney executives at a news conference in Beijing as they unveiled the Chinese Web site, www.disney.com.cn, late on Sunday.

SOURCE: http://biz.yahoo.com, 2002.

- ❏ Links to Usenet discussion groups and mailing lists that focus on ecotourism
- ❏ E-mail and e-newsletter on latest ecotourism news
- ❏ Online subscriptions to e-newsletters and mailing lists
- ❏ Links to other online travel reservation sites (do not be afraid to lose your customers; they will find other sites anyway)
- ❏ Links to other travel services

The idea is to keep the customers coming back again and again whenever they have any needs related to ecotourism or even outside ecotourism, as you have provided various types of links to travel services. Your customers can always come to your site first to look for the information they need. If they cannot find that information, they can still jump from your site to other travel-related sites to meet their needs. It saves them time and effort and provides them with a good reason to come back to your site.

A widely used strategy is to participate in an **affiliate marketing program.** An affiliate marketing program is similar to traditional partnership marketing, but they are very different in practice. An affiliate program is a form of part-nership in which a Web site owner or business pays or rewards other Web site owner(s) or businesses, called affiliates, for click-throughs on or leads from the advertisements displayed on an affiliate site. The affiliate marketing program is quickly becoming the dominant form of Web marketing and has been shown to have a positive impact on Web site marketing power.

An affiliate program can multiply marketing efforts since it acts as an extended sales force. By simply asking other Web sites to place a link to your site, you increase considerably your chances of being noticed by online visitors. You can enter into an affiliate program that allows displaying banner ads on each other's site.

One of the secrets of success for an affiliate program is to make sure that you and your partnered Web sites attract the kind of visitors who are most likely to be interested in the product or service you are offering. Web sites that are complementary or even competitive to your business are often the best candidates for affiliate programs. However, they need not be from the same industry or business. The critical consideration is the visitor's characteristics. If you are selling goods for women, then a Web site that is targeting women will be an excellent choice to be included in an affiliate program. You should think about Web sites that your target customers might visit. The more reciprocal links you have, the more the search engines will perceive you as popular and hence the higher your ratings.

The final strategy is to use *viral marketing.* It is the Internet version of word-of-mouth marketing. Viral marketing is quickly becoming one of the most important marketing techniques in e-commerce. There are many reasons for its popularity. First, the Internet has created many virtual communities and virtual social networks. Ideas and news pass among members of these online communities and networks much faster with a click than word-of-mouth. Second, it is much easier to spread the news and ideas from one consumer to another online since there are more communication tools available on the Internet to accomplish this task. Finally, the Internet is a network of networks and therefore the more people join the network, the faster the dissemination of information among the members of the network.

Viral marketing works under the assumption that people will pass on information to their friends and networked circles either conscientiously or unconscientiously if the information is of value, interesting, or entertaining. Viral marketing can be achieved in various ways. In the first situation, the consumer does not know that he/she is doing viral marketing for the company. For example, consumers who use Yahoo e-mail service help popularize Yahoo e-mail service when they send e-mail to other consumers since every Yahoo e-mail carries a message for signup at the end of the e-mail. We call this type of viral marketing incidental dissemination.

The second type of viral marketing is done by giving a consumer incentives to recruit new customers, so that the benefits to the consumer increases with more users signing on to the service or purchase the product. We call this type of viral marketing incentive networking. Finally, companies can pay to have consumers work as recruiters either on cash or commission bases. These paid recruiters are typically opinion leaders of social networks and virtual communities. Their referral and recommendation have significant impact on members of those networks and communities. We refer to this type of viral marketing as paid opinion leadership.

6.4 PUSH MARKETING

Push marketing techniques are widely used in traditional tourism marketing. Internet marketing incorporates the concept of push marketing and develops its own unique set of marketing techniques using Internet technologies. According to Webopedia (www.webopedia.com), a Web-based Internet dictionary for Internet technology, the word push, in client/server applications, means to send data to a client without the client requesting it. Technically, the Web is based on a pull technology where the client browser must request a Web page before it is sent.

On the other hand, traditional media, especially broadcast media, are push technologies because they send information out regardless of whether anyone is tuned in. There are many Internet technologies applying this type of push technique. One such example is e-mail, the oldest and most widely used push technology on the Internet. This is a push technology because you receive e-mail whether you ask for it or not (at least in theory, that is), as the sender pushes the message to the receiver.

Push marketing is a collection of Internet marketing techniques that are used to present and send data to online visitors. The idea is that data, as well as information, are presented in such an attractive and easy-to-access way that consumers will not be able to resist the temptation to ask for and receive them. In other words, the data and information should be available whenever consumers are looking for them. Some of the marketing techniques discussed in this chapter are part and parcel of this collection. In this section, we try to place those techniques and others under the rubric of push marketing for a simple reason: The term *push marketing* is widely used in the Internet marketing community and therefore deserves to be discussed separately. We will try to avoid redundancy in the following discussion.

PUSH MARKETING TECHNIQUES

One push marketing technique is the use of the **search engines.** Consumers use search engines to look for information they are interested in. Internet marketers should understand how search engines work and how consumers use them. If a company's name and information do not show up in a consumer's search engine result, it is unlikely that the consumer will use the company's service and product unless the consumer knows the company by memory. We call the use of the search engines a push marketing technique since we basically "force" or "push" our way through the competitive information to be viewed and noticed by the consumers.

Prior to the advent of the Web, it was not easy to search for information on the Internet. To find and share information on the Internet, users had to go through FTP sites, which were publicized and found by word of mouth, e-mail messages, or on message boards. In 1990 Alan Emtage improved search capabilities with a database client called **Archie.** Archie was able to obtain site listings of FTP files by scouring FTP sites across the Internet and indexing all the files found.

The first Web search engine was created by Matthew Gray who used an automated computer program called *robot* to gather URLs and stored them in a Web database. Gray also created the first robot on the Web. A search engine spider is a type of robot that performs search at great speeds on the Internet. A spider works by starting on a starter site and beginning exploring all of the links from that site.

The first browseable Web directory and searchable Web index was called Galaxy. It was designed in a hierarchal fashion and its listings were presented in a directory form and organized into categories. It was first introduced in 1994. Galaxy solved a problem that the previous spiders were facing: there was no intelligent way of indexing all of the information that the spiders were gathering. The same year witnessed Yahoo to come on the scene. Yahoo was basically following the same principals as Galaxy since it organizes its index in categories. The popularity of search engines prompted many newcomers.

We saw WebCrawler and Lycos in late 1994, Infoseek and Alta Vista in 1995, and HotBot, MetaCrawler in 1996.

Since 1996 many other search engines have emerged, giving consumers plenty of choices in searching for information on the Web. Prior to the advent of the search engine, people looking for a product or service were limited to their local yellow pages unless they were very technically savvy. Today, consumers have more choices in search engines than they can have time to try all of them. Some of the top search engines have become household names. According to Nielsen/NetRatings (2002), a company that measures the impact of the Internet and new technologies on commerce and marketing, the top five search engines during October of 2002 were Google, Yahoo, MSN, AOL, and Ask Jeeves. Table 6.4 lists the most popular search engines.

There are several types of search engines. One type uses categories or classifications. Yahoo is a good example of this type. Another type uses spidering or crawling technologies. Altavista (www.altavista.com), Infoseek (www.infoseek.com), and Excite (www.excite.com) belong to this group. This group uses an algorithm or a computer program to look for the information that an online visitor is seeking. For this reason, the concept of a Meta tag becomes very important. These search engines will look for these Meta tags for key words and terms that match the visitor's input key words and terms, even though each search engine has its own search criteria.

There is a temptation for Internet marketers to try to "cheat" search engines by creating or duplicating key-word lists in the Meta tag. Today,

| TABLE 6.4 |
The Most Popular Search Engines
Google.com
Yahoo.com
MSN
AOL
AskJeeves.com
Altavista.com
Goto.com
Netscape.com
Excite.com
Lycos.com
iWon.com
Overture.com
Looksmart.com
Hotbot.com

many search engines have developed smart technologies to punish these cheaters by totally ignoring these Web sites if caught. A better strategy for Internet marketers is to try to optimize their Web listings by looking for search engines that are most appropriate to their business. One of the cruel facts about search engines is that most Web sites will not get into the top 10 listings in the search results.

In using search engines as a tool for push marketing, a technique called search engine optimization (SEO) is the key to success. SEO is the process of designing and fine-tuning your Web site to ensure higher rankings in the search engine results. Essentially, SEO helps you to understand the criteria used by top search engines for ranking sites and then formulates strategies to take advantage of those criteria to increase the probability of higher rankings. There are five most widely used criteria employed by top search engines to rank a site. They are as follows:

1. Keywords in the title (META tags)
2. Keywords near the top
3. Frequency of keywords
4. Link popularity
5. Mechanism for penalty for repeat keywords

There are many companies that are specialized in SEO such as traffic-power.com. Through traffic-power.com, Lyon will be able to use their expertise and technological know-how to get top search engine placement:

❏ Their professionally trained technicians help you to choose the 20 keyword phrases that best reflect the main focus of your site.
❏ They use those keywords to optimize your Meta tags and build 280 HTML attraction pages designed to conform to the ranking criteria of the top search engines.
❏ Since many search engines now use link popularity in their rankings, they use systems developed by our programmers to build your link popularity.
❏ They manually submit your site to Web directories like the Open Directory Project. (They do not submit to spider-based search engine because recent studies indicate that these types of search engines give preference to sites that their spiders find through links.)
❏ Their online client reporting system puts tracking information at your fingertips so that you can monitor your site's progress.
❏ Free customer support is always available for active clients through their toll free customer support hotline.
❏ Active Traffic-Power.com clients can check their search engine keyword rankings with the Traffic-Power.com online reporting system.

A second push technology is the use of **banner ads.** A banner ad is a graphic image on a Web site that advertises a product, service, promotion, brand, or a combination thereof. Again, a banner ad tries to force its way into the attention of online visitors and hence is a push marketing technique. A banner ad is really a hyperlinked image displayed on the screen. When a visitor clicks on the banner, he or she will be directed to the home page or information Web page of the advertiser.

There are many types of banner ads. A **stationed banner ad** is one that stays on the same spot on the screen and never moves. What is displayed inside the banner ad will draw the attention of online visitors, but the ad may be totally ignored if the inside display fails to catch the vistor's attention. However, it is less intrusive and therefore less objectionable to visitors. A **moving banner ad,** as the name suggests, moves across the screen to try to stay visible to the eyes of the visitor as the visitor looks at the different parts of a Web page on the screen. It has the advantage of being hard to ignore and is always within view of the visitor. However, it is more intrusive and may interfere with the visitor's surfing experience, invoking feelings of resentment and annoyance.

There are 4 types of moving banner ads. The first one is the horizontal moving banner ad that moves from left to right screen or vice versa. The second type is the vertical moving banner ad that moves from top to bottom screen or vice versa. The third one is the random moving banner ad that moves around the screen continuously in random directions to draw the attention of online visitors. It is true that this type of ad is the hardest to ignore, but it is probably the most annoying type of banner ad from consumer's point of view. In choosing which type of banner ad to use, it is important that Internet marketers understand these negative impacts as well as the benefits.

The fourth type of moving banner ad is the ghost banner ad that follows your screen movement and stays visible no matter which part of the screen you are scrolling to. Both random moving banner ad and ghost banner ad will never leave your eyesight no matter which part of the screen you are on. They are intended to stay within your view as long as you stay on the same Web page. Finally, there is the touch-screen banner ad, which is typically half-hidden at the lower right corner of the screen and will rise to show the whole banner ad whenever your mouse happens to move over it.

The most common use of the banner ad is to entice a direct response. Such direct responses could be for membership enrollment, product purchase, or a combination of both. Other uses of banner ads can be for publicity, customer relations, or the introduction of a new Web site. One advantage of using a banner ad is that it can direct the online visitor to the exact Web page where actions will take place, saving time and effort for the visitor to find the information.

A third push technology is called **interstitials.** These are special banner ads that pop up on the screen to catch the attention of the online visitor. For this reason, they are also called **pop-ups.** Pop-ups usually come with incentives for the visitor to click on it and be led to a home page where the advertiser hopes to get action out of the visitor. Compared to regular banner ads, which have a click rate of about 1% or less, pop-up interstitials have a click rate of about 30%. However, since pop-ups interfere with the visitor's surfing experience, they can be annoying and frustrating. Therefore, the visitor may either close them before they are completely loaded or avoid the site where pop-ups occur. Major cons for the use of the interstitials are as follows:

❏ They interfere with the visitor's online experience.
❏ They slow down the visitor's loading speed.
❏ They give the visitor the impression that something is being pushed into his or her view, something that most visitors do not like.

To overcome this type of immediate reaction, a special type of interstitials was invented. These are invisible at first, as they pop under rather than up on the screen like a regular pop-up. These are called **invisible interstitials** or **pop-unders.** However, they will show up when an online visitor closes or minimizes the screen window, achieving the same effect as a pop-up but avoiding being shut down before fully loaded on the screen. Psychologically, they are less intrusive than pop-ups since they do not present immediate interference to the visitor's surfing experience.

A fourth push technology is the **e-promotion.** Technically, an e-promotion is a hyperlink special ad displayed on the screen. Like traditional promotion, e-promotion offers incentives, such as coupons, discounts, sales, and sweepstakes, to attract consumers to get action. However, e-promotion has the advantage of bringing the action and the incentives much closer to the consumer than traditional promotion. With a click of the mouse, the consumer takes action right on the screen. For advertisers, it provides a great way to track advertising instantly. Today, it is relatively easy to build or find a program to track the use of the e-promotion.

E-promotion is widely used by hospitality and tourism companies. Airlines offer incentives for booking online with frequent-flyer miles. Hotels offer frequent-stay points for reading e-newsletters and e-mail. Netcentives's Clickrewards (www.netcentives.com) program rewards online visitors with frequent-flyer miles for visiting specific sites. Expedia and Travelocity often run promotions on their own sites, offering discounts, special rates, free e-newsletters, and fare-watch e-mail alert programs. These promotions help draw visitors to a Web site and increase the chances of their buying the promoted service or product and having the site exposed to a larger audience.

A fifth push technology is the previously discussed affiliate marketing program. This is a type of promotion or advertising that sells or distributes products or services through allied partnerships. Affiliate marketing is particularly relevant for the hospitality and tourism industry. As we know, this industry is a multifaceted one, consisting of a group of interrelated businesses. Placing ads with companies in a related field increases the likelihood that the ad will attract consumers who would otherwise be missed.

A sixth push technology is **e-sponsorship.** Just like traditional sponsorship, e-sponsorship seeks to associate the advertiser to a brand name. In e-sponsorship, the advertiser identifies a Web site, an event, or a virtual community hosted by a Web site that attracts the audience the sponsors wish to reach. Instead of running a banner ad on the Web site or page, you become the official sponsor of the site, event, or community. Typically, the sponsor will be represented by a logo on the site rather than a banner.

Many traditional sponsorship ideas are being translated and modified into e-sponsorship. For example, a company can sponsor a Webcast event that discusses environmental conservation if that company is in the business of ecotourism. Sponsoring an e-newsletter can be an effective way to reach the target audience because the readers of an e-newsletter are those who have expressed interest in receiving the e-newsletter, so their interests are relatively clear. When a business sponsors an e-newsletter, it knows which audience it is targeting. For this reason, sponsorship of an e-newsletter can result in reaching a more targeted audience than can the other technologies discussed previously.

The benefits of e-sponsorship are the following:

1. It can provide a more directly targeted audience.
2. It gives more exposure than banner ads since the fee structures are based on a period of time rather than on per click.
3. It appears less commercialized than outright ads and may be more acceptible to the online visitors.
4. It is less intrusive.

A seventh push technology is so-called **rich media** (sometimes called **media-rich advertising**). Rich media refers to any online ad that allows for transactions, streaming media, and interactive communication directly in the ad space without leaving the home page where the ad is being placed. Rich media marketing tries to take advantage of one of the most powerful features of the Internet: interactivity. Unlike banner ads, which, when clicked on, will take an online visitor to a different home page (most likely forcing the visitor to leave the home page he or she is reading), rich media will not take the visitor away from the site. For this reason, rich media provide an attractive alternative to banner ads by offering a less interruptive communication channel. With rich media, a visitor need not leave the home page after clicking on the rich media banner window. Instead, the visitor can do all the transactions, interactive communications, or streaming video right inside the banner window.

▌ 6.5 PULL MARKETING

Traditional media marketing, such as television, radio, and magazine advertising, pushes marketing messages to the audience. They "scream" at the audience. **Pull marketing** asks for the target audience's permission to send a marketing message or to present the message in such an attractive way that the audience is pulled toward it. For this reason, pull marketing is also referred to as **opt-in marketing** or **permission marketing.** Opt-in marketing empowers users to explicitly request information from the Internet marketers through e-mail, e-newsletters, or other Internet communication tools for targeted information or advertising from businesses. Two of the most popular opt-in marketing tools are e-mail and e-newsletters.

Opt-in e-mail marketing is based on the notion that Internet users with an e-mail address will be interested in selected information at the user's discretion. The advertisers tell the Internet users that they have acquired their e-mail address and would like to send them information if the users give explicit permission. For example, a user might be interested in travel and recreation information. Instead of having to search for information themselves, the advertiser will send the information to the user on a regular basis or when it is available in the form of either e-mail or an e-newsletter.

Opt-in marketing can be a very effective marketing tool since it is highly targeted, and done in collaboration of the target audience. Such an audience is much more likely to click on messages and read them since these are the messages they have requested and regard as valuable. Unsolicited e-mails or e-newsletters are often considered junk by users and suffer the fate of deletion without being read. Opt-in e-mail and e-newsletters overcome this drawback and therefore are much more effective than other types of Internet marketing tools.

To be successful in opt-in marketing, follow these guidelines:

1. Obtain the target audience's e-mail addresses
2. Provide valuable information that the target audience wants
3. Offer incentives, if necessary, to add benefits
4. Provide convenient ways for the potential audience to sign up
5. Provide an option for the receiver to opt out of the program

One of the most critical issues in opt-in marketing is privacy. You likely have received direct-mail marketing materials in the past but never seriously thought about the issue of privacy, as most direct marketing mail comes from relatively well-known established businesses. However, with Internet e-mail marketing being so prevalent, the number of e-mail messages you receive every day from unknown sources might make you wonder how your e-mail address ends up with these businesses in the first place. You might not be sure whether these businesses are legitimate, and you may not be happy with all that e-mail. In addition, you might be concerned with Internet **cookies.** A cookie is a tiny program that a Web site places on your hard drive to collect information about you when you are visiting the site so that it can recognize you while you are visiting the site or when you return to the same site later. For these reasons, privacy has suddenly become a great concern to users of the Internet. Opt-in marketing is the direct response to this concern from Internet marketers.

Another strategy in pull marketing is the use of the **virtual communities.** A virtual community is composed of Internet users with similar interests and thus is a good target audience for advertisers. Tools that can be used to build a virtual community include portals, e-newsletters, and ad networks.

PORTALS

A portal is a Web site that serves as an opening page and main source of information for Web users. The idea is that when a user logs on to the Internet, the first page accessed and seen on the screen will be this portal, from which they can get the information they are most interested in. A portal holds a virtual community, which in turn is built by the members of the community. Members of the community can create their own contents, such as home pages, discussion forums, business transactions, chat rooms, e-newsletters, newsgroups, and so on.

Portals are highly targeted and interactive. For this reason, it is the dream of a business to make its Web site a portal. If your customers come to your site for information each time they log on to the Internet, your site will become important to them, and you will be able to keep customers and users loyal to your site. You will have an excellent platform for marketing and for distributing information. The time and money you save trying to identify and locate a target audience can be enormous.

Some specialized portals include Geocities (http://geocities.yahoo.com), now part of the Yahoo family; Travelocity (www.travelocity.com) for travel information and reservations; and Monster.com (www.monster.com) for job searches. The idea of using portals to reach consumers is well developed in Asia. In China, famous portals include sina.com (www.sina.com), sohu.com (www.sohu.com), and 163.com (www.163.com). Each portal has a USP to position itself in the vast sea of competition.

E-NEWSLETTERS

E-newsletters, especially opt-in ones, have come to be recognized as one of the most effective Internet marketing tools. Today, most Web sites offer convenient ways for their visitors to sign up for e-newsletters. Offering e-newsletters has many benefits for a business. First, they are an excellent way to provide customer service, as they keep customers or potential customers informed. Second, they are an inexpensive way to reach a target audience. The cost of sending out an e-newsletter compared to traditional mail is minimal. Third, thanks to the power of the Internet, users can respond to information or advertising messages instantly, achieving a higher response rate than traditionally mailed newsletters. Fourth, users feel in more control of the process since e-newsletters are more predictable and more easily organized by users, increasing the chances that users will keep and read them instead of delete them. Finally, e-newsletters can be a source of revenue or a type of e-commerce since they can be sponsored by related businesses that seek to reach their target audience or can carry advertising messages that generate revenue.

ADVERTISING NETWORKS

Advertising networks are Internet companies that allow businesses to place an ad with all the target Web sites in their networked or partnership companies. These networks typically represent those sites that are either too busy or too small to sell their own advertising. They act as ad agents for such sites. For example, www.doubleclick.com owns and operates a large ad network to increase its marketing coverage and power. For example, Disney would have a hard time identifying by itself all the Web sites that its potential customers visit. An ad network such as www.doubleclick.com could help Disney identify all the relevant sites and place Disney's ad on those sites, potentially saving time and money for Disney. If a business is looking for sports sites, an ad network could help find all those sites and place an ad for the business.

An ad network also specializes in tracking the use of an ad by Internet users. It has a mechanism to conduct research into the effectiveness of the ads placed and to improve that effectiveness by designing different types of ads to target different audiences. For a company that does not have its own information technology experts to track and monitor its advertising, an ad network offers one-stop shopping, providing both convenience and expertise. Table 6.5 summarizes the pros and cons of an ad network.

TABLE 6.5
Pros and Cons of an Ad Network

PROS

One-stop shopping: You deal with only one marketing agent.

Economy of scale: You pay more if you have to buy ads with individual Web sites.

Market research: Ad networks can optimize, serve, and track online advertising campaigns more effectively.

CONS

Expensive: If you do not need to advertise on many Web sites, you may end up paying more than necessary.

Less control: You have less control of your marketing campaign.

Customer database: You lose the opportunity to collect your own customers' information and build your customer database.

WEBCASTING

Webcasting is another online pull marketing tool. It may be argued that it is a push marketing technique rather than a pull one since it "pushes" the message to the audience. In fact, Webopedia (www.webopedia.com) refers to it as a push marketing technique. The reason it is called a pull marketing technique here is to be consistent with our notion of pull marketing. First, Webcasting often is done with pre-sign-ups online, so it is an event that online visitors agree to participate in and hence is permission based. Second, Webcasting presents the message in an attractive way so that visitors are "pulled" to view it. For this reason, we classify Webcasting as a pull marketing technique.

Webcasting uses **streaming media** to broadcast an event over the Web (Dietel et al. 2001). Streaming media is a technique for transferring data such that they can be processed as a steady, continuous stream. With streaming Webcasting, a visitor need not wait for the entire file to be downloaded before he or she can start displaying the data on the screen. This is important since the visitor wants to view the Webcasting right away, not wait for a long time for the complete file.

Webcasting resembles the traditional television broadcast in that it uses live visual images to present information and marketing messages. It differs from the traditional television broadcast in that it offers the capability of two-way communication and interaction rather than one-way communication. A Webcast audience is able to call or type in their response on screen and begin interacting right on-site, making it more interesting. Webcasts are great for introducing new products and educating consumers about products and services. They are also great for products or services that require more visual appeal than text information. Since they are innovative, Webcasts can be attractive to potential audiences (Table 6.6).

TABLE 6.6
Pros and Cons of Webcasting

PROS

Good for introducing new products and services and educating users about them

Good for products and services that require more visual appeal than text information

Interesting and attractive to potential audiences

CONS

Requires more sophisticated Internet users to use and appreciate it

Can slow down the download speed of the users, thus annoying them

Not yet a common feature for most users, so the audience is presently limited

---

6.6 CONCLUSION

Internet marketing is an important part of e-commerce. Knowing how to take advantage of these marketing tools can put a company ahead of the game and position it to succeed in the fiercely competitive world of e-commerce. Technology is ever changing, and Internet marketing techniques will change as well since every new development in Internet technology will bring about new ways and means for reaching consumers and marketing to them.

Internet marketing should be used in the broad context of a business's overall marketing plan. When and how to use Internet marketing or whether to use traditional means of marketing depends on the needs of a business. In fact, it often is necessary to use both as complementary tools. Some consumers are more apt to use the Internet and thus are more suitable targets for Internet marketing, while others are still traditional media fans and thus prime targets for traditional marketing media. Here, the principle of marketing still applies: targeting an audience with the appropriate channel of communication.

KEY WORDS AND TERMS

Unique Selling Proposition	Push Marketing
E-mail Marketing	Search Engines
Click–Through	Banner Ads
Customized Marketing Message	Stationed Banner Ad
Simpliers	Moving Banner Ad
Surfers	Random Moving Banner Ad
Bargainers	Interstitials
Connectors	Pop-Ups
Routiners	Invisible Interstitials (pop-unders)
Sportsters	E-Promotion
Opt-in E-Mail Marketing	E-Sponsorship
Response Rate	Rich Media/Media–Rich
Spamming	Advertising
Return of Investment	Pull Marketing
HTML Format	Opt-in Marketing/Permission
Application Service Provider	Marketing
Web Site Construction Plan	Cookies
Meta Tags	Virtual Communities
Portal	Advertising Networks
Web Portal	Webcasting
Affiliate Marketing Program	Streaming Media

SUMMARY

Internet marketing expands and complements the traditional marketing horizon. It offers many new opportunities to reach target customers and to attract and keep loyal customers. Internet marketing requires a vigorous approach, such as that used in traditional marketing. It also needs good planning and a research scheme. Finally, it needs to include an understanding of the needs and wants of consumers before any marketing campaign can be launched.

Internet marketing differs in many ways from traditional marketing in that it operates in a totally new environment in terms of time, speed, interaction, market segmentation, the means of collecting data and distributing information, and marketing message. The key to creating a sound marketing plan is to define a unique selling proposition, which defines what makes a business unique from competitors in a particular field. It spells out the precise niche a company seeks to fill and how it can aim to fill it.

There are many marketing tools you can use to achieve marketing objectives. These tools include e-mail, e-newsletters, Usenet and mailing lists, chat rooms, Web site portals and advertising and promotion. There are other special tools available as well, such as pull and push marketing. Internet marketing is an important part of e-commerce. Knowing how to take advantage of these marketing tools can put a company ahead of the game and position the business to succeed in the fiercely competitive world of e-commerce.

WEB RESOURCES

www.streamingmedia.com
www.macromedia.com
www.cyber-logics.com
www.real.com
www.apple.com/quicktime
www.internetworld.com
www.list.org
www.traffiz_power.com

CASE STUDY: "America Loves New York"

"America Loves New York": A hospitality e-mail marketing campaign in response to the terrorist attacks of September 11, 2001 (see Figure 6.1).

FIGURE 6.1
America loves New York campaign.

America Loves NY
The Big Apple Salutes You!

Travel agents have always contributed tremendously to NYC hotel business and we deeply appreciate your continuous support! Ask your clients to show their support for New York City by visiting the Big Apple and enjoying the world's best shopping, dining, hotels, theater and sightseeing! *Now is the time to visit the Big Apple!*

Big Apple Top Picks

THE WJ HOTEL
New York's Hippest Address! Hell's Kitchen!

Treat yourself and a friend to the WJ Get Away -$229.00 (plus tax) single or double occupancy; January 2 - March 31, 2002 includes: 2 nights/3 days, deluxe accommodations, welcome champagne/chocolates on arrival, breakfast for 2, *NY Times*, plus discount coupons. The WJ is a 132 room deluxe hotel conveniently located in the 'heart of restaurant row'; in a neighborhood made famous from West Side Story; within walking distance to Broadway theatre district, Times Square, Radio City and Rockefeller Center. Smart, stylish, sophisticated, the WJ is casual as it is cosmopolitan offering views of tree-lined streets, courtyard and goose down comforters! If you're planning to travel to New York for business or pleasure, let the staff at WJ pamper you! (*Sunday-Thursday, subject to availability) For Reservations, please call 1-888-567-7550 or visit the hotel Web site: http://www.wjhotel.com

Manhattan East Suite Hotels
WE LOVE NY WEEKEND
YOUR CLIENTS CAN ENJOY ALL THE CITY HAS TO OFFER, THEN RELAX IN A SPACIOUS SUITE

There's so much to love about New York City. Fabulous dining, award-winning entertainment, non-stop shopping and world-renowned arts. With the "We Love NY" weekend, your clients can enjoy all the city has to offer, then spread out and relax in a spacious suite in one of our eight distinctive hotels. They'll also receive special savings certificates for Bloomingdale's and Macy's. Rates start at $138 per night for studio suites and $178 per night for one-bedroom suites. To book, access "NY" on your GDS or call 1-800-ME-SUITE. For more information, click here www.mesuite.com.

Holiday Inn 57th Street
COLD DATES ....HOT RATES!

Come enjoy all that New York has to offer! Winter Special Starts at $129 from Now through Feb 2002. New Year's Special**Starts at $179 from Dec 28 through Jan 3, 2002. Rates are 10% commissionable based on single or double occupancy, per room, per night plus taxes and are subject to availability. Two night minimum stay. Book a room. Visit the hotel's Web site http:holidayinnmid57.citysearch.com/

The Warwick New York

No better location. Steps from Broadway, Rockefeller Center, Radio City, Carnegie Hall, and Fifth Avenue. Built by William Randolph Hearst for his Hollywood friends, and home to many celebrities, the European-style Elegance of The Warwick has been recently restored to reflect its glorious past. Its overly spacious rooms are beautifully appointed and the staff highly attentive. Reserve The Heart of New York starting at $179 per room. 800 223-4099 or sales.ny@warwickhotels.com

Holidays at The Algonquin
http://www.thealgonquin.net

The world-famous Algonquin Hotel has greeted generations of travelers for the past century, and as it welcomes its 100th year allows travelers to enjoy all New York City has to offer from one of the most prestigious addresses in town. Located at 59 West 44th Street--between Fifth and Sixth Avenues--The Algonquin is just steps from Broadway theater, fashionable shopping at the most exclusive shops and boutiques and attractions like Rockefeller Center, The Empire State Building and The Museum of Modern Art. During the months of January and February The Algonquin is offering rates from $149.00 per night single or double occupancy. Taxes are additional. Please call 1-800-555-8000 to reserve a guest room in this most venerable of New York City landmarks today.

Holiday Inn Wall Street
NEW YORK'S MOST TECHNOLOGICALLY SOPHISTICATED HOTEL

In the heart of the Financial District is New York's most technologically sophisticated hotel, designed for both the business traveler and leisure traveler, The Holiday Inn Wall Street. The first hotel where rooms have both high-speed T1 Internet connectivity through Plug and Play services, various rooms feature PCs as well as laptop computers, Web TV, direct dial personal phone numbers and cellular connect services. All 138 guestrooms and suites are "virtual offices," with eight-foot L-shaped workspaces and free office supplies. For leisure visitors we are steps from the South Street Seaport and convenient to the dynamic neighborhoods of Soho, Tribeca, Chinatown and Little Italy. Click here for more information: www.holidayinnwsd.com

The Ritz-Carlton New York, Battery Park
http://www.ritzcarlton.com

The Ritz-Carlton New York, Battery Park, opening in February 2002, is the only luxury hotel on the Manhattan waterfront and is conveniently nearby the fashionable Soho and Tribeca neighborhoods. The hotel will serve as the ideal place for both business and leisure travelers seeking the standard of superior service and accommodations set by The Ritz-Carlton worldwide. All 298 well-appointed guest rooms including 44 suites are designed in a 1920's art deco inspired style with luxurious details. All harbor view rooms feature telescopes to take advantage of the sweeping views of New York and the Statue of Liberty. www.ritzcarlton.com

Hotel Interactive
TIAA Leads New Ad Campaign Featuring President Bush
http://www.hotelinteractive.com

A new travel marketing campaign led by the TIAA features President
George W. Bush in a 30-second television spot promoting travel.

Hospitality eBusiness Strategies

Register today at **www.TravelTarget.com** and qualify to **WIN** your choice of $50,000 or a BMW-Z3.

SOURCE: Used with permission by Jason Price and Max Starkov of Hospitality
eBusiness Strategies, NYC.

BACKGROUND

The travel industry suffered insurmountable losses financially and in
consumer confidence after September 11, 2001. At the time of this writing,
some nine months later, the industry has yet to fully recover, and the
losses may deepen as long as the threat to national and global security
continues.

New York City was stigmatized not only from the vicious attack but
also by travelers and travel professionals who avoided the city in the
aftermath. Combined with a reduction in business travel (helped further
by a general recession), tourism in New York City, be it business or leisure,
slowed to a standstill.

The New York Convention and Visitor's Bureau acted quickly by
launching "Paint the Town Red, White, and Blue" to draw visitors who
could travel short distances by train, car, and bus. While this effort helped
attract day-trippers eager to spend money on Broadway shows and
restaurants, few converted to extended stays, thereby leaving the hotels
gasping for air.

INTRODUCING "AMERICA LOVES NEW YORK"

Recognizing an immense need to boost hotel occupancy in the city and
educate travel agents that New York City is stronger than ever, Hospitality eBusiness Strategies launched an ambitious hotel joint-marketing
campaign. An estimated 40 competing hotels joined forces by sharing
costs and being presented side by side in an e-mail marketing campaign
called "America Loves New York."

In the eyes of hoteliers, the campaign was an enormous success. It allowed hoteliers to experiment with rates and promotions, offer unique and bookable opportunities to travel agents, recognize that travel agents are a vital distribution channel, and allow the industry to help get itself back on its feet in the spirit of mutual cooperation.

Why do travel agents represent such an important group for e-mail marketing? Travel agents that use the Internet and e-mail are exactly the travel agents hoteliers must reach. These agents are likely to visit hotel Web sites, book online, and even boast hotel Web-only promotions in their own marketing efforts to preferred clients. Research from the most respected travel organizations, such as ARC, ASTA, IATA, and Plog Research, as well as leading travel industry trade publications, show that

- 96% of agents send and receive e-mail,
- 79% of agents receive e-mail travel requests from clients, and
- 54% of agents e-mail clients with special offers or incentives.

How the "America Loves New York" Campaign Worked

The travel agents received a listing of 10 hotels in any one mailing on a weekly basis for 10 weeks. The hotels' positioning rotated weekly. Each e-mail launch, or "blast," took place on each Tuesday for five months continuously. Participating hotels posted 100-word copy detailing the hotel and special room rate. The hotel logo hyperlinked, as did the reservation button, to the hotel Web site or reservation page. Usually a phone number and special rate code were provided.

HeBS partnered with Adval Communications for conducting such a blast with tracking and reporting capabilities. The 40,000 double-opt-in permission-based e-mail list came from a reliable and robust e-mail list provider. HeBS designed the campaign, and Adval launched and tracked results.

Campaign Results

"America Loves New York" was launched in early November 2001 and ran successfully for five months until occupancy rates began to improve citywide. According to Price Waterhouse Coopers, February 2002 housing occupancy rates for New York City surpassed February 2001 occupancy rates—a remarkable recovery in such a short period of time.

According to Adval, the campaign achieved a "view rate" as high as 25%, which is extremely high for a permission-based e-mail campaign. "America Loves New York" demonstrated (1) that travel agents are interested in what is happening in New York City, (2) that travel agents gain quick access to the hotel property for a commissionable booking, and (3) that the actual e-mail promotion serves as an effective communication tool to travel agents and helps them as they promote to preferred clients.

SOURCE: Used with permission by Jason Price and Max Starkov of Hospitality e-Business Strategies, NYC.

QUESTIONS TO PONDER

1. What is the purpose of the "America Loves New York" campaign?
2. Why did the marketer choose e-mail as the marketing tool?
3. How does the advertising campaign capitalize on the patriotic feelings of the Americans?
4. Why do travel agents represent such an important group for e-mail marketing?

REVIEW QUESTIONS

1. Why does Internet marketing require planning?
2. How important is it to have a USP? Why?
3. How can you use e-mail for marketing?
4. What issues are involved in e-mail marketing?
5. What is the difference between e-mail and e-newsletters when used for marketing?
6. What is the difference between a mailing list and an e-mail mailing list?
7. What is the difference between Usenet and mailing lists?
8. What do you need to know when considering chatroom marketing?
9. What is a WCP? What does it consist of?
10. How do you make your Web site a portal?
11. What is push marketing? Describe some of the techniques used.
12. What is pull marketing? Describe some of the techniques used.
13. Do you think Internet marketing is better than traditional marketing? If so, why? If not, why not?

REFERENCES

Deitel, H. M, P. J. Deitel, and K. Steinbuhler. (2001). *E-Business and e-commerce for Managers.* Englewood Cliffs, N. J.: Prentice Hall.
Fine, P. (2001). "E-Mail: The Unsung Marketing Tool". *Travel Counselor,* February 26, 8.

Nilsen/Net Ratings, (2002). www.nielsenNetratings.com.

Krishnamurthy, Sandeep. (2003). *E-commerce Management: Text and Cases.* Canada: Thomson/South-Western.

Schwartz, John. (2000). "Marketers Turn to a Simple Tool: E-Mail." www.nytimes.com.

Wilson, Ralph F. (2001a). http://wilsonweb.com.

Wilson, Ralph F. (2001b). *Slow-Loading Webpages* (e-newsletter). Vol. 3, Issue 61, April 25. www.doctorebiz.com.

For additional Travel and Tourism resources, go to
www.Hospitality-Tourism.delmar.com

7

THE IMPACT OF THE INTERNET ON THE HOSPITALITY AND TOURISM INDUSTRY

LEARNING OBJECTIVES

After you complete your study of this chapter, you should be able to:

- Understand the Internet's impact on travel suppliers.
- Know how the Internet impacts intermediaries.
- Understand the Internet's impact on destination marketers.
- Understand the Internet's impact on traditional brochure information distribution.
- Be acquainted with the emerging e-commerce marketplace.

7.1 INTRODUCTION

The hospitality and tourism industry has probably been the most affected industry by the Internet. This is to be expected, as this industry depends on the distribution of information about its products and services, which is exactly what the Internet is good for. Hospitality and tourism suppliers have been looking for new ways to expand channels of distribution so that they can reach target travelers in a more efficient and effective way. The rise of travel agents solved part of the problem. Travel agents are an effective (but not efficient) way to reach customers. Travel agents provide free service to travelers, but they charge hospitality and tourism suppliers commissions for the service they provide to travelers. It is not surprising that reducing the cost of information distribution and service has been a tempting proposition from the suppliers' point of view. The advent of the Internet provides an alternative, if not presently a better way, for the efficient distribution of hospitality and tourism information and services. The result of this impact is being felt far and wide beyond travel agents—it impacts the whole hospitality and tourism industry as well.

7.2 THE IMPACT ON SUPPLIERS

AIRLINES

For decades, airlines have been heavily dependent on travel **intermediaries,** such as travel agents, to disseminate information and sell tickets. It is not because airlines do not like to save money or market their services directly to travelers; rather, they have no other alternative for doing so, at least before the Internet arrived on the scene. The Internet has changed everything, enabling airlines to find a way to bypass intermediaries to reach their customers directly and save money at the same time.

From the early days when the Internet began to show its ability to market airline services directly to consumers, the airlines have stepped up their efforts to engage in e-commerce to cut costs. Their first move was to cut commissions they paid to the travel agents, typically from 15% to 10% and soon after to 8% and then 5%. On the other hand, airlines were investing in building their own Web sites as an e-commerce point-of-sale online storefront. The airlines use strategies such as **online pricing** and incentives to lure travelers to book and plan travel on their sites.

This ability to market travel services directly to travelers has created a new marketplace and changed the traditional relationships between travelers, **suppliers,** and intermediaries. In 1996, Northwest Airlines announced that it would cap commissions for tickets booked online by travel agents to 5%, or $25 per ticket. Other airlines soon followed suit. In 2001, Northwest again announced that it would no longer pay commissions to other third-party online travel agents, such as Expedia.com, for tickets booked on Expedia.com's Web site. It was paying 5% with a $10 cap before the announcement.

United Airlines is another company that has aggressively pursued its e-commerce strategies. In 2001, United announced that it had built a global e-commerce Web site, United.com, to cater to customers in different countries (from www.thestandard.com). The Web sites for its two largest overseas markets, Japan and Germany, can now accept local credit cards, display prices in local currency, and provide content of regional interest, such as information about United's airport terminals in those countries. Since the use of wireless devices is common in these two markets, United also provides flight-paging systems designed for local cell phone networks to alert travelers when flights are delayed or canceled. At United's other international sites, such as those for France, India, and Italy, static content is translated into the local language, and site users can book tickets with credit cards from their own country or from the United States. The prices are shown in both U.S. dollars and local currency.

Today, almost all major airlines own their own Web sites that are capable of taking reservations online as well as conducting other travel services. Some airlines are taking the technology to its fullest extent. Northwest Airlines has enabled its travelers not only to check in online but also to do last-minute changes to their itineraries either online or at kiosks available in over 40 airports. Travelers can book hotels or rent a car right at the site (www.nwa.com), making it a true one-stop travel shopping e-commerce portal. Austrian Airlines has made e-mail available on its long-distance flights between Europe and North America. Passengers can send text messages to fax numbers, mobile telephones, or e-mail addresses.

Other airlines are expanding their reach to their customers using the Internet. Delta Airlines now offers its U.S. **corporate clients** the ability to link directly and securely to delta.com from their respective **Intranet Web sites.** Delta.com will automatically recognize and associate with the client's applicable Delta corporate sales agreement, no longer requiring the corporate travel manager to submit SkyMiles numbers to Delta for traveler recognition. Before this technology, corporate travel managers had to submit SkyMiles numbers manually for processing by Delta. These online booking capabilities reduce costs by eliminating transaction fees and providing real-time reporting tools for travel managers to more efficiently track and supervise their travel budgets.

In fact, all major airlines are aggressively investing in the e-commerce, using all kinds of marketing strategies to lure customers to book and shop at their Web sites. The results are positive. While all sectors of e-commerce experienced a downturn in years 2000 and 2001, all major airline Web sites reported record online visits and revenues. In 2001, American Airlines (www.aa.com) reported more than three-quarters of a million daily visits—a 165% increase compared with the same time in 2000 (from www.eyefortravel.com). Southwest Airlines'

Web site is so successful that it refuses to pay commissions to any ticket booked on any third-party online travel Web site, such as Expedia.com and Orbitz.com. In fact, it has stopped the practice of listing its flight information through the **Airline Ticket Publishing Company,** an industrywide clearinghouse that provides data to U.S. travel agents. Instead, Southwest makes its listings available only through the computer reservation system of **Sabre.**

However, the airlines' most dramatic act came in 1999, when five of the largest U.S. airline carriers—American, Continental, Delta, Northwest, and United—announced that the consortium was going to launch a new independent Internet travel Web site for e-commerce. The Web site is called Orbitz (www.orbitz.com). With more than $100 million in backing from five U.S. airline carriers, Orbitz.com opened for business on June 2001, starting a new round of competition in the online travel market.

Not to be left behind, nine European airlines—Aer Lingus, Air France, Alitalia, Austrian Airlines, British Airways, Finnair, Iberia, KLM, and Lufthansa—announced in 2001 that they would get together and launch an online travel service site called Opodo (www.opodo.com), which stands for "opportunity to do." The move is not surprising when you consider the fact that Europe's online travel market is estimated to be worth $5.26 billion in 2001 and is expected to grow to $35.4 billion by 2005, according to Forrester Research (from www.eyefortravel.com). Opodo.com aims to offer cheap flights from more than 480 airlines, accommodations from 54,500 hotels and 23,500 car rental locations worldwide, as well as travel insurance. It would launch initially in Germany, the United Kingdom, and France and across Europe between 2002 and 2003 and will have local independent sites serving the European market, allowing customers to navigate and book in their own language. In June 2002, Opodo.com officially opened for business.

At the heart of the popularity of online booking and reservations is the idea of **customization** of travel products and services. Before the advent of Internet online reservations, this customization process was done through travel agents—in many ways a third party that stands in the way of customers and travel products and services. If travel suppliers can match their inventories directly with an individual's particular needs and wants on demand, travel suppliers will be able to better manage their inventories and personalize their products and services. Fortunately, airline products and services are not complicated to customize, so the Internet becomes a perfect channel for distributing them.

CRUISE LINES

In past decades, the cruise-line industry has witnessed a boom in business, partly because of the economic prosperity of the U.S. economy and partly because of their successful marketing efforts. With the emergence of Internet e-commerce in the travel industry, the cruise lines were tempted several times to follow the airlines in offering direct online marketing and reservations. But they managed to resist the temptation, keeping the base commission at 10%, which they used for more than 20 years (Hughes 1998).

The cruise industry's decision was definitely not an act of charity but rather a realization that customizing its products and services is much more complicated than an airline ticket and thus more difficult to sell directly to consumers. This is especially true with today's cruises, which are designed to replicate the large variety of amenities and activities available at the world's leading land resorts. To book a cruise requires the consumer to make a variety of major decisions that can include elements of three major travel categories: airlines, hotels, and cruises. For this reason, in 2000, 98% of the cruise business was still handled by travel agents (Dixon 2000).

However, the cruise industry has been looking for an opportunity to enter this cost-saving market, by selling cruises directly to consumers online. In fact, without much fanfare and in an attempt not to upset its traditional alliance (travel agents), the cruise industry is quietly experimenting with its e-commerce strategies. As early as in 1997, cruise lines sought to control distribution costs by eliminating or restricting bonus payments, keeping the base commission intact. It began to implement commission tiers for agencies that belong to consortiums. Previously, cruise lines paid overrides to members whether or not the agency itself produced a high volume of bookings for an individual line. By rescinding this practice, it required agencies to meet specific booking volumes to earn overrides.

In May 1998, a bold action in cutting commissions was taken by Renaissance Cruises, which announced the "Quik Pay" policy-a flat commission of $500 per cabin for all agent bookings. Although Renaissance Cruises did not offer an online booking strategy to go with this commissions cut, it was a move that certainly was influenced by the commission-cut frenzy by other travel suppliers, notably the airlines. By 1999, nearly every cruise line had its own Web site (Hughes 1999). Both agents and consumers could book online with Carnival Cruise Lines, and consumers could do so with Renaissance Cruises. Royal Caribbean International and Celebrity Cruises had an agent-booking engine and were considering consumer online booking later. Other cruise lines, such as Norwegian Cruise Line, Holland America Line, Princess Cruises, and Windstar Cruises, also had plans to launch an agent-booking engine on their Web sites.

For now, the cruise lines are walking a thin line between their online direct booking and avoiding losing the support of travel agents. There is evidence to suggest that cruise lines will keep their partnership with the travel agents for some time to come, even with the Internet's direct booking capability. For example, Royal Caribbean International and Celebrity Cruises have launched a new Internet tool, Partner Booking Link, to assist customers who visit a travel agent's Web site. A customer can click on a link to Royalcaribbean.com or Celebritycruises.com, where they can book cruises as well as view entertaining multimedia presentations. The cruise lines' Web sites automatically recognize the travel agent's Web site from where the visitor came and allows travel agents to earn full commissions on all bookings made through their site. **Amadeus,** a leading **global distribution system** (GDS) and technology provider, launched Amadeus Cruise in 2000, an advanced cruise-booking technology for travel agents and cruise providers. Online booking will be the trend. The question is, When will the cruise lines stop paying travel agents commissions? Table 7.1 provides a summary of e-commerce strategies used by the major cruise lines.

TABLE 7.1 A Survey of E-Commerce Strategies Used by the Major Cruise Lines		
CRUISE LINE AND URL	WHAT THE SITE OFFERS	DIRECT BOOKING? BOOKING WITH TRAVEL AGENTS?
Carnival: www.carnival.com	Benefits, gift shop, shore tours, destinations, guest services, group travel, agent finder, vacation planner, and specials	Yes. You can locate an agent in your location and customize a vacation to your needs.
Celebrity: www.celebrity-cruises.com	List of destinations; ship layouts with description, staterooms, guest club, rates; online reservations	Yes. You can locate an agent in your area, but you must contact the agent yourself.
Holland America: www.hollandamerica.com	Cruise search, online booking, shore excursions; request a brochure and virtual tours	Yes. There is a travel-agents-only section, where an agent can log in.
Disney: www.disneycruise.com	Entertainment onboard/onshore, members club, reservations, Walt Disney World; virtual tours of ships and accommodations; itineraries	Yes. There is travel-agents-only section, where an agent must log in.
Royal Caribbean: www.royalcarribean.com	Package reservation, destinations, ships, shore excursions that are described and priced, customer service, frequent cruiser, pictures of rooms, ships, and ports of call	Yes. You can locate an agent in your area. There is a section for reasons to contact an agent and also a link for travel agents only.

Princess: www.princess.com	Specials, voyage planning, cruise personalizer, virtual tour of the fleet; activities, dining entertainment, casinos	No. There is a travel agent locator to find an agent in your area.
Norwegian: www.ncl.com	Fleet, specials, itineraries, destinations, voyages/ pricing, bookings, e-mail sign-up	No. There is a travel-agents-only section.
Windstar: www.windstarcruises.com	Virtual tours, Internet offers, charter cruises, request a brochure, sign up for e-mail, booking, Windstar wear	No. In the travel agent link, know password to get information about how to sell Windstar.

LODGING

The lodging sector of the travel industry, though starting late in e-commerce, is fast catching up. The latest research shows that hotel industry room nights and revenue booked electronically in 2001 by travel agents and consumers grew at a rapid rate (from www.travelclick.net). Room nights were up 6% over the first quarter of 2000, and revenue was up a dramatic 10%. This growth in GDS booking both by consumers directly and through **third-party travel** Web sites occurred despite a slow market in the total U.S. economy. Such - third-party online travel Web sites, which include Travelocity.com and Expedia.com, represent approximately 17% of all consumer hotel online bookings made over the Internet.

Today, all major lodging chains have invested in e-commerce and information technology to various degrees. These investments include in-room high-speed Internet connections, online direct booking Web sites, and online procurement of services and products. The lodging industry has come to embrace the Internet, realizing that e-commerce is the future of the travel industry. Some companies are building so-called **e-hotels,** offering services, including 100-mb high-speed Internet access, video-on-demand systems, limited videoconferencing in all rooms, wireless access throughout the building; Internet kiosks in the lobby; and customized applications that let guests tap into the back-office systems to order food and services and to pay bills (Johnson 2000).

Other lodging properties are also beginning to pay attention to this emerging e-commerce market. Small bed-and-breakfast properties are either setting up their own Web sites or joining major bed-and-breakfast marketing sites. Finding information or even booking these small properties online is no longer a luxury—it is a common feature. Today, you can

TABLE 7.2 A Survey of the Major Lodging Web Sites		
COMPANY AND URL	WHAT THE SITE OFFERS	ONLINE BOOKING?
The Four Seasons Hotel and Resorts: www.fourseasons.com	Picture links to vacation getaways, business travel and rates, availability, residential properties, Four Seasons Hotel directory in five different languages	Yes
The Ritz Carlton Hotel and Resort: www.ritzcarlton.com	Reservations and exploration of hotels (each hotel link has extensive information on all hotel services and packages)	Yes
Embassy Suites: www.hilton.com/en	Reservations, check rates, find a hotel, special offers, hotel locator by city, state, or country	Yes
Marriott Hotel: www.marriott.com	Find a hotel, reservations, hotel directories, route planner, frequent visitors, links to all Marriott properties	Yes
Adams Mark Hotel: www.adamsmark.com	Locations of Adams Mark Hotels, reservations; search rates and availability by city, state, or country	Yes
Hyatt Hotels: www.hyatt.com	Rates and reservations, special offers, Gold Passport Program, Hyatt Resorts, Hyatt Extra Email Subscription Search for Hyatt's worldwide hotels by city, state, or country	Yes

log on to www.bedandbreakfast.com to find information on over 27,000 bed-and-breakfasts and inns throughout the world. The Internet has truly changed the way travelers plan their vacations. Table 7.2 provides a summary of the major lodging Web sites.

RENTAL CAR INDUSTRY

With its quiet start in the early 20th century, the rental car industry has gone a long way toward embracing technology. Beginning in the 1990s, the industry started to adopt technology to improve its reservation systems (Wood 2000a). National Car Rental made news in *Travel Agent* magazine when it adopted a new reservations system in 1999 (Wood 2000a). Almost at the same time, the rental car industry began to embrace Internet technology. Rental companies have realized that consumers are more interested in e-commerce and accordingly are putting more resources into online booking and marketing. Online booking and marketing of vehicles has helped rental companies streamline their business, increase its reach and efficiency and at the same time better serve the customers' needs and wants.

All major rental companies have set up their own Web sites with extensive offerings in e-commerce, marketing, customer service, and information distribution. From these sites, you can do a variety of activities, including viewing fleet photos to find out driving directions and making your online reservation. Most car rental firms have designated agent sections for incentive-program information and commissionable bookings.

Rental car companies are targeting their Web strategies not only at leisure travel customers but also at the corporate travel market. One by one, rental car companies are rolling out new Internet programs to facilitate and lure corporations to do business with them over the Web. In June 2000, Avis rolled out an Internet-based information system called **Avis InterActive** (www.avisinteractive.com) (Wood 2000b). This system allows its corporate customers to access complete, up-to-date information on their car rental usage, making the tracking of travel expenses and rental preferences easier for frequent business travelers.

In 2001, Avis provided an update to its Avis InterActive with Release 2.0, greatly increasing its capability and usability. Avis InterActive system has begun a trend in creating customized, Web-based reporting systems. Like airline products and services, rental car products and services are not too complicated to be customized. With Avis InterActive, corporate travel managers can use the "Data on Demand" feature to access corporate accounts with detailed, password-protected information on rental transactions as well as renters' car preferences (PR Newswire 2001).

A future development in the rental car industry will be to develop an online rental system that **streamlines** the rental process, including reservations, changes of schedule, signing agreements, checking in, and payment. In addition, the system will be Web based, customizable, and interactive. For instance, Alamo has already introduced a system called **QuickRent®**. This system allows online travelers to complete the entire rental process online. With QuickRent®, online travelers can bypass the counter by choosing all their options online, signing the rental agreement online, or using one of the ATM-style kiosks at one of the 36 Alamo rental locations in the United States. This type of system differs from those of the past, when online travelers were required to complete the rental transaction at the counter unless they were a special club member or frequent travel member. Table 7.3 provides a summary of the major rental car Web Sites. Table 7.4 provides a time line of the rental car industry's development.

TABLE 7.3		
A Survey of Major Rental Car Companies' Web sites		
COMPANY AND URL	WHAT THE SITE OFFERS	ONLINE BOOKING/ MARKETING STRATEGIES
Advantage: www.arac.com	Obtain quotes; reserve a car, airline tickets, or hotel; track flights; register a travel profile; dealers can purchase preowned vehicles; travel partners	Rent twice and earn a free day; Discover card coupon; discounts for AAA and AARP members, travel agents and airline employees; frequent rental and easy rental and return programs
Alamo: www.goalamo.com	Obtain quotes; make reservations (QuickRent(R)); get driving directions; weather	Internet discount, deals on certain cities
Auto Europe: www.autoeurope.com	Book car rentals, airline tickets, hotel reservations; rent cell phones; get maps and driving directions	Incentive for newsletter subscription; free cell phone rental for online booking; travel agent incentives; discount packages
Avis: www.avis.com	Obtain rates; make reservations; maps/weather; destination information	Online discount, earn bonus miles
Budget: www.drivebudget.com	Rate quotes; location listing; gift certificates; safety tip/moving guide	Online discounts; points program; loyalty program; awards for online booking
Dollar: www.dollar.com	Rates and rentals; airline and hotel reservations; flight tracker; and Palm-Pilot accessibility to Web site	E-mail specials; mileage or credits with travel partners; express rates
Enterprise: www.pickenterprise.com	City/airport locator; check automobile availability, make corporate reservations, purchase used cars, fleet management	E-mail specials
Hertz: www.hertz.com	Rates and reservations; obtain policies and procedures; find worldwide locations; vehicle guide	AAA member discount special offers; partnerships
National Car Rental: www.nationalcar.com	Rates and reservations, company information, links to travel partners	One-way specials, last-minute specials

| Payless:
www.800-payless.com | Rates and reservations, vehicles and policies, customer service, worldwide directory | Register to win a car, preferred renter club, 30th-birthday special, senior discount program |
| Thrifty:
www.thrifty.com | Rates and reservations; worldwide locations; car sales, franchise opportunities, travel partners | Business/government/ collegiate rates; GoldPoints rewards; e-mail programs |

TABLE 7.4
Major Timeline for Rental Car Industry Development

1939: Hertz begins to offer vehicles with automatic transmissions. The company was founded in 1918 by Walter Jacobs as Rent-A-Ford. In 1923, the company was purchased by John Hertz.

1947: National Car Rental is founded as an association called the National Car Rental system.

1958: Thrifty Car Rental is founded by L. G. Crane, with one location in Tulsa, Oklahoma.

1958: Budget Rent-a-Car is founded by Morris Mirkin in a storefront in Los Angeles. Mirkin offers rental rates as low as $4 per day and 4 cents per mile.

1962: Avis Rent-a-Car introduces the "We Try Harder" campaign, which is still used today.

1966: Dollar Rent-a-Car is founded by Henry Caruso.

1972: Avis introduces the Wizard computer system.

1973: Payless Rent-a-Car is launched.

1974: Alamo Rent-a-Car opens for business.

1980: Avis introduces the Wizard II system.

1984: Hertz introduces computerized driving directions for its rental customers.

1989: Thrifty Car Rental introduces FASTRAC.

1990: Alamo introduces its frequent-renter program, Alamo Express.

SOURCE: Adapted from Wood (2000a).

7.3 THE IMPACT ON TRAVEL AGENTS

By now, you might have come to the conclusion that the deepest impact of the Internet and e-commerce is on travel agents since almost all travel suppliers are marketing directly to travelers. You would not be far from the truth. With commission cuts, customers turning to the Internet for bargains, and a lack of resources and knowledge of technology, travel agents are learning e-commerce the hard way. The impact is so deep that many two-year travel schools that used to be a good employment source for travel agencies are closing their doors or are forced to revise their curricula to meet the needs of the employment market.

The fact is that suppliers such as hotels, airlines, rental car companies, and even cruise lines have already offered online real-time reservations. Indeed, they not only make reservations available online but also use incentives to encourage travelers to book online. For example, at one time, Northwest Airlines offered a new online booking program to small and medium-size corporations that featured incentives, including free tickets and upgrades, elite frequent-flier program status, airport lounge memberships, and travel management aids. United Airlines offered a bonus of 25,000 miles to participants in its frequent-flier program who stayed at least 10 times at Regent International Hotels by December 30, 2000; each stay must have been a minimum of three nights. Travelers also had to register with Regent and pay the corporate room rate. British Airways established a Web site on London as a destination (www.londontraveller.com) that contains in-depth information on the city from a variety of travel guidebooks as well as data on the newest restaurants, bars, clubs, theaters, and art exhibits. Visitors to the site can also buy airline tickets and book hotel rooms.

With increased interest by travelers in online travel information research and booking and the aggressive marketing efforts of travel suppliers to sell tickets online, travel agencies are being squeezed from all sides. As if this is not bad enough, suppliers, led by the airlines, began to cut their commissions as early as in 1997, which turned out to be a deadly blow to travel agencies.

Faced with this tremendous pressure to survive, travel agencies have used various strategies to cope with the new reality. Such strategies ranged from early denial of the Internet's impact to attempts to free themselves from the control of the traditional GDSs by setting up their own central reservations system.

Travel agencies are going through a period of restructuring and reorganization. Some of the small mom-and-pop travel agencies have closed, some have been taken over by large travel companies; and some have begun to take advantage of the Internet to turn it into a profit-making opportunity. In Chapter 8, we will discuss these impacts and their ramifications.

7.4 THE IMPACT ON TRADITIONAL BROCHURE INFORMATION DISTRIBUTION

Traditionally, travelers rely heavily on **print brochures** to obtain information on destinations and travel products and services. Each year, millions of dollars are spent by business and destination marketers to produce and distribute print brochures. With the increasing popularity of the Internet, the reliance on the print brochure as a major marketing tool is now in question.

Zhou and Lin (2000) conducted a survey on the use of the Internet versus the print brochure. Their findings show that the majority of the respondents have access to the Internet, with approximately over half having Internet access at home, followed by 34% at the library and 31% at the office. When asked how many hours on average they spent using the Internet per week, the answer ranged from 0 hours (30.1%) to 100 hours, with a mean of 6.39 hours. When asked which source(s) of information they will depend on the most for their future trip planning, about 43% of the respondents reported that they would use both print brochures and the Internet, followed by using print brochures (37.8%) and word-of-mouth recommendation from relatives, friends, or peers (23.5%).

However, if we add those who will use both print brochures and the Internet and those who will use only the Internet, we come up with a figure as large as 58%. In other words, nearly 60% of people will use the Internet either as a sole source of information or as a complementary source of travel information. Table 7.5 shows information source preferences for travel planning.

One thing that may catch your eye from Table 7.5 is that only about 7% of people use a travel agent for travel advice and planning. In fact, the biggest impact on the hospitality and tourism industry is in the area of travel information search and planning. A survey has shown that business travelers worldwide are increasingly embracing the Internet to research and book their flights (from www.iata.org). Almost two-thirds of the survey's approximately 1,000 respondents from Europe, North America, and the Asia-Pacific region said that they used the Internet to find flight information, a 50% increase over the survey's results from two years ago.

More travel companies and destination marketers have begun to realize that there is a huge online market for them to play. In the past, **convention and visitor bureaus** and other **destination marketing organizations,** relied

TABLE 7.5
Information Sources for Future Travel Planning

INFORMATION SOURCE	NUMBER	PERCENTAGE
Both print brochures and the Internet	335	42.8
Print brochures	296	37.8
Word of mouth	184	23.5
Internet	116	14.8
Travel agents	54	6.9

SOURCE: Zhou and Lin (2000).

mostly on print brochures to distribute information and conduct marketing. Research has shown that this domination is dwindling (Zhou and Lin 2000). The Internet has provided an excellent alternative (if not replacement) for distributing travel and destination information, including maps. With the price of a printer being so affordable, more people own printers at home, which makes printing online information easy and convenient.

Online travel brochures have several advantages over traditional print ones. First, they are more accurate since their information can be updated around the clock. This is especially true when it comes to pricing, events, weather, special promotions, and road maps. Second, they can be customized according to the needs of an individual online visitor. Customization is the key to the future development of destination information distribution. Third, information can be accessed 24/7, anywhere in the world. This will become even more important in the future when broadband wireless Web technology becomes widely available. At that time, travelers will have a **walking brochure** (a Web-based wireless device) in their hand wherever they travel. Using this device, travelers can access travel information anywhere, anytime they desire. Finally, online information distribution breaks the barrier of a brochure, which can carry only a limited amount of information. With the Internet, the only limit is the Web server's storage space. Theoretically, destination marketers can place as much information as they want online on their own Web site. In addition, the hyperlinks of the Web dramatically increase and expand the amount of information that can be made available to online travelers.

▆ 7.5 THE TRAVEL E-COMMERCE MARKETPLACE

The potentially lucrative online travel market has attracted other players into the competition. A number of **online-only travel Web sites** have loomed large in travel information distribution and travel reservation (Table 7.6). All these sites have strong financial and marketing clout from some of the largest corporations in the United States. Expedia.com (www.expedia.com) was originally owned by Microsoft, while Travelocity.com (www.travelocity.com) is owned largely by Sabre, one of the largest GDSs.

Other online-only travel reservations sites include Priceline.com (www.priceline.com), a company that claims that consumers can name their price; Lowestprice.com (www.lowestprice.com); and the airline-backed Orbitz.com (www.orbitz.com), which went into operation in the summer of 2001. Table 7.6 describes some of the most popular sites in operation in 2003. Some of these players are trying to establish themselves as a **one-stop shopping portal** for travel needs, supplying travel information as well as

TABLE 7.6			
New Players in the Online Travel Marketplace			
URL	WHAT THE SITE OFFERS	PROS	CONS
www.bedandbreakfast.com	Search/book a room at a bed-and-breakfast or inn by address, amenity, or key word	Very detailed and informative; some pictures; some have online reservation requests; some have links to home pages	Some inns may just have a contact number with no online reservations available
www.cheaptickets.com	Search/book hotels, flights, cruises, rental cars, specials	Customer service agents available to help with your search; specials via e-mail	Web address denotes airfare only; must be a member to fulfill a search
www.expedia.com	Book/research flights, cruises, rental cars, and hotel rooms; search for packages and deals; read	A one-stop site to arrange a trip; find relatively good priced fares	There is no connecting flight option; fares are not discount prices
www.fodors.com	Vacation guide site with several reservations sites connected to it; print a map; find night life, attractions, and activities	Link to Yahoo currency converter; links for booking airfare, hotel, and so on; find restaurants and attractions in area	Limited cities/ destinations to choose from; not all properties rated; no direct reservation
www.lonelyplanet.com	Plan a vacation here by searching for information by various points of interest	Helpful information, several countries to choose from	Cannot book anything here, just research and get information
www.lowestfare.com	Search/book a flight, cruise, vacation; read up on travel news; find deals and specials	Search process is relatively easy; multiple-leg travel available; competitive pricing	No hotel reservations, may come in contact with several search errors

TABLE 7.6			
New Players in the Online Travel Marketplace			*(continued)*
URL	WHAT THE SITE OFFERS	PROS	CONS
www.orbitz.com	Comprehensive site for online booking on tour packages, rental cars, cruise lines, and hotels; multicity flight tickets	Many specials backed by its airline owners; one-stop shopping; quick flight search right on the first screen	Still in its development; some areas are not fully functioning and user friendly
www.opodo.co.uk	One of Opodo's local sites offers comprehensive travel services from travel guide to flight and car rental reservation	Another comprehensive Web site backed by Europe's nine leading airlines	German, UK, and French sites are open in 2002
www.priceline.com	Book/research/ purchase airfare, hotel rooms, rental cars, new cars; name own price	Name own price; get results within one hour by e-mail; searches several companies to find you a deal	Need credit card information to see any results; will charge your card if your request is granted; many restrictions
www.frommers.com	Budget travel search site; search from several countries for hotels, restaurants, and shopping; tips and resources for budget travel; links for some forms of travel	Informative site for international travel; good for students or backpackers across Europe; name-brand links to find and book specifics	Find limited results with very general descriptions; seemingly outdated rates; Web pages listed but no links

TABLE 7.6 New Players in the Online Travel Marketplace *(continued)*			
URL	WHAT THE SITE OFFERS	PROS	CONS
www.hoteldiscounts.com	Book/research room rates only in select cities throughout the United States; read about features; get more information on a property; plenty of pictures to give you an idea of the accommodations	Can read up on each and every hotel on-site; hotel rating system on various services; search by rate; receive about 15 listings per search; claims to be the lowest price and highest quality "guaranteed"	Can book/ search for rooms only in select cities, and even then, you cannot choose loca- tion; need to log in to make a reservation; no links to hotel's home page
www.hotwire.com	Book/search for hotel rooms, flights, and rental cars; view others' searches; receive travel information	Discounts airfare; you have an hour to purchase once selections have been made; can have special deals e-mailed to you	Does not give name of hotel or airline or flight times until after you have made the purchase; some- what lengthy registration process
www.travelocity.com	Book/research flights, cruises, train, hotel rooms, rental cars, and vacations; search for deals and e-travel savings; receive customer service	One-stop site that is user friendly; excellent customer service; can hold and save inquiry for 24 hours; name own price and search three-legged itineraries	Site is somewhat cluttered, so making a search could take a long time if this is your first time using the site
www.travelweb.com	Book/research room rates and airfare; get specific travel information; check availability of several items	Very informative site; gives some pictures to help user gain insight; able to check availability before trying to book	For flights, the site sends you to Expedia.com; it really searches only for hotel rooms; prices are not shown until booking stage; longer process

booking for all types of services, ranging from lodging to airlines and from entertainment to transportation. Some of these are being provided by traditional travel service companies.

This **e-commerce marketplace** is still in its development and, in fact, is going through some rapid changes. With technology changing almost daily and new players entering the travel e-commerce marketplace, we are bound to see some major shakeups in the competition. Even Microsoft, a company with much financial clout, had to sell its Expedia.com to USA Networks in 2001 despite the fact that for the first time Expedia.com was beginning to make a profit. The latest development in this marketplace is the entry of Orbitz.com and Opodo.com, each backed by powerful airline consortiums in the United States and Europe respectively, raising the questions of monopoly and unfair competition. The winners of this intense competition are consumers, who will determine which of these e-commerce Web sites will survive the competition.

7.6 CONCLUSION

The impact of the Internet on the hospitality and tourism industry is far reaching and multifaceted. It affects both the supply side and the demand side as well as those in between. And then there are newcomers—those travel dot-coms who serve as the new electronic intermediaries, competing aggressively with both the suppliers and the old intermediaries. The suppliers of hospitality and tourism products and services saw the opportunity to market directly to consumers, and consumers are eager to use the Internet to assist their travel needs. In the meantime, those in between are at a loss, struggling to find the right approach to defend their markets.

The key to the success of any travel e-commerce is the ability to provide customization, easy access, a friendly interface, 24/7 customer service, value information, interaction, online transactions, and global appeal. All these elements must be considered carefully in making the Web site construction plan as discussed in Chapter 6. In the age of the Internet, the rules of the game may have changed, but the core business principles remain the same.

KEY WORDS AND TERMS

Intermediaries	Intranet Web Sites
Online Pricing	Airline Ticket Publishing Company
Suppliers	Sabre
Corporate Clients	Customization

Global Distribution System
Third-party Travel Web Sites
E-hotels
Avis Interactive
Streamline
QuickRent®
Print brochures

Convention and Visitor
   Bureaus (Destination
   Marketing Organizations)
Walking brochure
One-stop Shopping Portal
E-Commerce Marketplace

SUMMARY

The hospitality and tourism industry is embracing the Internet to cut costs and increase efficiency and effectiveness in e-commerce, marketing, and customer service. Airlines are the most aggressive in adopting Internet technology since they want to save on the commissions they pay out to their traditional ally: travel intermediaries. The lodging industry is determined not to be left behind in this rush to embrace Internet technology. From in-room service to reservations, the lodging industry is implementing Internet technology solutions to increase its reach to new markets and better serve its customers.

The cruise lines are still relying heavily on travel agents and tour operators and is reluctant to break the ties since cruise-line products are more difficult and complicated for consumers to book on their own. However, the cruise lines are beginning to experiment with online e-commerce and marketing strategies and are making online booking an alternative for consumers. The future is still unclear, but the trend is for the cruise lines to move closer to adopting new technologies.

The Rental car industry has witnessed leaps and bounds in adopting technology. Consumers and corporate travel managers are now able to conduct a whole range of e-commerce activities on rental car company Web sites. The trend is toward creating a system that can streamline the online booking process and other customer service functions.

The hospitality and tourism e-commerce marketplace has heated up as more third-party online travel Web sites enter the competition. The latest entry by Orbits.com and the future development of Opodo.com, both backed by powerful airline companies, demonstrates the attractiveness of the online travel market. However, it also raises questions as to which direction the marketplace will go and who will survive this intense competition. The impact on travel agents is obvious from what has been discussed in this chapter. Its impact is so deep that it deserves a separate chapter.

▋WEB RESOURCES

- www.opodo.com
- www.businesstravel.com
- www.btnonline.com

CASE STUDY: The Colony Beach and Tennis Resort

The Colony Beach and Tennis Resort is a world-renowned resort for its beautiful surroundings, top-notch tennis facilities, and award-winning restaurants. The Colony is located in Longboat Key, Florida, an island community on the Gulf coast of Florida. The Colony takes pride in pampering its guests with many complimentary features. The resort offers tennis on 21 courts with round-robin and match-play tournaments; a state-of-the-art fitness center; full-service health spas with whirlpool, saunas, and steam room; and year-round supervised children's programs.

The Colony Beach and Tennis Resort was started in 1969, when Dr. M. J. "Murf" Klauber purchased what was the Colony Beach Club. It was an 18-acre patch of sand, about 110 little bungalows, and a couple of concrete tennis courts. After a large investment in the resort, workers began to transform the small club into what is now the Colony Beach and Tennis Resort. The resort now has 208 fully equipped villa suites and 26 specially accommodated penthouses, along with 21 hard and soft tennis courts, two award-winning restaurants, a pool, and a brand-new aerobic and fitness center.

The Colony Beach and Tennis Resort has been named the number 1 tennis resort in the country by *Tennis magazine* several times in the past decade. The resort has set itself apart from its competitors by great management and advertising. The Colony was quick to realize the importance of the Internet during the Internet boom in the 1990s. The company knew that, to increase its hold on the market, it would need to implement online advertising to its marketing scheme.

The Internet has been a helpful tool for the resort. However, because of the limited technology resources inside the company, the resort outsourced the entire Internet and information technology operation to a consulting company, including domain name registration, troubleshooting, upgrades, new product research, and third-party information technology vendors. The Colony feels it is important to outsource its network operations so that it can receive professional assistance and not tie down its employees by dealing with these issues.

The Colony is currently using a wireless direct connect with Static IP. It has Web hosting outsourced through a third-party vendor, Colony Resort, which provides fast, flexible bandwidth that not only exceeds domain needs at an excellent cost but also allows potential for the unused bandwidth to generate revenue through service offerings to Colony clients. The Colony was previously using the basic 56K modem system on its own, but the system failed to provide the desired results.

After careful consideration, the Colony decided to outsource to meet its needs. This was because outsourcing Web hosting allows specialists to do what the Colony lacks in expertise at the fraction of the cost of hiring a full time Web designer and a dedicated server for it. The Colony is dedicated to progressing with information technology, with a priority to use it to increase revenue and margins. In addition, the new system also allows the resort to get into business-to-business e-commerce. The Internet and information technology solutions have given the Colony the ability to provide service that is faster, better, and more economical.

The Internet has been a large part in the Colony's success as a world-renowned resort. The Internet allows the resort to communicate efficiently and effectively to both customers and business partners. In the past, the resort had to use traditional methods of sales and marketing, such as cold phone calls or obtrusive door-to-door sales. Today, with Internet solutions, the Colony can communicate and market its products and services to almost anyone, anywhere in the world, reaching markets that were previously impossible or too expensive to approach.

While the Internet offers many benefits and advantages to the Colony Resort, there are still some problems and issues with its use. One problem is trying to prevent the nonproductive use of the Internet by employees in the workplace. Another problem is trying to find a balance between security and flexibility. The resort is taking measures to resolve these issues.

The Colony sees a great future using the Internet. The resort plans to increase its funding for Internet marketing and hopes to increase revenue through selling its excess bandwidth capabilities to advertising opportunities and possible Internet-based client services. In the future, the Colony feels that with a sound backbone of bandwidth, there are many things that it can do to increase its profitable usage. The resort has high hopes of continuing to use the Internet and information technology to help maintain the resort as one of the world's finest.

QUESTIONS TO PONDER:

1. What are the reasons for the Colony to outsource its Internet and information technology solutions?
2. Why did the resort opt for broadband?
3. In what ways did the Internet help the resort market its services?
4. What are some of the problems the resort has? What do you think is the best way to solve those problems?

REVIEW QUESTIONS

1. Why were the airlines the first to cut commissions to travel agencies?
2. What are the factors that make the hospitality and tourism industry so adaptable to the Internet?
3. Why were the cruise lines hesitant to go fully with the online reservation?
4. What are some of the strategies used by the lodging chain companies to sell their products and services in different locations of the world?
5. Do you think the rental industry will become the leader in taking advantage of the Internet for e-commerce solutions? If so, why? If not, what is the evidence?
6. Give one major reason why travel agencies are struggling to hold on to their market.
7. Describe the benefits of using online information distribution and online brochures.
8. Do you think that third-party Web sites will dominate the online travel reservations market? Support your argument with evidence.

REFERENCES

Dixon, P. (2000). "Fare Game, Airlines, Travel Agents Duke It Out over the Web." *San Diego Union Tribune*, January 9,

Hughes, L. Q. (1998). "Changing Tide." *Travel Agent*, August 3,

Hughes, L. Q. (1999). "Untangling the Web." *Travel Agent*, April 26, 3.

Johnson, A. H. (2000). "E-Hotel." www.computerworld.com.

PR Newswire. (2001). "Avis Upgrades Its Comprehensive Tracking System for Corporate Travel Managers." www.Prnewswire.com.

Wood, Danielle. (2000a). "Driving through the Decades." *Travel Agent*, July 31,

Wood, Danielle. (2000b). "Getting Connected". *Travel Agent*, June 10,

Zhou, Z. Q., and Li Chun Lin. (2000). "The Impact of the Internet on the Use of the Print Brochure." Proceedings of the CHRIE's 2000 annual conference, July 19–22, New Orleans.

For additional Travel and Tourism resources, go to
www.Hospitality-Tourism.delmar.com

A Special Case Study: The Past, Present, and Future of Travel Agents

Learning Objectives

After you complete your study of this chapter, you should be able to:

- Gain a historical perspective on the role of travel agents.
- Describe the attitude of travel agents toward the use of technology.
- Understand why travel agencies' business models no longer fit the Internet age.
- Explain why travelers leave travel agents.
- Understand new strategies for the future of travel agents.
- Explain why marketing orientation, combined with individualized service, is the viable business model for the future of travel agencies.

■ 8.1 INTRODUCTION

According to the Travel Industry Association of America (2001), more than 59 million Internet users in the United States went online last year to gather information or to check prices and schedules, growing 395% over the past three years. Of that group, 25 million actually purchased travel products or services online, a 384% increase from 1997. Other research also supports the scenario that more travelers are logging on to the Internet for travel information, trip planning, and online reservations and purchasing of travel products and services (Zhou and Lin 2000).

In 1999, according to the search engine AltaVista, 10,602,880 Web pages contained the key word "travel." On July 22, 2001, there were 51,093,044 Web pages containing the key word "travel," a five-fold increase over 1999. According to Nielsen/Netratings (www.nielsen-netratings.com), over one-third of all e-commerce transactions are now attributable to travel, and online travel advertizing ranked fourth in 2002, reflecting the fierce competition in the online travel market for consumers. (www.nielsen-netratings.com, Dec. 2002) In just one month (March 2001), it was estimated that a massive $1.03 billion was spent on online travel—an increase of almost 60% over the March 2000 figure. It is estimated that by year's-end 2002, it will reach $8.9 billion (from www.nielsen-netratings.com).

Travel agents have never seen such a major challenge to their survival. They are being hit from all directions. Both the availability of online booking and the commissions cut and cap by travel suppliers and carriers put considerable pressure on travel agents. As if this was not enough, third-party online travel stores, such as Expedia.com, Travelocity.com, Orbitz.com, Priceline.com, and Travelweb.com are competing with them and taking customers away. The global distribution systems, GDSs, the former allies of the travel agents, are reaching out to consumers themselves.

Despite the event of September 11, there is increasing consumer interest in e-commerce that, in turn, is fueled by consumers' increasing online accessibility. In addition, there has been increasing consumers trust in various online payment methods as well as in credit card transactions over the Internet. A study of why and how travel agents have ended up in this situation and the future direction this might take can shed light on the impact of the Internet on the hospitality and tourism industry as well as the underlying reasons for the impact. Identifying these problems and issues can help travel agents as well as other sectors of the industry develop strategies to cope with new changes in the market. For those travel agents who can harness the new technology, the Internet can be a blessing in disguise. For others, it can prove to be a deal with the devil, costing both money and the life of their business.

8.2 A HISTORICAL PERSPECTIVE

THE HISTORICAL ROLE OF TRAVEL AGENTS

Historically, travel agents played an essential role in hospitality and tourism. They were a leading intermediary between the **traveling public** and travel carriers and suppliers. Travel agents were supposed to be trained professionals with extensive knowledge of the hospitality and tourism industry. They were there not only to sell tickets but also, supposedly, to provide advice and recommendations on every aspect of a trip, from planning to onsite visitation. Travelers recognized this knowledge as an asset and called on these agents for a variety of services, including the arrangement of transportation, preparation of itineraries, and booking accommodations and flight tickets.

Travel agents do not actually produce these travel products and services; rather, they simply act as the **retailer** and **promoter** on behalf of the service providers, that is, the travel carriers and suppliers. Agents sell these products and services directly to the traveling public and in return receive a **commission** from the travel carriers and suppliers. In essence, the travel public receives "free" service from travel agents.

TRAVEL AGENTS AND THE VALUE OF INFORMATION ACCESS

Travel products are unique in that they are not of a **tangible nature**. Information constitutes the bulk of travel products and transactions. In addition, travel is about the experiences and memories that tourists will have for a lifetime. Travel agents are therefore crucial in the tourism world, as they provide the key to an unforgettable travel encounter in providing critical travel information that leads to a satisfactory travel experience.

In the past, travel agents were held in high esteem because they were virtually the most important, if not the only, medium through which consumers could gain travel information and make advanced travel purchases. Travel service providers and customers alike rushed to their doors for business. In 1985, it was believed that "without travel agents, it would be practically impossible for the traveler or tourist to shop for the most convenient flights at the best price; for tours, cruises packages, hotel and resorts; or for any other travel related product" (Stevens 1989). At that point in time, travel agents were the "messiah" of the hospitality and tourism industry. Their expertise and vast array of travel resources kept people coming back repeatedly. The key to success was their access to travel information not available directly to the public.

TRAVEL AGENTS AND THE AIRLINE INDUSTRY

Travel agencies work in conjunction with a broad array of travel service providers, but one stands out from the rest. Travel agents relations with airline carriers create many impacts within the industry. In the past, one could not feasibly exist without the other. Travel agents relied heavily on the commissions they received from airline ticket sales to stay in business. At the same time, airlines conducted a majority of their ticket sales through agents. Although this was not the most profitable of alternatives, airlines did so because of the agents' great popularity and visibility in the eye of the public. Airlines and travel agencies have experienced many difficulties establishing their relationship, which remained relatively unchallenged before the advent of e-commerce. Many issues faced by agents have come about because airline commissions have such a great effect on travel agents. Any changes in the distribution of the travel and ticketing information would have directly affected travel agents as well.

Travel agents have not always been present since the airlines began shuttling travelers around the world. Historically, airlines were dependent on any person who had contact with the traveling public to sell their tickets. Obviously, this was not the safest or the most effective method. A major change occurred in 1945, when the **Air Traffic Conference** (ATC) was established by the airline industry to alleviate this unorganized method of distribution. The conference system was responsible for establishing agreements and standards that would regulate the activity of domestic airlines and the dispersion of their tickets. It also established the modern-day travel agent.

TRAVEL AGENCY AND AIRLINE REGULATIONS

The ATC Passenger Agency Program was developed to determine the conditions for the authorization of agents. This system protected airlines from dealing with unqualified distributors (Meyer and Oster 1987). Under this program, only agencies appointed by the ATC were authorized to sell airline tickets for member airlines. ATC **accreditation** was based on several standards, including business practices, financial requirements, personnel training, and agency location.

A major provision of the Passenger Agency Program was the "20% rule." This rule required that an agent must do less than 20% of its annual air transportation business with itself or other businesses under its control (Meyer and Oster 1987). This rule was essential for preventing large corporations from forming agencies to regulate distribution of their own business travel. Not long after the establishment of the ATC, the **International Air Transportation Association** (IATA) was formed for the regulation of international air travel. The IATA has the same basic functions of the ATC: security, safety standards, and appointment of travel agencies to represent member airlines. The ATC and IATA worked in conjunction with each other in many aspects.

For example, all revenue incurred from the IATA was deposited into banks that were established by the ATC.

The ATC and IATA were voluntary conferences governing air travel, but there was also regulation at the federal level. The **Civil Aeronautics Board** (CAB) regulated air travel from 1938 to 1978 (Stevens 1989). During its 40-year tenure, this branch of the U.S. government took on many roles, especially granting airline routes, controlling fares, and protecting the interest of the public. Airlines were under tight scrutiny by the CAB. The area of CAB's greatest control was airline fares. Airlines themselves had little control in pricing their own tickets. Any price commanded by the CAB was dictated to travel agents for sales. All airlines were required to charge the same fare for flights to and from the same city.

The CAB allowed minimal experimentation with discounts or promotional fares and controlled all revision of ticket prices. Thus, **prederegulation** procedures encouraged competition not by price but solely by the unique services they offered. Such was the climate of the airline and agency industries through the late 1970s. Regulation was enforced on every aspect of air travel, from airline routes to the agencies that dispersed tickets to the public. By 1973, with a majority of airlines on the brink of bankruptcy, it was evident that major changes were needed in the airline industry.

AIRLINE DEREGULATIONS

In the winter of 1973, worldwide oil supplies were condensed by petroleum exporters seeking to profit from exceedingly high prices (Foster 1990). Airlines had no choice but to surrender to these price increases in order to deliver their services to the traveling public. They were injured severely by this action. Under CAB regulation, airlines were not allowed to increase the cost to passengers to compensate for these unexpected operational costs. Caught in a frenzy of turmoil, the airline industry came close to collapsing.

Gradually over the next four years, the CAB loosened its grip on the industry. Recognizing the negative side effects of its tight regulation, by 1977 the CAB had departed from its restrictive policies enforced in previous years. This administrative **deregulation** allowed discount fares and advocated total airline deregulation. From 1976 to 1978, a boom in the airline industry resulted from these changes. Airlines were experiencing financial success as they had never seen before, in turn spurring the growth and success for travel agencies.

AIRLINE DEREGULATION ACT AND ITS IMPACT

The final step to the complete liberation of the airline industry came with the passage of the **Airline Deregulation Act,** signed by President Carter in 1978. The act removed all remaining obstacles to route entry by established carriers, opened up entry to new carriers, and phased out all fare regulations

(Meyer and Oster 1987). There were two major components of this law that led to serious effects in the years following deregulation. The first was the gradual dismantling of the CAB by 1985, thus eliminating any prospect of further airline regulation. The second was the scope of antitrust legislation that was entered into on the freedom to competition and protection from monopolies gained by the industry. These changes brought both airline and agency into the realm of the modern business world.

Airlines experienced a period of unlimited freedom following deregulation. Ticket prices rose and fell on the basis of individual airline instruction, competition accelerated, and the general trend in air travel was overwhelming. With this independence came many positive and negative outcomes for both airlines and travel agencies. Along with the abundance of positive effects of airline deregulation mentioned previously, new selling techniques arose that gave way to major increases in airline ticket purchases. The variety of price and service combinations available to the public greatly expanded. Discounting, promotional events, and rebating became common practice. The importance of travel agents to the travel public was obviously increased since travelers were depending more and more on travel agents for deals and for understanding the complicated rules of airline ticket pricing.

Negative side effects that echoed throughout the airline industry were apparent as well. The harsh reality that airlines could indeed succumb to bankruptcy became evident in the years to follow. Airlines could no longer rely on the CAB to protect them, and many fell prey to this misfortune because of increased competition and price wars. Greater responsibility on the part of agents to protect their clients from minimizing personal losses stemming from airline's potential bankruptcy followed accordingly (Gregory 1989). Another downfall was felt mainly by travelers. Airlines no longer had the need to work with one another. Thus, passenger baggage would no longer be automatically transferred from one carrier to another, and airlines would no longer honor one another's tickets on same routes.

THE RAPID GROWTH OF TRAVEL AGENCIES

Travel agencies experienced unprecedented economic gain as airlines prospered in the wake of deregulation. The number of travel agencies around the country multiplied at an alarming rate. Increases in commissions were a result of the confusion that airlines felt with their newfound freedom and were readily accepted by agents. For the time being, the travel agent industry was a prosperous one that appeared to have limitless opportunities.

Disputes arose in the agency industry not long after deregulation planted its roots. Before the CAB was dismantled, issues dealing with the validity of the ATC conference system were discussed. Travel agent exclusivity and agency accreditation procedures were greatly disliked. Despite efforts made by trade associations to support the longevity of the conference system and its components, the travel agency industry experienced its own deregulation in December 1982 (Stevens 1989).

TRAVEL AGENCY INDUSTRY DEREGULATION

In the aftermath of the deregulation, airlines had the added freedom of allowing non-ATC agencies to sell tickets. Business travel departments would be permitted to function as full agencies, and protection from antitrust would become obsolete for agencies. The largest change resulting from agency deregulation was the implementation of the **Airline Reporting Corporation** (ARC). In 1984, this corporation replaced the ATC while maintaining most of its functions.

One major difference resulting from this switch involved the representation of airlines. The ARC allowed airlines to decide for themselves who represented them and their ticket distribution, a function formerly controlled by the ATC. As a result, the airlines gained enormous power in the distribution of air travel information and ticketing. This also sowed the seeds for the strained and hostile relationship between the airlines and the travel agencies over the structure of commissions in the age of e-commerce.

IMPACT OF THE DEREGULATIONS ON TRAVEL AGENTS

Both airline and travel agency deregulations affected every facet of airline-agency relations in the late 1970s and early 1980s. Many hardships and opportunities ensued for both industries, but travel agencies were affected most adversely. Both deregulations set the tone for the industry standards and practices that were followed up to the birth of Internet e-commerce. In fact, deregulation was the largest issue faced by airlines and agencies throughout their history. Without airline deregulation, the airlines may have had a much more difficult time jumping on the Internet distribution channel and freeing themselves from the influence of travel agents.

COMMISSIONS AND TRAVEL AGENTS

The **commission structure** of travel agents with travel carriers and suppliers as well as travelers is such that potential troubles for travel agents were already planted. In many service-oriented businesses, it is customary for some sort of service charge to be added on to the final total cost for the time and effort made by the service provider. Such is not the case for travel agents. The commissions accumulated from the products sold are the primary means of revenue for an agent. Travel agent commissions are unique in that they are subtracted from the selling price of a ticket rather than added on the final cost for the customer. Travel agents' monetary compensations come solely from the service providers, not the customers they work with. Therefore, agencies are at the mercy of those who direct commission payouts; these people determine the financial success of an agency. With heavy reliance on airlines, the greatest effects of agent revenue are generally felt by the decision of air travel suppliers.

Airline commissions account for approximately two-thirds to nine-tenths of a travel agency's total income (Foster 1990). Over time, commissions have risen and declined to fit the changing desires of the airline industry. In the earliest days of commercial air travel, the typical commission was set at 5%. In the 1960s, a series of studies were conducted, revealing agents' strong belief that they were being undercompensated. Regardless of agents' pleas for higher commission rates, airlines forged ahead in their mission to decrease commission costs to 3% (Stevens 1989). By 1969, a somewhat complicated formal structure for commission rates was established that was more realistic than former rates. Typical commissions under this structure ranged from 5% for point-to-point domestic flights to 13% for flights arranged for advertised tours (Stevens 1989).

Deregulation freed airlines from structured commissions. Contrary to what one might think, rates typically rose following this change because of the increasing competition between the airlines for customers. Since the agents were almost the only effective channel of distribution, the rise in the commission structure was not surprising. Soon, a commission rate of 10% became the industry standard, though it was subject to frequent fluctuations because of varying airline ticket prices that spawned from deregulation. The increase in commission was necessary for airlines to stay competitive with rival carriers and keep partner agents loyal to selling their product. This is the philosophy behind the frequent fluctuations and changes of the airline ticketing commissions.

In the heyday of air travel, airlines were very generous with travel agents since airlines depended on travel agents to move the flight seats. **Overrides** and **incentives** became commonplace for agents. These systems provided the means for agents to receive additional income. Overrides are rewards presented to agents when they show exceptional sales performance. Incentives come in the form of cash bonuses and reduced-rate tickets for agents, which inspires the determination for excellence on behalf of the travel agent. These programs are the airlines' way of saying thank you to travel agents for showing exemplary selling skills and helping such airlines make considerable profits.

THE FAILURE OF A BUSINESS MODEL

Commissions have always been a high-priority issue for agents. Without a reasonable commission structure, agencies would surely come face to face with bankruptcy. Amicable conditions permeated the airline and agency industries throughout the 1980s because of the airlines' reliance on agents. However, relationships between travel agents and the airlines have been dictated largely by the airlines since it is the airlines who control the commission structure, not the agents. In other words, when airlines feel they need travel agents, they will try to improve the relations, typically by increasing the commissions they pay out to the agents.

On the other hand, when airlines feel they do not need travel agents for their success, they can decrease and cut the commissions. There is strong incentive for airlines to reduce the commissions since it is a considerable part of their operating expenses in selling tickets. It is not surprising that when the Internet provides an alternative for airline ticket and information distribution, airlines were the first ones to capitalize on it. A commission cut seemed to be a logical step for airlines since they were relying less on their old-time partners, travel agents, to complete sale transactions.

8.3 TECHNOLOGY AND TRAVEL AGENTS

It is not only in recent times that airlines have felt the effects of advances in information technology. With the extensive amount of information that airlines deal with on a daily basis, from flights and fares to seat inventory and passengers, information technology has become critical to organize and maintain every aspect of the industry. In the years preceding such information technology advances, agents had to access information through various channels. Phone calls to central locations, using wall-sized availability boards, and a manual method called the "lazy Susan," which stored colored cards with pencil markings on them to record bookings, were the norm of the past (Sheldon 1997).

COMPUTER RESERVATIONS SYSTEMS

Obviously, these manual methods had their inefficiencies and led to the researching of computerized methods. As for the airline industry, computer technology was first introduced in the 1950s with the advent of the **computer reservations systems (CRS)**. These systems have traditionally been organized by individual airlines to handle reservations, ticketing, schedules, and seat inventories and have created great advances in speed and accuracy for the booking of airline flights.

The first CRS was officially introduced in 1953. Organized by a partnership between American Airlines and IBM, this system later became known as Semi-Automated Business Research Environment, better known as **Sabre** (Sheldon 1997). Sabre is both a CRS and a global distribution system (GDS) of travel information and ticket reservations. A GDS is basically a computer reservations system that contains a vast database of inventories and travel

FIGURE 8.1
Travel information distribution prior to the advent of the Web.

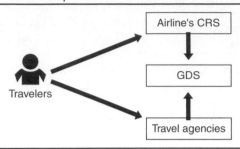

information of participating travel carriers and suppliers who pay a fee to subscribe to the GDS service (see Figure 8.1).

Soon, other airlines followed suit and developed their own CRSs. While CRSs were beneficial to agents compared to the old methods of researching information and securing flights, it was impractical for travel agents to subscribe to different CRSs owned by different airlines. A system would be needed to collect all airline information into one mass database. These systems are the GDS systems.

There are four main GDS systems existing today: **Sabre** (www.sabre. com), **Galileo/Apollo** (www.galileo.com), **Amadeus** (www.amadeus.com), and **Worldspan** (www.worldspan.com). Travel agents typically use only one of these systems to connect to airlines and other suppliers of travel services, such as resorts, hotels, and car rental companies. These GDSs serve as central repositories for all kinds of data and information, ranging from databases of reservations to information about the travelers who made reservations with them (see Figure 8.2).

Today, all these GDSs have set up Web sites that are linked to their databases, allowing travelers to view their booked reservations and itineraries (Table 8.1). For instance, a traveler who made a reservation through Orbitz.com and Expedia.com, which use Worldspan GDS, or through travel agencies that subscribe to the Worldspan GDS can go to www.mytripandmore.com to view their reservations and itineraries. Similarly, reservations made through travel agencies subscribing to Sabre can go to www.virtualthere.com to view and print their itineraries (see Figure 8.3).

GDS has enabled agents to access complete information listings for all airlines through one system. However, in the whole process of adopting technology, travel agents have always been passive receivers: They will use whatever is given to them and tend to resist new technological changes since they require new training and expenses. Most of the travel agents are operating under thin margins, and cost of the technology is a barrier to their adopting new technologies.

FIGURE 8.2

GDS databases and technologies are still the main sources of reservation systems.

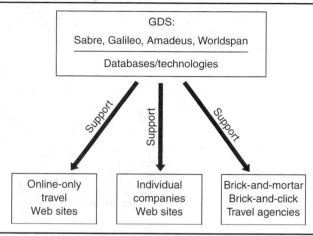

TABLE 8.1			
A Brief Overview of Global Distribution Systems			
COMPANY/ WEB SITE	INTERNET GATEWAY FOR CORPORATE AND/OR TRAVEL AGENTS	INTERNET GATEWAY FOR INDIVIDUAL TRAVELERS	OWNERSHIP IN 2000
Sabre:www. sabre.com	www.getthere.com	www.virtuallythere. com	Publicly owned; former owner: AMR
Galileo/Apollo: www.galileo.com	www.travelgalileo. com	www.viewtrip.com	Cendant, a large franchising company that owns Ramada, Avis, and other brands.
Amadeus: www. amadeus.com	www.e–travel.com	www.checkmytrip. com	60% publicly owned; Air France 23%, Iberio 18% and Lufthansa 18%
Worldspan: www. worldspan.com	www.tripmanager. com	www.mytripand– more.com	Delta Airlines 40%; Northwest 34%; America Airlines, Inc. 26% (inherited from TWA)

FIGURE 8.3
Multiple channel access of travel information and reservation.

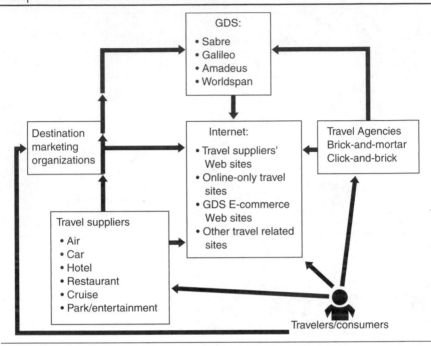

8.4 TRAVEL AGENTS AND THE INTERNET

Facing this new challenge, travel agents had several different responses. The first was to blame the airlines, accusing them of breaking the traditional partnership and practicing bad business ethics. The second was to shrug their shoulders and shut their eyes to the changes by saying that people will never leave travel agents since they always need live, human help. They claimed that Internet was a fad and that it would go away as the frenzy died down. The third was to simply give up, claiming that doomsday had come for the travel agents. The final one, this time positive, was to look for ways to survive, compete, and ride the tidal wave of e-commerce.

While all these reactions have some facts to support them and may be justified in specific circumstances, there are three things travel agents need to do before they subscribe to any particular visions or claims. First, they need to ask the questions about their business:

- ❏ Why are customers leaving us?
- ❏ Are we meeting the changing needs of our customers?
- ❏ How can we keep and grow our customer base?

Second, they need to ask questions about the use of technologies:

- ❏ What can the Internet do for us and our customers?
- ❏ What can I do to take advantage of the Internet to meet the needs of my customers?

Finally, they need to come up with strategies. Table 8.2 summarizes answers to the first two questions. Travel agents have to realize and admit the following facts about themselves before they can realistically comprehend their current situations:

- ❏ They have always been passive receivers.
- ❏ They have always been at the mercy of suppliers and technology.
- ❏ They are not receptive to technological innovations.
- ❏ They have not really defined their roles. If they have, however, they have incorrectly done so.

What is behind this rush to online travel shopping? First, the Web is revolutionizing the way consumers plan and buy their travel. For the first time, Web technology makes it possible for intangible hospitality and tourism

TABLE 8.2	
Questions and Answers for Travel Agents	
Why travelers leave travel agents	• Convenience factor (not accessible 24/7)
	• Illusion of cheaper fares
	• Glamour of shopping online
	• Curiosity of technology
	• Customer service (unhappy with travel agents' service)
	• Marketing of services (travel agents neglect marketing their services)
	• Image problem: agents and low-tech
Motivating factors for the use of the Internet	• 24/7 accessibility
	• Information: rich and updated
	• Seeing/comparing options
	• Global reach
	• Control over decision
	• Dollar driven
	• Instant gratification

products and services to be tangible, that is, only a click of the mouse away. The richness and instant accessibility of travel information online has made the Web more appealing to the travel consumers.

Second, the novelty of multimedia and the interactive capacity of the Web captures the imagination of millions of computer users. Consumers can now "fly" the skies, "cruise" the seas, "climb" the mountains, "sleep" on the hotel bed, "drive" the road, "hear" the roar of tigers, and "explore" the cities, towns, and countries around the world and then book their trips instantly from the comfort of their personal computers.

Third, the competitiveness of the hospitality and tourism industry requires, on the one hand, that companies better manage their information systems with less of their financial resources and, on the other, that they are pressured to increase the speed of responding to customers and raise the satisfaction level of their customers. The central issue is how to reach customers with the most efficiency and cost effectiveness, and the Web is regarded as such a possible solution to this age-old problem. A Web site for a specific travel destination can be created with relative ease and for a fraction of the cost of advertising in a major national magazine.

Fourth, the perception of getting a deal by bypassing the middleman, in this case, the travel agent, and buying directly from service suppliers has generated plenty of excitement among consumers. Combine this with the awareness and publicity generated by increasing competition between online travel services, and it is not surprising that the Web has attracted so many consumers to the market.

Finally, the traditional travel agents' **business model** needs to be revamped. A business model that was based totally on commissions and at the mercy of a single source was pitiful at best and vulnerable and risky at worst. Travel agents need to change from a ticket retailer to a travel information and service provider, from a product-oriented business to a service-oriented one. Each travel agency must redefine its role and relationship to its customers.

The impact of the Internet is far reaching and can be felt by many sectors of the travel industry, but the travel agencies feel it the most. Recall that airlines have not always particularly enjoyed having travel agents around, but agents have been a necessary intermediary for ticket distribution. In 1995, this essential role became antiquated when the Web gave airlines a new and powerful way to communicate directly with consumers.

Many alarms have been sounded as to the survival of the travel agent in the face of this technological shake-up. The truth is that travel agents will probably never go away, but not all travel agents will survive this tidal wave. Travel suppliers will continue to seek ways to save money and market directly to their customers. It is true that the Internet will not replace the value of human service, but, like any other technological innovation, it will reduce the dependence on human service.

8.5 STRATEGIES FOR TRAVEL AGENTS IN THE AGE OF THE INTERNET

In previous sections, we mentioned that travel agents are vulnerable in several areas. First, they are almost totally at the mercy of travel suppliers for their revenue. Second, they have never been active participants in any technological advancement. Third, they have never clearly defined their role in relation to consumers. By changing their attitudes toward technology and defining their new role, travel agents can create strategies to take advantage of the Internet and better serve the needs of their customers.

Many strategies arise based on the understanding and the answers to the questions asked in the previous section. In fact, travel agents have many competitive advantages in terms of understanding customers' needs and wants. They have their existing customer database that they can use to market their services. To do this, however, they need to change from the old **product-oriented** sales approach to a **service-oriented** sales and marketing approach. The Internet has created a new demand for better service and service alternatives. If consumers were considered to be kings in the past, they are now the kings of all kings. This new found freedom of choice and ever increasing consumer power is not necessarily good or bad to anyone in the travel industry. To a large extent, it is unbiased toward anyone. The difference it makes is in the responses travel agents take to harness this power of freedom to choose.

STRATEGIES

Understanding customers is the first step in deriving strategies. To serve customers' needs and wants, travel agents need to understand what technologies can do for them in servicing customers. Why do customers leave for the Internet? Travel agents must ask that question of themselves. If customers want convenience, give them convenience and in the way they want it, in this case, with Internet service. If they want the instant gratification of being able to search travel information and buy tickets online, give them that gratification. If they want perceived cheap online fares, give them the power to do so and educate them about the ability of travel agents to give them that power with a special touch of human service.

Trying to prevent customers from using the Internet is like trying to prevent a person from ordering french fries when they are at McDonald's. It is better to harness the power of consumers than to stop them from using their power. The initial reaction of many travel agents to the Internet was exactly trying to stop people from using the Internet. Table 8.3 presents some strategies for travel agents to compete and succeed in the new marketplace.

TABLE 8.3 Strategies and Opportunities for Travel Agents	
QUESTIONS AND ISSUES	STRATEGIES AND OPPORTUNITIES
Understand customers	1. Use your existing customer database to understand your customers' needs. 2. Ask your customers what you can do for them to keep them as loyal customers. 3. Reassess your relationship with your customers.
Convenience	1. Have a presence on the Internet. 2. Try to make a portal for your customers. 3. Choose the appropriate Internet communication tools. 4. Provide your own travel information and links to all major travel information sites.
Perception of cheap fares	1. Travel agents need to educate the public that online travel service providers are not providing cheaper fairs but simply an alternative. 2. Be pro-technology but emphasize travel agents' "human touch."
Glamour of shopping online	1. Build your own online booking capability. 2. Link your home page to online booking Web sites. 3. Provide valuable travel information online.
Marketing of services	1. Change from product orientation to marketing orientation. 2. Emphasize the human factor. 3. Add value to your service.
Image problem: low-tech	1. Provide better training. 2. Be pro-technology. 3. Vocational schools revise curriculum to include technology courses. 4. Geography is irrelevant on the Web. Companies should think globally when they go online.
Improve customer service	1. People who are not happy with customer service are always looking for alternatives. 2. The Internet offers excellent tools for improving customer service. 3. Think globally but act locally.

8.6 THE FUTURE

MARKETING ORIENTATION COMBINED WITH INDIVIDUALIZED SERVICE

Despite all the hoopla about the death of the middleman caused by the Internet, many travel agents are still surviving and, in fact, doing quite well. This is not to dispute the fact that many small mom-and-pop travel agencies have closed their doors since Internet reservations became available. We have to admit that even until today, the Internet is just beginning to be understood and its power and potential revealed. There are no certain ways to predict the future of its development and impact on travel agents. However, we can use some general guidelines to help us better cope with the future. We can, as a general rule, predict the following:

❏ Technology will not totally replace human service, but it will considerably reduce dependence on it. Travel agents are not going away, but they will feel the pinch from now on.

❏ The travel information distribution system will undergo major shake-ups, and so will travel agents. Restructuring and forming new partnerships are inevitable. Fee-based and value-added services will be combined. Only the fittest will survive.

❏ Travel agents must find their niches in customer service—areas where human service is superior to nonhuman interaction—to find new customers and at the same time to keep the old ones.

Consumers are not using the Internet for cheap tickets and inexpensive reservations. They are looking for value and experience in their total travel package—the travel information search, travel planning, and the actual purchase of travel products and services. Whoever can provide value and good experience will win the minds of the consumer.

With the currently strained relationship between airlines and travel agencies, agents can no longer rely on airlines for their revenues. Lower and zero commissions from airlines and higher Internet bookings have helped reduce the ranks of traditional U.S. travel agencies by 16% in the past six years (Reckard 2000). Airlines have discovered the advantages of the Internet and e-commerce and are milking it for all it is worth.

There is really no single party to blame for the current situation. In any industry, increasing profits and lowering the cost associated with marketing has always been a central issue, especially in a competitive environment. To a large degree, the quest to cut costs is not an impulsive one for businesses but rather a way of life. E-commerce has provided the tool to endorse this way of life.

A look at the brief history of commissions will show that efforts to reduce cost is a new phenomenon. In 1991, commissions held steady at about 10.83%. By 1999, those rates had nose-dived to an approximate 6.43%, if not lower (Reckard 2000). In 1994, 32,913 brick-and-mortar agencies were in operation, but this number dwindled to 27,729 in 1999 (Reckard 2000), four years after the Web first enabled online booking.

The travel agency industry was partly to blame for this initial decrease in agency numbers. Deregulation in the travel agency industry loosened the accreditation requirements in the ownership of travel agencies. Hobbyists—people who had retired and conducted their business mainly as a leisure activity—operated many agencies. These agents were simply selling tickets rather than providing meaningful services. When the Internet was able to provide avenues for travel information and booking capability, these agents were the first to close their doors. But without good service, active participation in technological changes, and sound marketing strategies, travel agents may soon become an endangered species.

8.7 CONCLUSION

The Internet acts only as a change agent, not as a technological barrier, as some people would like to think. It is the attitude toward change that makes the difference. Travel agents have realized that denying or ignoring the change will not do them any good. They need to reexamine their relationship with travel carriers and suppliers and with their customers in a totally new Internet environment.

A historical perspective is important to travel agents since history can help shed light on both the current situation and future directions. History has shown that a business model based on commissions and depending too much on one source of suppliers is subject to the mercy of the controlling party and will not fare well in a time of radical change.

Travel agents have much to offer consumers in hospitality and tourism. Their knowledge of the industry, their human touch and personal relationship with consumers, their vast base of existing customers, and their traditional role of being a neighborhood store provide them with a solid foundation to play competitively in the market. It is critical for travel agents to bring out these strengths while avoiding their weaknesses. A willingness to take advantage of new technologies will help them catch up with the times and with consumers' needs and wants. Travel agents must learn how to turn their human touch to a golden touch in an ever increasingly competitive world.

KEY WORDS AND TERMS

Traveling Public

Retailer

Promoter

Commission

Tangible Nature

Air Traffic Conference

Accreditation

International Air Transportation
   Association

Civil Aeronautics Board

Prederegulation

Deregulation

Airline Deregulation Act

Airline Reporting Corporation

Commission Structure

Overrides

Incentives

Computer Reservations System

Sabre

Galileo/Apollo

Amadeus

Worldspan

Business Model

Product Oriented

Service Oriented

SUMMARY

There are many developments in travel e-commerce that travel agents should be worried about. These developments include the increasing number of online travelers, the desire of travel suppliers to market directly to travelers, and the increasing amount of money spent on online travel transactions.

A historical perspective revealed that travel agents have always been at the mercy of travel suppliers (airlines in particular) because of their commission-based revenue structure. The role of travel agents with their customers has never been clearly defined. Many agencies are product and sale oriented rather than service and marketing oriented.

Travel agents have never been active technological participants and fail to understand the implications of technological advances. Their slow and often resistant attitude toward the Internet contributes partly to their less popular position with consumers.

Strategies can be derived to cope with changes by looking at the roots of the problems. The most fundamental change that travel agents need to take is to shift from a product-oriented business model to a service-oriented one. Travel agents will probably never go away, but their roles will certainly change and be reduced to meet the new changing needs and wants of consumers.

▮ WEB RESOURCES

- www.astanet.com
- www.counciltravel.com
- www.asiacyberholidays.com
- www.nielsen-netratings.com
- www.travelmole.com

CASE STUDY: *The Only Way to Travel, Inc.*

The Only Way to Travel, Inc., was established in 1991. Donna and Arthur (Art) Wickerham started the business as independent contractors working part time from their home. In 1994, Donna began working as a travel agent full time. In 1995, The Only Way to Travel became a member of CLIA and began operating as an independent agency. In 1995, the agency brought on its first employee and in 1996 moved into an office space. In 1998, the agency was endorsed by IATAN as a Travel Service Intermediary. In August 1999, the agency moved into a retail location.

Today, the agency employs two full-time travel counselors in addition to Donna. Art works full time as an electrical engineer and spends his "free" time working as the agency's Webmaster. The agency is 100% leisure based, with annual sales under $2 million. In 1999, total Internet sales revenue made up 36% of the agency's sales. In 2000, the agency's Internet sales revenue was up 80% over 1999, comprising 40% of its total sales.

In 1997, The Only Way to Travel was trying to decide what it should do about this thing called the Internet. Embrace it? Ignore it? Would it go away? Then Donna, the president of the agency, went to the annual meeting of the agency's consortium. Another agency owner stood up and said that her cruise-only agency had done $3 million in sales the previous year and that $1 million of it had come from the Internet. Wickerham was sold. She went to the phone at the next break, called the agency's vice president, and told him to go to the other agency's Web site and see what they were doing because The Only Way to Travel needed to do it, too.

The vice president took the time to learn HTML and created The Only Way to Travel's Web site. One year later, in May 1998, the agency's site, www.onlywaytotravel.com, was launched. "We thought we were going to be really smart and give away a cruise. We just knew that would bring people to our site. We were right. People came in droves. We were getting 500 entries an hour for the free cruise," said Wickerham.

The agency had not anticipated this kind of response and was not adequately prepared to handle the flood of e-mail. It knew it had to capture the information it was receiving, and it took some time to figure out how to automate the process. But it was accomplished.

The agency's site also had a form that people could use to request pricing for up to three different cruises at a time. The agents in the office did not feel as though they were getting well-qualified leads from these forms. An analysis was performed, with the result that the agents thought that perhaps they were not getting the requested information back to potential clients quickly enough.

As a test, an additional agent was hired to come into the office for three months. That agent's job was solely to respond to those forms. As a result, each inquiry was responded to within 24 hours. This test was an eye-opener. No sales were closed from those leads. The agents surmised that the anonymity of the form allowed people to request prices, even if they were just curious and not truly interested in purchasing a cruise. The request form was removed from the site.

On the other hand, the agents found that people who called the agency as a result of finding its Web site were much more interested in purchasing travel. Agents were closing sales with at least 30% of the people who called. The agents found that if they could get people on the phone, they had a much better chance of closing the sale.

After the request form was removed from the site, the agency was still getting e-mail from people. Usually the e-mails were vague and did not provide enough information to get a price quote. The agents developed a form letter that was used to cut and paste into a reply e-mail. The responses were customized, depending on what the clients had included in their first inquiry. The reply requested the names and ages of the travelers, and a phone number was required for a response. If clients did not provide the required information in two replies, they were not provided with the information they requested.

The information requested by e-mail is always provided by phone. This allows the client to realize that it is not a computer on the other end just spitting out prices. Most important, it allows agents the opportunity to build a rapport with the client and increases the odds of closing the sale.

The Only Way to Travel continued to give away a three-night Carnival cruise each quarter for a year. At the end of the year, the giveaway program was reevaluated. The agency's owners realized that the people who were entering to win the cruise were interested only in winning a cruise. They had no desire to purchase a cruise, but if they could get one for free, they would take it. They were not the prequalified shoppers the agency was looking for. Whenever an entry for a free cruise was received, a reply would be sent to confirm the entry and then ask the person if he or she wanted to receive a free monthly travel e-newsletter. Many people did, but surprisingly a number of people responded with an emphatic, "No! And don't contact me again unless I have won the cruise!"

The Only Way to Travel had just made a video—"Prepared for Your Cruise . . . The Only Way to Travel"—for first-time cruisers and decided to give away one video each month. As a result, all the people who entered this drawing were interested in taking a cruise. Almost every one of these entrants responded yes when asked if they wanted to receive the monthly travel e-newsletter. The agency had prequalified its audience.

People could sign up for the free travel e-newsletter without entering the drawing for the video. There is a form on the Web site where people can easily sign up for the e-newsletter, which has purposely been kept informational in nature. It is not a place where travel specials are advertised. In fact, there is no advertising in this e-newsletter. The agency has had numerous businesses requesting information on charges for advertising in the e-newsletter. The Only Way to Travel has steadfastly refused any advertising, and it has paid off. Many subscribers of the agency's e-newsletter forward it on to others who in turn have subscribed.

In the summer of 2000, the agency members had a staff meeting and did some brainstorming. The vice president asked the agents, "When you talk to someone, what is it they are asking for?" A common theme was discovered: People always want to know what kinds of good deals are out there. As anyone in the retail travel industry knows, agencies receive many faxes each day from cruise lines and tour companies. Sometimes, these faxes have some really great prices. How could The Only Way to Travel get this information out to potential clients? Then the answer came to the staff. They had thousands of names on their e-newsletter list. In the next e-newsletter, each recipient would be asked if they wanted to sign up for the agency's last-minute-deals e-mail.

This idea really hit home. At least one last-minute deal is sent out daily. The people who are on this list must request to be on it. (It is easy for subscribers to unsubscribe if they choose.) The last-minute-deals list quickly built up to over 10,000 e-mail addresses. The response was exactly what the agency desired.

People were responding to these great deals, deals to which every other agency in the country had access to. The difference was that The Only Way to Travel was getting this information out to potential clients. The agents were somewhat hesitant as to whether the really cheap cruises should be sent out as specials. The agents did not know if it would be worth their time. They found that people were purchasing four or more cabins at these great prices. So even though the commissionable portion or the fare was less than the port charges and taxes, the volume of sales made it worthwhile.

Contrary to what most people believe, people searching for travel on the Internet are not looking for cheap products and services. What they are searching for is a good value and good service. To prove this point: The Only Way to Travel's average Internet sale is approximately $400 more than its average non-Internet sale. Clients who come for service as a result of the Internet come from all over the world, including local communities. Internet clients purchase everything from the upscale Radisson Seven Seas Cruises to budget-priced Carnival Cruises.

The Only Way to Travel continues to use the Internet as a primary source of marketing the agency. The agency continues to look for more ways to successfully use this medium to grow its business.

SOURCE: Donna Wickerham, President, The Only Way to Travel, Inc.

QUESTIONS TO PONDER:

1. How was the owner of The Only Way to Travel convinced to adopt the Internet into its business operation?
2. What types of research did The Only Way to Travel undertake to understand its customers?
3. How does The Only Way to Travel use the Internet as a communication and marketing medium?
4. Do you agree that people use the Internet not for cheap tickets but because what they are searching for is a good value and good service?
5. What lessons can be learned from The Only Way to Travel about small business?

REVIEW QUESTIONS

1. Why should travel agents be worried about their businesses?
2. What is the historical role of travel agents?
3. What made travel agents so valuable both to travel suppliers and consumers before the advent of Internet e-commerce?
4. What was the relationship between the airlines and travel agents before Internet e-commerce?
5. What was the impact of airline deregulation on travel agents?
6. Why did the travel agency industry grow so rapidly after airline deregulation?
7. What was the role of commission structure in the well-being of travel agents?
8. What was the business model of travel agencies in the past? Do you think it was a good one? Why?

9. Why is the traditional business model not a viable one in today's environment?

10. What is the difference between a CRS and a GDS?

11. What are the four main GDSs?

12. What are the major questions travel agents need to ask themselves in coping with Internet e-commerce?

13. What are the strategies that travel agents can use to take advantage of Internet e-commerce?

14. How can travel agents turn their human touch into golden touch?

REFERENCES

Foster, D. (1990). *First Class: An Introduction to Travel and Tourism*. New York: Macmillan/McGraw-Hill.

Gregory, A. (1989). *The Travel Agent: Dealer in Dreams*. Elmsford, N.Y.: National Publishers.

Meyer, J., and C. Oster, Jr. (1987). *Deregulation and the Future of Intercity Passenger Travel*. Cambridge, Mass.: MIT Press.

Nielsen/Netratings. (2001). www.nielsen-netratings.com.

Reckard, S. (2000). "Threatened by the Web, Travel Agents Adopt New Tactics," *Los Angeles Times*, p. C1.

Sheldon, P. (1997). *Tourism Information Technology*. New York: Civil Aeronautics Board.

Stevens, L. (1989). *Guide to Starting and Operating a Successful Travel Agency*. Wheaton, IL.: Merton House Travel and Tourism Publishers.

Travel Industry Association of America. (2001). *www.tia.org*.

Zhou, Z. Q., and Li-Chun Lin. (2000). "The Impact of the Internet on the Use of the Print Brochure." Proceedings of the CHRIE's 2000 annual conference, July 19–22, New Orleans.

For additional Travel and Tourism resources, go to www.Hospitality-Tourism.delmar.com

9

A New Paradigm for Internet Research

Learning Objectives

After you complete your study of this chapter, you should be able to:

- Know how to search for information on the Internet.
- Understand how to collect data on the Internet.
- Know how to analyze the data you collect from the Internet.
- Be familiar with the major measurements used in Internet market research.

9.1 DEFINING INTERNET RESEARCH

Internet research is, for the most part, no different from traditional research in that it is the process of seeking, collecting, and analyzing data to arrive at information that aids decision making. It is, however, different from traditional research since it uses different media and measurements that have been made possible by Internet technologies. Furthermore, Internet research differs from traditional research in that it deals more with dynamic information than with static information. It is fast paced, ever changing, and evolving.

9.2 INFORMATION SEARCH ON THE INTERNET

The Internet is a vast sea of information. It is hard to measure the scope and the depth of this wealth of information since countless people throughout the world contribute to it. To look for the information you want, you need to know where the data are stored and how to access them. As discussed in previous chapters, the Internet consists primarily of a variety of access protocols. These include e-mail, **Mailing Lists,** HTTP, and Usenet news. Many of these protocols have their own programs that allow you to search for and retrieve material made available by a specific protocol.

For this reason, the Internet is not really a library in which all available items are identified and can be retrieved by a single catalog. Rather, it is a network of libraries, each of which may require different IDs to allow access. For instance, many search engines and tools exist for different types of information needs.

There are a number of ways you can search for or gain information on the Internet:

- ❏ Conduct a search using a Web search engine
- ❏ Participate in an e-mail discussion group or Usenet newsgroup
- ❏ Use a known URL to directly access information

CONDUCT A SEARCH USING A WEB SEARCH ENGINE

Search engines share a common characteristic; that is, they all rely on some sort of **search logic** to find the information you request. One of the most commonly used search principles is **Boolean logic,** which refers to the logical relationship among search terms.

Boolean logic is a method of combining terms using "operators," such as AND, OR, and AND NOT. AND requires that all terms appear in a record, OR retrieves records with either term, and AND NOT excludes

TABLE 9.1 How Boolean Logic AND Works	
SEARCH TERMS	RESULTS
"Tourism"	4,800,000
"Technology"	43,300,000
"Tourism and technology"	618,000

terms. For example, if you type "tourism and technology" into a search engine, it will return with all records in which both of the search terms are present. Therefore, the more terms or concepts you combine in a search with AND logic, the fewer records you will get. Table 9.1 shows the results of this search (using the Google search engine) as compared to the results of using either "tourism" or "technology," alone.

If you type "tourism or technology," the search engine will return with all the records in which at least one of the search terms is present. OR logic produces all the unique records containing one term, the other, or both. Therefore, the more terms or concepts you use in a search with OR logic, the more records you will get. If you are interested in synonymous terms or concepts, you can use OR logic to accomplish the search goal. Table 9.2 shows the outcomes of an OR search as compared with other methods.

If you want only information about tourism but avoid getting anything about technology, you can use Boolean NOT logic. By using NOT logic, you will retrieve only records in which "tourism" is present. NOT logic excludes records you do not want to see from your search results. Table 9.3 illustrates the results of such a search as compared to other types of searches.

There are many search engines in the Internet. The following are some of the more popular ones:

- ❏ About.com (www.about.com)
- ❏ AltaVista (www.altavista.com)
- ❏ Academic Info (www.academicinfo.net)
- ❏ Excite (www.excite.com)
- ❏ HotBot (http://hotbot.lycos.com)

TABLE 9.2 How Boolean Logic OR Works	
SEARCH TERMS	RESULTS
"Tourism"	4,800,000
"Technology"	43,300,000
"Tourism or technology"	4,150,000

TABLE 9.3	
How Boolean Logic NOT Works	
SEARCH TERMS	RESULTS
"Tourism"	4,800,000
"Technology"	43,300,000
"Tourism not technology"	461,000

❑ Google (www.google.com)
❑ Infomine (http://infomine.ucr.edu)
❑ Librarians' Index (www.lii.org)
❑ Northern Light (www.nlsearch.com)
❑ ProFusion (www.profusion.com)
❑ WebCrawler (www.webcrawler.com)
❑ Yahoo! (www.yahoo.com)

PARTICIPATE IN AN E-MAIL DISCUSSION GROUP OR USENET NEWSGROUP

An effective way to obtain information on any interest is to join an e-mail discussion group (Mailing List) or a Usenet newsgroup. When you subscribe to a list, your name and e-mail address are automatically added to the list. You will receive a standard letter of welcome via e-mail describing the list. From that time on, you will receive all mail postings sent to the list by its members. You may follow the discussions or join in on them. If you respond, you can send your response to the list, and all members of the list will receive it. As you know from previous chapters, you can sign off or unsubscribe from a list at any time. You can also get a listing of all the members of a list and their e-mail addresses.

Experts in certain fields of interest start many of these Mailing Lists. People joining the list are those who share common interests. By joining these e-mail discussion lists, you can get up-to-date information about what is happening in your field of interest. In Chapter 3, we introduced a Mailing List called InfoTech Travel, where subscribers participate in discussion of all topics related to tourism information technology. To search for a discussion group, go to www.liszt.com or www.alabanza.com/kabacoff/Inter-Links/ listserv.html. Another specialized Mailing List is the GREEN-TRAVEL list, which is dedicated to sharing information about culturally and environmentally responsible or sustainable travel and tourism worldwide, including ecotourism and adventure travel. To sign up for this Mailing List, go to www.green-travel.com.

Usenet newsgroups provide another great place to look for information you need. These are bulletin board–like discussion forums where people post information and then read and respond to the information. These discussion forums also are often organized by interest and topic. The best place to go to search for newsgroups is http://groups.google.com, where you can find the following newsgroups:

❏ alt: Any conceivable topic
❏ biz: Business products, services, and reviews
❏ comp: Hardware, software, and consumer information
❏ humanities: Fine arts, literature, and philosophy
❏ misc: Employment, health, and much more
❏ rec: Games, hobbies, and sports
❏ sci: Applied and social science
❏ news: Information about Usenet news
❏ soc: Social issues and culture
❏ talk: Current issues and debates

USE A KNOWN URL TO DIRECTLY ACCESS INFORMATION

If you know the **URL** (Universal Resource Locator), the Web site address of an information source, you can type in the address bar of a browser and go directly to the source. Sometimes, you can click on a link even though you do not know the URL. Most browsers now offer the capability of using the major part of the URL to carry out the search. For instance, instead of typing **"http://www.expedia.com"** to go to the site, you can simply type **"www.expedia.com"** or simply **"expedia.com"** to go to the site.

Most established businesses have been able to use their company's name as their domain name or URL. In the early days of the Internet, domain registration was not regulated and was not subject to the same strict rule of registering a traditional business name or copyright. Many domain names were snapped up by people who hoped that large, wealthy corporations or some business that liked their registered domain names would pay big bucks to buy their domain names. Some did succeed in selling some of the domain names and got rich, but the government and Congress soon stepped in and outlawed this practice. Today, as long as you are not deliberately registering a domain name for profit, you are safe in registering any name you want as long as it is still available.

▮ 9.3 COLLECTING DATA ON THE INTERNET

Collecting data has been one of the most important but difficult steps in any type of research. Traditional data collection typically takes a long time to accomplish, and often the response rate is not high. The Internet offers an

FIGURE 9.1
Log files data collection and analysis.

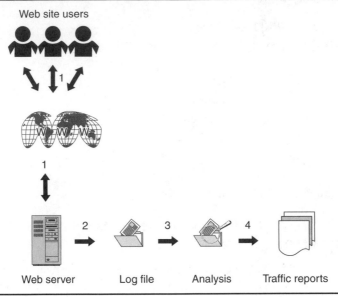

Web site users

Web server   Log file   Analysis   Traffic reports

SOURCE: WebSideStory, Inc.

alternative for data collection that promises to be faster and more convenient and to yield a higher response rate. One area that Internet research can be applied to help you understand consumer behavior is in e-commerce. For instance, it is critical for e-commerce companies to be able to measure the traffic to their sites and identify visitor activities in order to determine and enhance the effectiveness of their sites.

One approach to data collection uses the servers **log files** (Figure 9.1) to get visitor information. A log file is created by a Web server, containing every request received by the server from every user. These log files typically are raw data and require extensive data manipulation and analysis in order to arrive at intelligent information. However, since it is inexpensive and fast, log file data collection and analysis is still widely used today, even though many software programs are available that do more sophisticated data collection and analysis.

Specialized data collection and analysis software can handle more sophisticated data and are capable of collecting and analyzing extensive, detailed traffic and visitor information directly from the browsers of individual users and delivering this information instantly in real time to site owners all over the world (Figure 9.2).

FIGURE 9.2
Specialized software online data collection.

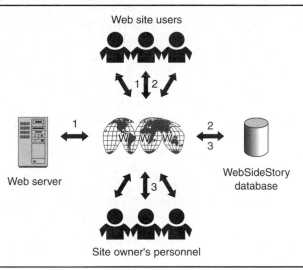

SOURCE: WebSideStory, Inc.

In a log file analysis, the Web visitor issues requests (typically by clicking the mouse) to view specific pages on a site. When the Web server receives these requests, it serves the requested pages back to the visitor. In the meantime, the Web server records each visitor's request in a chronological log file. In order to see and analyze these records, the Web site owner must use proprietary **log file analysis software** to extract useful information from these log files. The reports generated from the analysis can then be distributed to the parties concerned.

In the case of specialized online data collection software (Figure 9.2), the Web visitor issues requests to view specific pages on a site. When the Web server receives these requests, it serves the requested pages back to the users. When a page is displayed on a browser, a special HitBox code that the site owner has embedded in the page sends a variety of anonymous information about the page and user to WebSideStory (www.websidestory.com), where it is immediately integrated into the HitBox database for the site. Anyone who is authorized by the site owner can log on to the WebSideStory site and request HitBox audience information.

There are many other ways to collect data on the Web. The first way is to use **cookies.** A cookie is a message sent from a Web server to an online traveler's local computer and stored by the browser on his or her computer. When the online traveler visits the originating Web server next time, the cookie is sent back to the server, allowing it to respond to the online traveler according to the cookie's contents.

In other words, cookies are used by a Web server to collect information from a computer about its user—the online visitor. This cookie will be reactivated each time the visitor who uses the same computer revisits the same site (Deital et al. 2001). Although all browsers allow the visitor to disable the cookies from their browser, most people do not choose to do so since more Web sites require the visitor to turn the cookies function on before the visitor can access customized information. This is because cookies are used to provide customized Web pages according to a profile of the visitor's interests. When the visitor logs on to a customized Web site to fill in his or her name and other information, a cookie may be created on his or her computer that the Web server he or she is visiting will access to get to know the visitor and therefore provide the kind of contents and information the visitor wants. Some ad rotation software uses cookies to see which ad the user has just seen so that a different ad will be rotated into the next page view.

A second way to collect data is to ask online visitors to fill out a form about themselves in terms of their interests and other important demographic information. Many visitors will take the time to fill out these forms if they are assured of the security and privacy of their information and if incentives such as sweepstakes, coupons, or a promise of sending relevant information with an e-newsletter are offered for completing the forms. In previous chapters, we talked about the importance of using e-newsletters to communicate with customers. To send e-newsletters to your customers, you need to know about their interests and their e-mail addresses. You should place an e-newsletter invitation on your Web site for those visitors who care for your products and services. They will be asked to fill out the invitation form for the e-newsletter.

A third way to collect data is by searching the Internet for the specific information you are looking for. Data collected this way is called **secondary data.** Today, most competitors have their own Web sites that post a lot of information. By simply taking a look at the information provided on their sites, you can gain valuable information. There are also many not-for-profit as well as government agency sites that provide analytical and statistical data about specific products and services as well as specific industries. Compared to firsthand data collection, secondary data collection can be cheaper and less intrusive.

A final way to collect data is to use online survey instruments. Traditionally, surveys can be conducted by mail, face-to-face interviews, or telephone interviews. Many of these methods have the problem of being regarded as intrusive, time consuming, and costly. Internet surveys can be constructed in such a way that makes filling out the form both easier and less formidable.

Many commercial **Web authoring programs** come with such a capability. Microsoft Frontpage 2000, for instance, comes with a survey form wizard to guide the user in building a survey instrument. It also provides many options for the user to select the kind of format in which to store the data collected. For instance, the user can choose to store the data in text form, in HTML form, or in a database form. The user can export the database form to a spreadsheet or database program. If the user has installed the right Microsoft server extensions, the user can also do statistical analysis right away, providing instant analysis of the data collected.

Besides commercial Web authoring programs, there are many tourism consulting and research companies and organizations beginning to offer online survey research service. One of these companies is Ipsos-NPD (www.ipsos-npd.com). Some of the services it offers include the following:

❏ Web site evaluation
❏ Customer profiling
❏ Attitude and use testing (also called habits and practices)
❏ Customer satisfaction measurement, spanning a range of applications and experiences, including incentive reward programs, membership registration and log-in, customer service, purchase experience, community/ support group experience, and e-mail marketing programs

Another company, Thruport (www.adjuggler.com), provides online survey software called **Demographica,** a platform-independent, browser-based application for creating online surveys and polls. Demographica provides Web sales and marketing professionals with the ability to quickly and easily create surveys customized with their own questions, to manage accounts, and to schedule intervals for results to be e-mailed. Demographica is available either in an ASP model or for installation on a local server.

Other Internet research firms include some of the biggest names in media research. These companies provide services ranging from data collection and market analysis to online consumer behavior studies. Table 9.4 presents some of these companies.

TABLE 9.4 Internet Media Research Companies	
COMPANY	WHAT THE COMPANY OFFERS
Jupiter Media Metrix: www.jmm.com	Analyzes and measures the end-to-end impact of the Internet and new technologies on commerce and marketing
Media Metrix: www.mediametrix.com	Provides demographic data about Web, Internet, and online service usage as well as computer hardware and software trends. Merged with Relevant Knowledge
AMR Research: www.amrresearch.com	A Boston-based research firm that provides information for the selection of manufacturing software applications

TABLE 9.4	
Internet Media Research Companies	(continued)
COMPANY	**WHAT THE COMPANY OFFERS**
ActivMedia Research: www.activmediaresearch.com	Includes statistics and research information from semiannual studies of Web marketers as well as news and tips from the Web marketing world
Nielsen/NetRatings: www.nielsen-netratings.com	Syndicated service that provides advertisers, site publishers, and media planners with Internet audience information
SRC: www.extendthereach.com	Provides demographic and market analysis tools through custom Internet and intranet applications
E-valuations Research: www.e-valuations.com	Online market research facilities and services
eMarketer: www.e-land.com	Provides statistics and demographic data about Internet users, usage patterns, advertising, e-commerce, and market size, growth, and geography
MarketTools: www.markettools.com	Provides technology products and consulting services for conducting research online
Jupiter Communications: www.jup.com	Research, consulting, and publishing firm that specializes in emerging consumer online and interactive technologies

9.4 ANALYZING DATA ON THE INTERNET

Analyzing data collected from the Internet is not that much different from analyzing data collected by traditional means. The principles underlying data analysis, such as reliability, statistical measurement, and sampling bias, still apply. However, there is no consensus so far regarding the criteria governing these principles. For example, how do we define a probability sample? The same visitor may log on to a Web site using different names and from different computers in different locations and take the survey more than once. The anonymous nature of the Internet makes it even more difficult to apply the results of the research to a general population.

Other issues concerning the analysis of data stem from the fact that the Internet is a unique medium. In secondary data online research, you need to be careful about the accuracy of the data collected from online sources since they can be published by anyone who knows how to publish on the Internet. In Chapter 2, we pointed out that anyone with an IP address can host a server and become an online publisher. Compared with traditional research, where the accuracy of data is a major concern, the issue becomes even more prominent in Internet research since publishing information on the Internet is much cheaper—sometimes it can be free—and easier.

There are many companies that provide statistical analysis data for the hospitality and tourism industry. Some of the companies are mentioned in the previous section. They include Jupiter Communications and Nielsen NetRatings. One company that also specializes in online customer behavior research and visitor statistics is StatMarket (http://statmarket.com), a division of the Internet market research firm WestSideStory (www.websidestory.com). Some of the main services StatMarket provides, besides offering online data analysis, include the following:

- ❏ Top referring search sites—From Yahoo to Excite and Lycos, it monitors all the top search sites. See what percentage of referrals each one is generating worldwide.
- ❏ Referring domains—See what the top referring sources of traffic to Web sites consist of, broken down by search sites, direct navigation/bookmarks, and links from other sites.
- ❏ Visitor countries—See what countries have the most surfers on the Web per day.
- ❏ Top Internet Service Providers (ISPs)—Find out what percentage of surfers are connecting through each of the top ISPs.
- ❏ Loyalty index—What percentage of surfers visit a site for the first time every day? What about additional visits? They break it all down.
- ❏ Frequency index—What percentage of surfers visit a site once a month? Twice a month? This list details how often the average Web site worldwide is visited.
- ❏ Major visitor domains—Give a percentage breakdown of all the major domains of Web surfers worldwide, including how much traffic is coming from non-U.S. domains.
- ❏ Referring countries—See what percentages of non-U.S. Web surfers use the domain extension of the country they are in.
- ❏ Referring major domains—Learn which major domains are responsible for referring the most traffic to other sites.
- ❏ Day of week—Find out which days of the week are the most popular for Web surfing.
- ❏ Time zones—Which time zones are most wired? See a breakdown of each time zone by percentage.
- ❏ Rush hour–Review a list of which hours of the day generate the most surfer traffic, both locally and globally.

Many airlines, including Northwest and Alaska, are beginning to look at special software programs to help them to track their online visitors' behavior in the hope of increasing customer conversion rates and improving visitor satisfaction and loyalty (WebSideStory 2001). This trend will continue to spread into other sections of the hospitality and tourism industry since more companies are realizing that e-commerce has become a marketplace and that customer service and satisfaction are key to attract and keep customers.

9.5 MEASUREMENTS FOR E-MARKETING AND ONLINE CONSUMER BEHAVIOR

An important part of Internet research regards online consumer behavior and marketing and advertising effectiveness. The Internet has offered a whole new set of tools to measure these activities. Most of the terms discussed here are special terms used only in Internet marketing and advertising research. Table 9.5 lists and explains these terms.

| TABLE 9.5 |
| Internet Marketing and Advertising Measurement Terminology |

TERMINOLOGY	EXPLANATION
Banner	A banner is really an ad in the traditional sense. It is typically a graphic image or set of animated images displayed on a Web site. Banners and other special advertising that include an interactive or visual element beyond the usual are known as rich media.
Impression	An impression is a measure of how many times an ad is served on a sponsoring site. It is sometimes referred to as an "ad view." In other words, if a single ad appears on a Web page 100 times, when the page arrives at the viewer's display, it has 100 impressions. Many Web sites charge advertisers by number of impressions.
Click	A click, as its name suggests, means that a visitor clicks on a displayed ad banner. It does not mean that the visitor actually follows the click to arrive at the advertised Web page; rather, it simply means that the visitor actually clicks on the ad banner.
Click stream	A click stream refers to a recorded path of pages a visitor has clicked through. This is important information since it can help Web site owners understand how visitors are using their site and which pages are getting the most use. It also provides advertisers with valuable information regarding how users get to the clients' pages, what pages they visit, and how they order a product or service.
Click-through	A click-through often is used interchangeably with "click." However, by using the word "click-through," the sponsoring site wants to convey the idea that the visitor not only clicks on the banner but also follows through to the linked Web page. Many advertisers want to pay only for click-throughs, not just the click or impressions.

TERMINOLOGY	EXPLANATION
Click-through rate	The click-through rate measures the percentage of impressions that results in click-throughs. It is important for advertisers to know how many visitors actually click on their ad banners, even though ad impressions have their own value in terms of visibility and branding. A click-through rate measures not only the number of the eyeballs of a visitor (impressions) but also, to a certain degree, how effective a banner is.
Conversion	Another term for "click-though." It measures a visitor's completed action—that is, a visitor clicking on a banner—which often is the goal of a marketing campaign. A second use of conversion refers to the "look-to-book ratios" in online travel reservations.
CPM	A measurement used by ad agencies or site owners to charge advertisers. CPM stands for "cost per thousand" online ad impressions. The traditional advertising industry uses the same measure; the online advertising community simply borrows this term. Note here that "M" has nothing to do with " mega" or million. It is taken from the roman numeral for "thousand."
Pay per lead	When an advertiser places a banner on a site and a visitor clicks on the banner to complete what the banner intends him or her to do, the advertiser pays accordingly. An advertiser, for instance, will pay for every visitor who clicks on a banner that asks the visitor to sign up for a newsletter and the visitor does.
ROI	Stands for "return on investment." It is a measure of how successful an ad campaign is in terms of what the returns, sales revenue, or fulfillment of the ad campaign objectives were for the money invested.
Run of network	An ad network enables you to place your ad on all its associated sites, giving you the power of large-scale exposure. It is a selling point for the ad network to advertisers. An ad placed in such an ad network is commonly referred to as a run-of-network ad.
Unique visitor	A unique visitor is someone who visits a Web site with a unique IP address for the first time in one day or a specified period of time. It is used to investigate how many different visitors a site has for that day or for a specified period of time. A visitor with the same IP address who returns within the same day is counted only once as a unique visitor.
Hit	A hit is a record of a requested file from the server. Requesting a single Web page can bring with it a number of individual files (e.g., text, graphics, or sound), thus several hits. A hit is not a good indicator of actual use (number of visitors) but is a good indicator of traffic flow on a site.

TABLE 9.5
Internet Marketing and Advertising Measurement Terminology *(continued)*

Internet technology has opened up a new horizon for marketing research with its instant, interactive 24/7 capabilities. With increasing competition in the e-commerce marketplace, the need to understand online visitors and keep them as loyal customers is increasingly vital to the success of any e-commerce business. The old saying that if you build, they will come, has proved to be invalid in the e-commerce marketplace, as can be attested by the failure of so many dot-com e-commerce companies in the past few years.

There are other issues related to Internet research. These issues include but are not limited to privacy, copyright, ethics, and rights of individual online visitors. We will discuss these issues in Chapter 10 when we discuss the future of e-commerce.

9.6 CONCLUSION

The Internet has provided a new paradigm for consumer as well as marketing research. It is a new paradigm since the markets and the players are different from traditional research. It is a new paradigm also because the measurements and methodologies involved are different from what they used to be. Just as retail checkout scanners help retailers understand shoppers better and manage their inventories more efficiently, Internet research tools enable hospitality and tourism companies feel the "pulse" of the online visitors' behavior faster and better, allowing them to respond and market to online visitors in an intelligent, customizable way.

As Internet technology changes, the tools available for Internet research will change, too. In the years to come, we will see new measurements and methodologies being developed to better serve the needs of online marketers and various research interests. In the meantime, issues will arise since Internet research is a brand-new field of study, and traditional concepts about research might not be readily adaptable to this new medium of communication and research.

KEY WORDS AND TERMS

Internet Research	Log Files Analysis Software
Search Logic	Cookies
Boolean Logic	Secondary Data
URL	Web Authoring Programs
Log Files	Demographica

SUMMARY

Internet research is the process of seeking, collecting, and analyzing online data to arrive at information that aids decision making. It deals more with dynamic information than with static information. It is fast paced, ever changing, and evolving. There are a number of ways to search or gain information on the Internet: (1) conduct a search using a Web search engine, (2) participate in an e-mail discussion group or Usenet newsgroup, and (3) use a known URL to directly access information.

Collecting data has been one of the most important but difficult steps in research. Traditional data collection typically takes a long time to accomplish, and often the response rate is not high. The Internet presents many tools for data collection. These include the use of log files, cookies, specialized data collection software, online surveys, e-newsletter subscriptions, and secondary data collection.

Data analysis can start from basic, simple log file analysis to specialized tracking software. Many large media companies are involved in analyzing data collected from the Internet. Other specialized research companies are also involved in producing software for online visitor data analysis and Web site traffic analysis. The ability to analyze these data has increased as the technology has become more sophisticated and powerful.

There are many specialized terms used in Internet marketing research. It is important to know the difference between these terms since each measures only one aspect of online visitor research. You need to be careful when interpreting the results of analysis when such terms are involved. Internet research is a vital part of any e-commerce business since increasing competition dictates that understanding the needs and behavior of online customers is the basis for a successful e-commerce enterprise.

Like traditional research, Internet research involves issues that concern privacy, rights of the individual, and other ethical issues. However, Internet research, because of its intrusive ability, makes these issues more important than ever and, in the meantime, brings other issues into focus. As a researcher, you need to pay attention to these issues.

WEB RESOURCES

- ❏ http://searchebusiness.techtarget.com
- ❏ www.hitboxenterprise.com
- ❏ www.positionresearch.com
- ❏ www.surveyagent.com

CASE STUDY: *Major Airline Web Sites Take Flight with WebSideStory's Real-Time E-Business Intelligence Service (www.hitboxenterprise.com)*

WebSideStory, Inc. (www.websidestory.com), the world's leading provider of outsourced e-business intelligence services, has helped the major airlines, Northwest and Alaska, integrate HitBox Enterprise (www.hitboxenterprise.com) into their online operations to help improve customer acquisition, retention, and conversion. Geared for sites with high volumes of traffic or sophisticated needs, HitBox Enterprise is a best-of-class e-business intelligence service that helps companies increase revenue and improve profitability by providing detailed information about online visitor behavior in real time. The service requires no hardware or software expenses and does not drain valuable information technology resources. Using HitBox Enterprise, the airlines are able to improve their return on marketing campaigns, improve customer loyalty, increase the effectiveness of affiliate relationships, and drive sales through enhanced site design and usability.

Alaska Airlines, the first U.S. carrier to sell tickets over the Internet, is using the service to streamline its online flight reservation process by pinpointing areas where customers have difficulty in the purchase path. The airline is also using the service to track the effectiveness of various online promotions in driving ticket sales.

"We take functionality and ease-of-use very seriously on our Web site," said Mark Guerette, director of Web content for Alaska Airlines. "HitBox Enterprise's clickstream analysis helps us in developing a better, more efficient site for our customers. We expect these changes to have an impact on our conversion ratios."

Northwest Airlines is using HitBox Enterprise to analyze in real time the behavior patterns of visitors to both its online WorldPerks Mall, a shopping section of the site, and its WorldPerks Elite Program, a special area for frequent fliers. Based on visitor behavior information, Northwest is able to adjust promotions, improve usability, and better understand the needs of its visitors. This has resulted in an increase in sales, membership, and overall customer loyalty. The airline is also using the service to identify which affiliates drive the most traffic to its site and would be the best partners for joint promotions.

"The success of our online business comes down to our customers and how satisfied they are with our products and services," said Brian Ficek, manager of e-commerce for Northwest. "With its ease of use and detailed, real-time analysis, HitBox Enterprise makes it very easy to determine where we should focus our efforts."

"The smartest businesses understand the importance of knowing how visitors interact with their Web site," said Meyar Sheik, senior vice president and chief marketing officer for WebSideStory. "Our best-of-breed services can help any business immediately identify areas of opportunity and risk on their site."

SOURCE: WebSideStory, Inc.

QUESTIONS TO PONDER:

1. What can airlines benefit from using Hitbox?
2. How does the Alaska Airlines use Hitbox to help its business?
3. In what ways can Hitbox help Northwest Airlines?
4. Why do you think the airlines are paying for this kind of service?

REVIEW QUESTIONS

1. Is Internet research different from traditional research? If so, why? If not, give reasons.
2. List three ways to do research on the Internet.
3. How many types of search engines are there?
4. What can you do to increase the probability of being found and listed by search engines?
5. Describe how Boolean logic works.
6. What is a log file? How do you use a log file to do research?
7. How does proprietary log file analysis software work?
8. List at least three research companies, go to their Web sites, and provide a brief description of their services.
9. How do you look for secondary data on the Internet?
10. Why do consumers allow cookies to stay in their computers?
11. What do you think is the most important measurement tool in tracking the behavior of online visitors as well as tracking the effectiveness of online marketing?

REFERENCES

Deitel, H. M., P. J. Deitel, and K. Steinbuhler. (2001). *E-Business and E-Commerce for Managers.* Englewood Cliffs, N. J.: Prentice Hall.
WebSideStory. (2001). www.websidestory.com.

For additional Travel and Tourism resources, go to www.Hospitality-Tourism.delmar.com

10

THE FUTURE OF HOSPITALITY AND TOURISM E-COMMERCE AND INFORMATION TECHNOLOGY

LEARNING OBJECTIVES

After you complete your study of this chapter, you should be able to:

- Describe new technology trends.
- Understand new e-commerce paradigms.
- Grasp new e-commerce strategies.
- Understand the issues, problems, and barriers in hospitality and tourism e-commerce and information technology.
- Understand the implications of all those changes.

10.1 NEW TECHNOLOGIES, NEW PARADIGMS, AND NEW STRATEGIES

While much dot-com e-commerce has either disappeared or merged and the market is experiencing a major shake-up in adopting the new reality, there are plenty of indications that consumer interest in e-commerce is actually picking up. The hospitality and tourism industry has not only survived the downturn in e-commerce and related technologies but also flourished when other industries are having a difficult time.

New technologies are being introduced into the market almost on a daily basis, which in turn opens up new territories and new possibilities in hospitality and tourism e-commerce. With new technologies, new paradigms are being created, and therefore new strategies are being formed to compete in this ever changing but profitable world of e-commerce in the hospitality and tourism industry.

10.2 NEW TECHNOLOGY TRENDS

In considering development trends in technology, you need to understand the needs of humankind for communication, information distribution, and business transactions. Just as the Internet is the result of our relentless quest for instant, real-time, and 24/7 communication, future developments in technology will need to solve the remaining issues for communication and business.

BROADBAND AND SPEED

The dial-up modem connection to the Internet has become a bottleneck for the complicated needs of human communication. Large chunks of data transmission, such as video, graphics, and other multimedia, require a lot of bandwidth, which the traditional dial-up telephone line was not designed to handle. Broadband will be key in solving this problem. The diffusion of broadband technology among Internet users will greatly increase the appeal of hospitality and tourism e-commerce since the intangible nature of hospitality and tourism services requires much more visual information and interaction over the Internet than any other industry.

Broadband technologies such as DSL, ISDN, cable, fiber optics, satellite, and radio wireless will become the norm in the future. At that time, the question will change from 'What can you put onto the Web that consumers can view without difficulty?' to "What can you do to make your presentation and communication more effective?" As competition heats up in providing these services and prices drop as a result of this competition, consumer adoption of broadband technologies will rise quickly.

At the same time, hospitality and tourism businesses will continue to look on broadband technologies as their major offering for consumers demanding broadband services. Today, most major hotel chains have installed broadband high-speed Internet connection in their hotel rooms and business centers. Increasingly, travelers are expecting every hotel to have such a connection, just like they expect cable television in every room.

MOBILITY AND ACCESSIBILITY

Travelers need to access information not only 24/7 but also wherever they have a need to do so. Mobility and accessibility are key in meeting the needs of the consumers. Wireless and satellite communication provides such a solution to solve the problem. Handheld devices, such as PDAs (personal digital assistants) and cell phones will take the market lead in the years to come.

A more advanced wireless technology that seems to be made just for the travelers has evolved: **location-based technology.** With this technology, travelers who either know their location or where they are headed input their address or the destination address. The service provider that uses this technology can then find restaurants, stores, theaters, and so on for the traveler. This technology can also provide interactive functions that permit people in different locations to communicate via IM, play tic-tac-toe together, or view restaurant listings together to decide where to meet (Gutzman 2001).

INSTANT MESSAGING (IM)

IM is a live chat and e-mail service that enables you to find your friends when they are online and send messages or talk via a private chat room. With IM, each user has a private list of instant messaging addresses, and the instant messaging system can be set to alert you when someone on your list is online. You can leave an e-mail message for a user who is not available online. Hospitality and tourism e-commerce can use this technology to send customized information ranging from travel conditions to flight cancellation.

CONVERGENCE OF TECHNOLOGIES

Another development will be the convergence of all communications media through the Web. This does not necessarily mean that all communications will take place on the Web; rather, the Web will serve as a **central communication platform** where means of communications merge with each other to create the most powerful and convenient information distribution, communication, and e-commerce channels.

Convergence refers to the integration of voice, data, and video into a single, IP-based network. We have already seen the process of convergence happen before our eyes. The wide spread use of Intranet and Extranet by hospitality and tourism businesses has speeded up this convergence process. **Destination marketing organizations** (DMOs) begin to use the Internet as a central platform for streamlining functions of marketing, travel information distribution and customer service. Hotels' **property management systems** (PMS) are not only transformed by the use of Intranet, but also become accessible to customers by way of extranet, providing 24/7 customer service.

As a whole, twenty-six percent of the Global 2000 are already migrating towards a converged network, and 42 percent plan to do so within the next two years (Blacharski, 2002). There is a good reason for this trend. Companies not doing so could be in a serious competitive disadvantage. It's true that infrastructure investments can cost a lot of money, but they can save revenue by reducing the total cost of ownership. In addition, there are other benefits in terms of business empowerment, which includes increasing organizational speed and efficiency, flexibility, and better support for a mobile workforce. Furthermore, with the same IP network, companies can run video over the network for teleconferencing, a feature that can potentially accrue tremendous savings in travel.

INTEGRATION OF BUSINESS AND E-COMMERCE TECHNOLOGIES

Related to the trend of the converging of different technologies is the trend to integrate e-commerce technologies into the daily operations of hospitality and tourism businesses. The motivation behind this trend is twofold. First, the development of new technologies has made it possible for businesses to use Internet technologies to transform their old business technology solutions into an integrated system. Second, and more important, is the drive to cut costs in the adoption of new technologies.

The need to reduce costs is urgent. As technology plays an increasingly important role in maintaining competitive advantage by increasing efficiency and effectiveness in business operations and customer service, the need to adopt new technologies is no longer a luxury but a life-and-death issue for most businesses. The question is how to strike a balance between spending and adopting new technologies.

The answer is not an easy one, but a general rule can be applied. Only when the adopted new technologies become integrated into a business operation can it save money and increase productivity. Failure to do so will result in costly expenses and inefficient and ineffective use of technology.

VOICE RECOGNITION

Another technology that has been around for a while but is receiving new interest is voice recognition, part of the artificial intelligence quest of humankind since the introduction of the computer. With voice recognition, travelers can free up their hands while driving or doing fun things by speaking to voice recognition devices, such as handheld computers, instead of typing on a keypad. For instance, through a voice command service, a traveler can use a wireless device (either a handheld computer or a PDA), get e-mail and have it read or receive a response, and get headlines and make reservations.

TRACKING TECHNOLOGIES

Yet another technological development will be tracking technologies. These technologies are needed by e-commerce companies to get users to visit their sites, allow shoppers to easily find and buy the products they need and enable **electronic customer relationship management** (e-CRM) by customization and personalization.

With these technologies, new paradigms and strategies arise that will determine whether an e-commerce business will survive and profit from the great potential that the Internet has to offer. In the next two sections, we discuss some of these new paradigms and strategies.

WIRELESS COMMUNICATIONS

The Internet has speeded up the process of globalization and technological innovation. As a result, wireless technology is growing at great speed worldwide. As pointed out elsewhere in this book, the United States lags behind other nations in terms of the popularity of wireless usage. However, this is changing. It is estimated that 137 million Americans are now equipped with some type of wireless service (Hospitality Sales and Marketing Association International 2002), and the possibilities that this presents for the hospitality and tourism industry are far reaching and endless.

Key wireless technology applications are emerging quickly to meet the needs of the travelers. Already in use or being improved are applications such as **location based services** (the ability to locate cell phones to send information), **voice command service** (basic voice recognition technology), **multimedia** (viewing short videos, like trailers for movies and videos taken on vacation), speed (faster wireless networking—an Ethernet connection at 11 megabytes per second that can match the speed of broadband), and **interoperability** (improving the ability to talk to one another).

The hospitality and tourism industry will continue to look for ways to increase productivity through wireless extensions of e-commerce. With wireless technology becoming more mature and shifting from voice to data and from limited personal usage to mobile e-commerce and personalization, it is foreseeable that more companies will be taking advantage of wireless technology.

In the future, as convergence trends continue, the wireless device might become **point of access** for all sorts of information, such as news, sports, maps, entertainment (e.g., music), graphics and games, communications (e.g., e-mail), **instant messaging** and **SMS** (short messaging service), and transactions such as banking, shopping, and reservations.

10.3 NEW PARADIGMS

For hospitality and tourism, information has been the king. The Internet has made it even more so. From the traveler's point of view, the ability to access information anytime, anywhere, is always something to dream about. However, the most important thing for consumers is probably the ability to make intelligent choices, that is, the **freedom of choice** based on an informed decision. For business, the ability to gather information from travelers so as to understand their needs and wants is key in providing satisfactory customer service. In addition, the ability to market directly to consumers has been a goal for hospitality and tourism marketers, and that goal was made possible with the introduction of the Internet.

INFORMATION AS ASSETS

With the advent of the Internet, a new **information paradigm** has arisen: Customer information has become part of a business' assets. When customers trust a business with their personal information, they expect the business to take good care of it, just as they trust a bank with their money. In this regard, they also expect to get something valuable in return for their trust and to be able to withdraw that trust any time they desire.

The idea that customer information is part of a business' assets means that the business will have to find ways to invest these assets. One simple way to do so is to make sense of those assets and customize the information so as to be able to provide valuable services to customers. In e-commerce, this is called e-CRM, one of the hottest trends in hospitality and tourism management.

Once we use the terms *assets* and *investment* to refer to customer information, we are accepting the idea that a long-term relationship with customers is more important than any temporary gain. Any time you abuse your customers' trust and handle their information against them, you will be penalized by losing their trust and thus their loyalty.

PERSONALIZATION AND CUSTOMIZATION IS KING

In the Internet age, mass marketing and commercialization are out, and personalization, customization, and target marketing are in. Long before the Internet, market segmentation played an important role in marketing and information distribution. The difference now is that Internet technology has made it much easier to do target marketing in a faster, more accurate way. Hospitality and tourism businesses have realized that while it is important to deliver targeted and personalized information to existing and potential customers, they also know that not everyone needs the same information, nor will they use it and receive it in the same way. A more difficult challenge is to customize the information for the end user, delivering high touch in a high-tech world.

For years, the hospitality and tourism industry has realized the importance of customization and personalization in delivering marketing information as well as service, and there was no easy, economical way to do it. The Internet has changed all that. With Internet research and communication tools, delivering personalized and customized information is no longer a time-consuming, costly proposition. In fact, it is cheaper and faster to deliver such information today than it was with a mass mailing in the past.

The tracking technology discussed in Chapter 9 is an important tool in helping a business achieve the goal of personalization and customization. For instance, many e-commerce sites install shopping wizards that can help visitors find what they want quickly and easily. More important, when these visitors return to the site, the site will have remembered their interests and preferences to provide a personalized experience for the customers. Personalization and customization make up the future of e-commerce.

THE WEB SITE AS A 24/7 OFFICE

In the fierce competition for Web dominance in e-commerce, the site that not only can attract visitors but also convert them into loyal customers will be the winner. Since online visitors can come to a Web site at any time of the day from every corner of the world, a business Web site must serve as a **24/7 office** or an **extension branch** of the business. Only when visitors can find what they need quickly and easily and when their visiting experience is satisfactory will they become repeat visitors and therefore possible customers.

The concept that the Web site is a 24/7 office is critical to e-commerce. It means that you have to be present at the site all the time to respond to customer needs and questions. This can be done by several means. One way is to try to understand these visitors as soon as they come to your site and give them what they want, which requires a high degree of personalization and customization, discussed in the previous section. A second way is through the design of the Web site, that is, anticipating the needs and wants and providing the needed information in an easy-to-find and easy-to-understand manner. Another way is to create as many interactive communication channels as possible so that visitor questions can be responded to and answered instantly and satisfactorily. Throughout this book, we have discussed many communication tools that can accomplish this goal.

PERMISSION MARKETING IS EVERYTHING

Related to the personalization and customization is permission marketing and selling. As the Internet makes communicating with and reaching customers more easy and less expensive, the sensitivity of customers to privacy and consumer rights also increases. Hospitality and tourism e-commerce businesses must make sure that they get consumers' explicit permission to send marketing or any type of information. Furthermore, they will need to provide an option for consumers to opt out in case they decide not to continue the relationship.

DISINTERMEDIATION AND RE-INTERMEDIATION

The Internet has been blamed for much of the death of middlemen. It is true that the Internet provides an excellent alternative for direct marketing and selling, thus putting most of the traditional middlemen out of business. This process of cutting off the middlemen is what has been referred to as disintermediation. In the meantime, the Internet creates a new platform for introducing new e-commerce businesses to fill the void left by traditional middlemen. The emergence of online-only travel Web sites such as expedia.com illustrates this process of re-intermediation. The fact is that it is not that travelers do not need travel agents, the middlemen; it is that consumers need a more efficient and effective way of accessing travel information and reservation.

10.4 NEW STRATEGIES

New technologies and new paradigms require that hospitality and tourism e-commerce businesses adopt new strategies. Some of the fundamentals of doing business will not change, but the way in which business is conducted will have to change to adapt to the Internet environment.

SERVICE ORIENTATION

The first e-commerce strategy for hospitality and tourism enterprises is to focus on customers and customer service rather than on products. A customer-and-service-oriented company tries to understand the customer needs and find solutions to meet their needs. A product-oriented company tries to sell features of its products and lets customers decide what they want. A customer-and-service-oriented travel agency, for instance, understands customer needs and preferences, personalizes solutions to meet those needs and preferences, and builds a long-term relationship with the customer.

A product-oriented travel agency, on the other hand, simply tells the customer what the customer can get from the agency, such as airline tickets, hotel reservations, or cruise-line bookings. It leaves the customer to decide where to go and what to buy. In this case, the travel agency becomes a ticket retail store. When people can get tickets quickly and easily from the Internet, they bypass the travel agent. This spells the decline of the popularity of the travel agent if the role of the travel agent is just to sell tickets.

BUILDING VIRTUAL COMMUNITIES

Another strategy is to build virtual customer communities. The Internet has provided every imaginable tool for businesses to offer opportunities for their customers to communicate and share information about their products and services. Tools such as mailing lists, Usenet, discussion forums, chatrooms, and Web site portals are great communication vehicles for people with the same interests to gather in cyberspace to communicate and share information.

One of the most exciting and promising marketing techniques in Internet marketing is based on this idea of virtual consumer communities. It is called **viral marketing,** which refers to a process in which consumers voluntarily spread a message about a company, a product, or a service based on their own experience. It is the Internet version of word-of-mouth marketing.

When your satisfied customers recommend your Web site or service to their friends in virtual communities, the impact of that recommendation will be much more powerful than if it comes directly from your business. If that customer passes his or her recommendation to his or her friends and so on, you get a viral marketing effect. All this is made possible because passing information on the Internet is much easier and more convenient than through any traditional means.

PARTNERSHIP

We all know that **partnership** is one of the important elements in traditional hospitality and tourism marketing in addition to the classic four Ps of marketing: price, product, place, and promotion. Partnerships are important because of the nature of the hospitality and tourism industry, which is an interrelated group of businesses that serve the needs of travelers. Hotels benefit from partnering with airlines, and small businesses benefit from partnering with large, reputable corporations.

There are many benefits derived from partnership in hospitality and tourism, particularly in marketing. These benefits include a large pool of resources for marketing, expansion of customer base, utilization of the partner's unique products and services to increase product and service value to customers, and the customer's conception of convenience and value.

In e-commerce, partnership is assuming its old role and in the meantime taking a new name. The role of partnership assumes a more important role than ever. The shake-up of the hospitality and tourism industry due to both technological changes and the terrorist attacks of September 11 intensifies competition by placing a priority on cutting costs and increasing revenue. Consolidation is happening in every sector of the hospitality and tourism industry, especially in the travel information distribution sector. For small businesses to compete in this market, partnership is an alternative to being consolidated by large corporations.

Another new dimension of partnership is being made possible by Internet technologies: The affiliate loyalty program, or affiliate marketing, discussed in Chapter 6. This e-commerce strategy is based on the fact that the Internet is basically a Web of information: Everything is linked to everything else. By identifying Web sites or Web pages that attract potential customers for your product or service, you can exchange links or pay to be linked to or advertised in another Web site.

MULTICHANNEL COMMUNICATIONS

This strategy uses **multichannel communications** for marketing and customer service. By multichannel communications, we mean the utilization of a combination of traditional media and Internet technologies in marketing and customer service. You need to realize that not all your customers have the same technological skills and may not prefer to use the same communication vehicle. In addition, technology does break down, but today's consumers are notoriously impatient. If they cannot find what they want or cannot ask the question they need an answer for before buying a product, they can click away and vanish in cyberspace.

BUILDING BRAND WITH TRUST

A final strategy is to build a brand with trust. Compared with brick-and-mortar businesses, e-commerce is relatively intangible and mysterious since a consumer cannot see who is behind the Web site and cannot see how the information he or she types into the computer gets transmitted through cyberspace. The Internet has made trust an overriding factor in the consumer's choice of services and products. A Yahoo survey has shown that 84% of consumers would be more likely to buy from a Web site that has been certified and is thus trustworthy (PITA 2001).

Established, well-known brands can play catch-up so quickly with Web entrepreneurs and in many cases outperform the latter because consumers feel safe in dealing with these brands, even in cyberspace. The old rule that if you build it, they will come, does not apply to e-commerce. Another old rule of e-commerce in the age of dot-com boom, "He who comes first will win", is no longer true with today's sophisticated online travelers. Earning the trust of consumers will become a vital strategy for successful e-commerce businesses.

10.5 ISSUES, PROBLEMS, AND BARRIERS

The Internet has given the hospitality and tourism industry great opportunities, but at the same time it has produced many challenges. For many small businesses, the cost of adopting new technologies becomes a big issue.

Related to the cost issue is that of deciding on managing technologies in house or out of house, that is, **outsourcing** to technology companies.

There are many other issues for the hospitality and tourism industry to face, and one of these is the problem of **standardization** of technologies. Because the Internet is a decentralized structure and does not dictate what type of technologies can be used with it, various technology vendors have produced different technology standards, resulting in confusion at best and incompatability at worst. Without a system of standardization, the hospitality and tourism industry cannot reap the potential that various innovations in technology can bring to their businesses and e-commerce. The hospitality and tourism industry has other barriers to face. One of these is online payment methods. E-commerce requires a complete system for online financial transactions so that online travelers can pay for products and services instantly as they see fit. Only when business and online travelers feel that they can pay or accept payment easily, reliably, and securely can you convert more lookers into buyers.

10.6 CONCLUSION

The Internet has revolutionized the way we communicate, expanded the horizon of our thinking, and presented countless opportunities for various human activities that include e-commerce. More important, the Internet is here to stay. Just like electricity and the automobile have become part and parcel of our daily lives, the Internet is bound to permeate every facet of our activities.

The Internet is like water in the ocean, to use a Chinese metaphor. It can keep a boat afloat and carry the boat to the destination; it can also engulf the boat and sink it to the bottom of the ocean. For the hospitality and tourism industry, understanding and learning how to control and take advantage of the Internet (the ocean) may very well determine the course of business success in the years to come.

E-commerce is not an option that we can safely predict but rather a necessity of life for every business in the coming years. This might not seem obvious since e-commerce is not doing as well as it should. However, this is not the fault of the Internet. Indeed, it reinforces the point that we have tried to make throughout this book: We need to gain a better understanding of the potential of the Internet and learn how to take advantage of it. The fact is that the age of e-commerce is just beginning. The potential of the Internet has yet to reveal its greatness and capacity.

We will soon see e-commerce as commonplace as our neighborhood automobile repair shop. And the biggest beneficiaries will be the hospitality and tourism industry and travelers since the Internet and this industry, as we stated at the beginning of this book, is a marriage made in heaven.

▌ KEY WORDS AND TERMS

Location-Based Technology
Central Communication Platform
Electronic Customer Relationship
  Management
Location-Based Services
Voice Command Service
Multimedia
Interoperability
Point of Access
Instant Messaging
SMS

Freedom of Choice
Information Paradigm
24/7 Office
Extension Branch
Viral Marketing
Partnership
Multichannel Communications
Outsourcing
Standardization
Corporate Travel Specialists

▌ SUMMARY

Internet technology will undergo many changes, but these changes will most likely be in the direction of providing solutions for human communication needs. Just like the Internet is the result of humankind's relentless quest for instant, real-time, and 24/7 communications, future technology development will need to solve the remaining issues for communication and business.

New technologies will most likely focus on improving communications speed, increasing the accessibility of information, and making communications more mobile. Broadband, wireless communications technology will witness tremendous growth in the years to come. We will see a convergence of all technologies with the Internet as the major communications platform. In addition, tracking systems will become more sophisticated and highly valued.

New paradigms arise as a result of the development of new technologies. Customer information becomes part of a business' assets. Personalization, customization, and target marketing proclaim the death of mass marketing. By the same token, permission marketing will dominate Internet marketing.

New technologies and new paradigms require new strategies. The first strategy is to focus on customers and customer service rather than on products. The second strategy is to build virtual customer communities, which lays the foundation for viral marketing, or Internet word-of-mouth marketing. Partnership takes a new form and name in the age of the Internet; the affiliate loyalty program, or affiliate marketing. Trust is also an important strategy to win over consumers to a business brand.

To better serve the diverse needs of customers, you will need to develop a multichannel communications strategy.

As Internet technology matures and its potentials are better understood by both consumers and businesses, we will witness leaps and bounds in adopting this technology for all facets of our lives.

■ WEB RESOURCES

- www.broadband-guide.com
- www.everythingDSL.com

CASE STUDY: The Hotel Reservations Arena:
An At-a-Glance View from Around
the Globe

In today's technologically advanced environment, no hotelier can afford to ignore the explosive growth of electronic bookings from travel agents, third-party Web sites, and tour operators around the globe or avoid the rapidly growing consumer demand for direct electronic access to the hotel product. The reservations process has moved from faxes and phone calls made directly to the property to call centers and international representation services, connections to global distribution systems (GDSs) and access to the Internet via computers, wireless phones, and personal digital assistants (PDAs).

In this ever changing marketplace, the challenge to hoteliers around the world is to learn how to operate effectively, efficiently, and economically in this complex multichannel distribution environment. Tapping the proper technology services to manage the reservations process is the secret to achieving profitable results, leaving hoteliers to focus on their core competency—a superb guest experience.

A VISION FOR AN ELECTRONIC FUTURE

The idea of electronic hotel bookings most likely would not have become a reality if a group of 16 of the world's leading hotel and travel-related companies had not shared a collective vision for the future of the reservations process: automation.

In 1988, this forward-thinking group founded Pegasus Solutions to create a streamlined and automated hotel reservations process for the hotel industry. The company's pioneering technology provided a seamless electronic connection between a hotel's central reservations system

(CRS) and the GDSs, such as Sabre and Galileo, which travel agents use to book airline reservations. Through this connection, travel agents could easily reserve hotel rooms from the same desktop computer terminal used to book flights.

This industry milestone dramatically improved the efficiency of the entire hotel reservations process and was the foundation needed to build additional technology platforms for today's global hotel reservations arena, including reservation systems, Internet reservations and hosting services, call center services, travel agent commission processing services, and marketing representation services.

THE IMPORTANCE OF THE INTERNET

In the mid-1990s, Pegasus recognized the importance of the Internet as a distribution channel for making hotel reservations and is credited with launching the first online travel agency site to provide real-time hotel bookings for a variety of hotels in 1994. To provide consumer-friendly hotel information and photos through the site, Pegasus created what is now one of the largest property information databases, containing detailed, descriptive property information for more than 44,000 hotels. The data are managed directly by the hotel chains, ensuring a high level of accuracy.

Today, the Online Distribution Database and Internet booking engine that Pegasus created in 1994 and has continually upgraded and enhanced are used worldwide, "powering" thousands of travel-related Web sites, including HotelHub, Ebookers.com, Lastminute.com, Hotwire, and Orbitz. As the Internet continues to gain wider acceptance as a means to both shop for and make hotel reservations, Pegasus' online distribution service is well positioned to take advantage of this escalating trend. Two reasons for the success of this expanding online segment are the ability to easily access the CRSs of more than 44,000 hotels and the high caliber of the property information.

Pegasus also identified that for non-English-speaking customers to maximize the opportunity from their Pegasus hotel booking solution, ideally the hotel content within the Pegasus database would need to be in various European languages. Since June 2002, Pegasus has provided the ability for its member hotels to start loading their hotel content in French, German, Spanish, and Italian.

With hotels looking to increase the proportion of their reservations that are made online, consistency of information across the brand is essential. For example, the Ritz-Meridien in Madrid would like to know that a corporate traveler in Barcelona would see the same information about its property regardless of whether the traveler is using Lastminute.com or Ebookers.com or any other travel booking site.

GLEANING THE GLOBAL ELECTRONIC DISTRIBUTION TRENDS

As a provider of hotel industry technology services, Pegasus Solutions is in a unique position that enables it to anticipate industry change and recognize market issues. Pegasus has identified several industry challenges and has developed solutions used by industry players such as travel agencies, hotel booking agencies, corporate travel specialists, middleware companies, and tour operators. Following are some examples:

- Both leisure and corporate travel agencies are reviewing their online hotel booking solutions in order to provide their customers with direct access to negotiated rates and real-time availability. By using Pegasus' online booking system, agents are not limited to the functionality provided by the GDSs. By connecting to Pegasus, they obtain better property data, can view pictures of the properties and an unlimited number of rates, and can access real-time availability.

- Large hotel booking agencies, such as Hotel Reservation Service (HRS) in Germany, no longer want to manually update their proprietary booking systems. These companies want an automatic interface to the hotels' CRSs and have enlisted the services of Pegasus to achieve this goal. For example, hotels that work with HRS do not have to manually update the HRS database but just ensure the HRS rates and room allocations are featured in the hotel's CRS.

- Like the rest of Europe, corporate travel specialists in Spain are thriving. Sercotel, Keytel, and Utell are among those that directly or indirectly service the corporate market. Many corporations are demanding that their travel agencies make their corporate rates available over their company's intranet. Some travel agencies use a GDS-based corporate travel offering, while many others are considering using alternative hotel distribution channels that are connected to Pegasus. For example, Finland-based Hotelzon International is tapping Pegasus to provide a booking solution that allows other companies using the unique Hotelzon booking system to view and book their negotiated corporate rates online in real time. Similarly, NetBook in Sweden and KDS in France are using Pegasus as their booking engine and to access to corporate-negotiated rates stored in the hotels' CRSs.

- Tour operators want to access real-time hotel room availability so that they can dynamically create tour packages and no longer need to store hotel inventory in their proprietary reservation systems. Even the tour operators who decide to continue to manage their contracted room inventory on their own proprietary system are looking for a way to automate the delivery of hotel reservations directly into the hotel's CRS, eliminating the need to manually fax the reservation information to the hotel.

- Tour operators are also seeking an automated solution to manage and process the payments due to the various travel suppliers with which they have contracted. Pegasus is working with several tour operators to help automate their exchange of reservations with the contracted hotel and recently launched PegsPay™, a payment processing solution that helps tour operators manage and pay their travel suppliers for the sales that the tour operators made on their behalf. Additionally, PegsPay will help facilitate tour operators' payment transactions to travel agents that secured guest bookings.

THE "WIRELESS" WAVE

The worldwide availability and affordability of wireless phones is certain. For the hotelier, the question is "what" is being accessed. Is a wireless phone a distribution channel in itself? This is not the case—the wireless phone is a communications tool giving access to a distribution channel. If so, who are the accommodation providers, and from where are they sourcing the availability?

To help answer these questions, Pegasus capitalized on its aggregated supplier direct connections to systematically enhance its connectivity to the lodging industry and expanded its services to enable hotels to take advantage of emerging distribution channels, such as the Internet, via wireless devices.

Pegasus has pinpointed that in Finland, the United Kingdom, and Germany, the corporate traveler wishing to book a negotiated rate is the first sector using the wireless phone to book a hotel online. Pegasus addressed this trend two years ago through its working relationship with Hotelzon International, an expert in the conversion of CRS data to "thin messaging" required for the mobile Internet. Therefore, hotels connected to Pegasus for electronic distribution are secure in knowing that as travelers may move toward the use of PDAs and other wireless devices, Pegasus has already developed the required interface and is processing bookings today via this medium.

TOOLS TO HELP MANAGE HOTEL INVENTORY AND BUSINESS GENERATOR RELATIONSHIPS

While Pegasus Solutions continues to remain active in enabling its hotel customers to access more and more distribution channels, the increasing challenge for the hotelier has been not only how to discover and evaluate emerging channels but also how to best manage the inventory across these various channels. It is commonly accepted that the hotel CRS is the repository for inventory for distribution channels, whether traditional GDS, GDS-sourced online offerings, overseas call centers, and non-GDS-reliant online solutions.

Utell, a wholly owned subsidiary of Pegasus Solutions, established itself in the Spanish market over 25 years ago, being the first to market with a call center serving travel agencies that wished to make instant reservations for a growing portfolio of hotels worldwide. Equally, Utell gave hoteliers a cost-effective way of reaching independent corporate and leisure individual travelers in overseas markets by way of its expanding voice reservations network for travel agencies around the world.

Today, the Utell representation service has expanded far beyond a voice reservation service and can provide independent hotels and small chains with even more distribution opportunities via all four GDSs as well as access to all the distribution channels mentioned previously—access that the hotels would never be able to achieve on their own. Utell provides the tools and service staff to help its hotel members manage and maximize the presence of their room inventory on all the various distribution channels as well as sales and account management service to assist them with promoting their hotels to travel agencies around the world and the electronic marketing of their hotel rooms. Examples of agencies that frequently book Utell hotels are Viajes El Corte Ingles, GBTA, Barcelo, and Halcon. More than 250 hotels in Spain are members of Utell.

ON-PROPERTY SYSTEMS

Pegasus has expanded its offerings to include another industry first, *PegasusCentral*™, a new Web-based hospitality management solution. Hotels using the *PegasusCentral* property management system can manage daily on-site operations of all hotel departments, such as guest checkin and checkout, sales and financial tracking and forecasting, comprehensive guest profiles, and inventory management. A Spanish-language version of ASP-based *PegasusCentral* is expected to be available by the end of 2002. Interest in *PegasusCentral* is growing strong from a number of hotel groups operating across Europe with properties in Spain as well as from independent properties.

In addition, Pegasus Commission Processing, the hotel industry's largest travel agent commission processing service, continues to see growth in its European business and maintains a Member Travel Agency Support Center in Europe. With tens of thousands of travel agencies subscribers in more than 200 countries, Pegasus processes an average of $41 million in travel agent commissions per month for more than 180 hotel brands. Serving both travel agencies and hotels, Europe represents Pegasus' second-largest penetration of travel agency membership, reinforcing the value that Pegasus brings to hoteliers' worldwide business generators.

In summary, there are many positive changes taking place in the development of technologies that offer new distribution channels and inventory management solutions in regard to the reservations process. It is clear that hoteliers need to enlist the support of a robust technology services provider to help them navigate the ever changing landscape of the hotel reservations arena and to ensure that they leverage all the emerging distribution channels.

SOURCE: This case study was written by Peter Fitzgerald, vice president of International Sales Pegasus Solutions, Inc. Printed with permission.

QUESTIONS TO PONDER:

1. What is the biggest challenge to hoteliers?
2. What is the vision of an electronic future? Do you agree with the vision?
3. What are the industry challenges that Pegasus has identified?
4. What are the solutions developed by Pegasus to meet the challenges?
5. Describe the major functions of Utell.
6. What on-property solution does Pegasus provide to manage daily on-site operations of all hotel departments?

REVIEW QUESTIONS

1. What are the major new technology trends?
2. What are the new e-commerce paradigms?
3. Describe the new e-commerce strategies.
4. What is the difference between personalization and customization?
5. Do you agree with the author that wireless has a great future in the hospitality and tourism industry? Justify your answer.
6. Why is partnership so important in the new Internet environment?
7. Why does trust become a critical issue for e-commerce and brand building?
8. What are the major issues, problems, and barriers for using technology?
9. What do all these trends, paradigms, and strategies mean to the hospitality and tourism industry?

REFERENCES

Gutzman, Alexis D. (2001). "Location-Based Services for PDAs."
    http://e-commerce.internet.com.

PITA. (2001). www.pitaonline.com.

Blacharski, Dan. (2002). "Convergence Impacts the Entire Enterprise."
    www.itworld.com.

Hospitality Sales and Marketing Association International. (2002).
    www.hsmai.org.

*For additional Travel and Tourism resources, go to
www.Hospitality-Tourism.delmar.com*

Glossary

Accreditation Recognized as having met set standards for a specific reason.

Advertising Networks/Ad Networks Internet companies that offer the advertising service that allows businesses to place an ad with all the target Web sites in their networked or partnership companies. These ad networks are typically representing those websites that are either too busy or too small to sell their own advertising.

Affiliate (Marketing) Program A form of partnership in which a Web site owner or business pays or rewards other Web site owner(s) or businesses, called affiliates, for clickthroughs on or leads from the advertisements displayed on an affiliate site. Affiliate Marketing Program is quickly becoming the dominant form of Web marketing and has been shown to have a very positive impact on Web site marketing power.

Air Traffic Conference (ATC) Was established in 1945 by the airline industry to alleviate the unorganized method of distribution for airline tickets.

Airline Deregulation Act An act signed by President Carter in 1978, which removed all remaining obstacles to route entry by established carriers, opened up entry to new carriers, and phased out all fare registrations.

Airline Reporting Corporation (**ARC**) Replaced the ATC in 1984 and maintains most of its functions.

Airline Ticket Publishing Co. An industry wide clearinghouse that provides data to U.S. travel agents.

Amadeus One of the four main GDS systems existing today.

Applets A Java application. Applets adhere to a set of conventions that let them run within a Java-compatible browser. It uses the client's Web browser to provide a user interface.

Application Service Provider (**ASP**) An information technology company that offers a complete access solution over the Internet to applications and related services that would otherwise have been located in an individual's or organization's computers.

Applications Standalone computer programs designed for a specific task or use.

ARPA Stands for the Pentagon's **A**dvanced **R**esearch **P**rojects **A**gency. Introduced the first version of the Internet called the "ARPANET."

ASCII   American Standard Code for Information Interchange. A code for information exchange between computers made by different companies; text files that were used for communication and publication on the Internet before the birth of the Web.

Asymmetric Encryption   A type of public-key Encryption, the sender encrypts the data with a public key, which requires a private key as the corresponding pair. The receiver uses the paired private key to decrypt the data to read it.

Avis Interactive   An Internet-based information system brought out by Avis that allows its corporate customers to access complete, up-to-date information on their car rental usage, making tracking travel expenses and rental preferences easier for frequent business travelers.

B2B e-commerce   Any business process between two companies that uses web-based network technologies.

B2B Exchanges   The exchange of information and business transactions on a Web-based network from business to business.

B2C e-commerce   The business process between the business and the consumer that uses a Web-based network techonology.

Bandwidth   The amount of data that can be sent through a given communications circuit per second. The more bandwidth there is, the faster it can receive and send data through the same communication channel.

Banner Ads   A banner ad is a graphic image on a website that advertises a product, service, promotion, brand, or a combination of all or some of them. A form of push technology.

BillPoint   An electronic payment system that simplifies and facilitates person-to-person and person-to-small business payments over the Internet. Founded in October, 1998 and acquired by eBay in 1999, Billpoint provides a payments solution that could be seamlessly integrated into the overall eBay transaction experience.

Boolean Logic   Search technique based on the logical relationship among search terms. Believed to be named after the British mathematician George Boole.

Broadband Communications   A communications network that allows for simultaneous transmission of signals such as voice, data, or video.

Business Model   Shows what composes a business and by what it stands by. Travel agents need to change from a ticket retailer to a travel information and service provider, from a product-oriented business to a service-oriented business.

Central Communication Platform   Where means of communications merge with each other to create the most powerful and convenient information presentation and communication on the Web.

Certificate Authority A third party who issues digital certificates for authentication and authorization for secure interactions over the network.

Civil Aeronautics Board (CAB) Regulated air control from 1938 to 1978 and took on responsibilities such as: granting airline routes, controlling fares, and protecting the interest of the public.

Click-through A click-through is often interchangeable with a click, referring to the process of clicking on an online advertisement. It is what is counted by the sponsoring site as a result of an ad click. A click-through, however, tends to imply that the user actually gets to the destination site that the ad is for.

Commission Percentage of money made from selling a product or service that the salesperson or company gets to keep for making the sale.

Computer Reservations System (CRS) Organized by individual airlines to handle reservations, ticketing, schedules, seat inventories, and have created great advances in speed and accuracy for the booking of airline flights.

Convention and Visitors Bureau (CVB) An organization in most cities that promotes travel and tourism to the represented destination to increase awareness and attracts guests for leisure and/or business travel.

Cookie A tiny program or a file on a Web user's hard drive that is used by Web sites to record data about the user.

Cookies A message sent from a Web server to an online traveler's local computer and stored by the browser on his/her computer. When the online traveler visits the originating Web server next time, the cookie is sent back to the server, allowing it to respond to the online traveler according to the cookie's content.

Corporate Clients Consumers that are businesses themselves: the B2B ecommerce.

Corporate Travel Agencies Travel agencies that are housed in the corporation or are specialized in business travel.

Corporate Travel Specialists Professionals that specialize in business travel.

Customization The process of providing information and service according to the needs and wants of individual consumers.

Customized Information Information tailored to meet the specific needs of individual consumers.

Customized Marketing Message Promotions or messages sent to target audiences to market a product or service that is personalized with their name or other fields that makes them feel like they were specifically picked.

Demographica A platform-independent, browser-based application for creating online surveys and polls. It provides Web sales and marketing professionals with the ability to quickly and easily create surveys customized with their own questions, manage accounts, and schedule intervals for results to be emailed.

Destination Marketing Organization (DMO) Organizations that are involved with marketing tourism destinations to targeted travelers to help increase the tourism traffic to a certain area.

Digital Certificate Serves the same purpose as a digital signature, but it is issued by a certificate authority.

Digital Signature A digital code attached to the electronic message being sent over the Internet to uniquely identify the sender.

Discussion Forum An Internet-based interest group that shares and exchanges ideas and information over a bulletin board system. It is sometimes called a newsgroup in which participants with common interests can exchange open messages.

Domain Name The address identifying a specific site on the Internet. Domain names are derived from a hierarchical system with a host name followed by a top-level domain category.

Domain Name System DNS, a distributed database used by TCP/IP applications to map between hostnames and IP addresses. It works behind the scenes to translate Internet domain names (such as

example.com) to their corresponding IP addresses (such as 128.143.7.185), and vice versa, allowing Internet users to use familiar names rather than IP addresses.

Dot-com Internet companies that conduct e-commerce purely online without a physical business location.

Dynamic Information Information that changes over time; information such as the 'clicks,' the number of visitors to a specific site in a certain hour or day, weather condition, daily hotel pricing, and the interaction of instant feedback and communication.

e-Cash An electronic payment system that uses electronic money designed to be used over a network or stored on cards similar to credit cards.

E-commerce Marketplace The Web-based business environment in which online companies compete with each other for business.

E-commerce A system of conducting business activities using the Internet and other information technologies. Refers to using computer networks to conduct business, including buying and selling online, electronic funds transfer, business communications, and other activities associated with the buying and selling of goods and services online.

E-communities Another term for Virtual Communities which is based on the Internet where people from all over the world group together by common interests.

EDI Electronic Data Interchange. Before the Internet, the electronic communication process enables business transactions, such as orders, confirmations, invoices, and payments between two organizations.

E-hotels Hotels that offer services ranging from 100mb/sec. high-speed Internet access, video-on-demand systems, limited videoconferencing in all the rooms, wireless access throughout the building, Internet kiosks in the lobby, and more.

E-mail Electronic Mail. A system of electronic transmission of digital messages over the Internet.

E-mail Marketing Sending marketing promotions and messages through the channel of E-mail. It can be an inexpensive yet effective way of bringing marketing information to a target audience.

E-marketing Bringing information of the products and services to the targeted consumers in a timely and accurate fashion through the Internet.

E-marketplace The place where two companies that use web-based networks exchange information to conduct the exchange.

E-Promotion A hyperlink special ad displayed on the screen that comes with an incentive to entice the online visitor to click on it and act right away.

E-Sponsorship Just like traditional sponsorship, e-sponsorship seeks to associate the advertiser to a brand name. In e-sponsorship, the advertiser identifies a website, an event, or a virtual community hosted by a website that attracts the audience the sponsor wishes to reach.

Ethernet A type of networking technology for LAN; it was originally developed by Xerox Corporation and quickly became one of the most popular LAN standards.

Extension Branch An extension of a company to handle customer service online and offer the accessibility that consumers now demand.

Extranet An Intranet connected to the Internet, allowing people from outside the organization to access it. A private network that not only connects to the Internet but also uses the same special set of rules for communication.

FAQs Frequently Asked Questions. A FAQs section placed on your website can be viewed twenty-four hours a day and save a lot of time and labor.

Firewall A set of related programs located at a network gateway server that protects the resources of a private network from users on other networks.

FTP File Transfer Protocol. Software programs that enable a user on one computer to transfer files to and from another computer over the Internet or a TCP/IP network.

Galileo/Apollo One of the four main GDS systems existing today.

Global Distribution System (GDS) Basically a computer reservations system that contains a vast database of inventories and travel information of participating travel carriers and suppliers who pay a fee to subscribe to the GDS service.

Hardware The mechanical, magnetic, electronic, and electrical components making up a computer system. In Internet technology, it is the physical infrastructure that includes things such as the telephone, networks, cables, routers, computers, servers, and satellites.

HDML Handheld Device Markup Language. One of the two main programming languages that make up the Wireless Web. It is similar to HTML and runs on a micro-browser designed for handheld devices.

HTML HyperText Markup Language. It is a collection of platform-independent styles indicated by markup tags that define the various components of a World Wide Web document.

Hyperlink Text and information that can be linked in such a way that a simple click will lead you to the next level of texts or information.

Hypertext Text and information that can be linked in such a way that a simple click will lead you to the next level of texts or information.

ICANN Internet Corporation for Assigned Names and Numbers. A not-for-profit organization that handles IP address space allocation, protocol parameter assignment, domain name system management, and root server system management functions.

Incentives Comes in the form of cash bonuses and reduced rate tickets for agents, which inspires the determination for excellence on behalf of the travel agent.

Information Superhighway A metaphor used for the Internet because it provides a physical infrastructure through which communication is made possible. It is like a highway system on which all kinds of transportation vehicles pass through.

Instant Messaging A live chat and e-mail service that enables you to communicate instantly with your friends when they are online and send messages or talk via a private chat room. Each user can set up a private list of the IDs from friends so that an alert system can be created to alert the user when a friend on the list comes online. You can also leave an e-mail message for a user who is not available online.

Interactive Information Dynamic information that requires two-way, fast and instant communication to allow for meaningful communication.

Interface A program that translates and presents information on your computer screen so that the user and the computer can interact with one another.

Intermediaries The connecting business of the manufacturer or supplier to the consumer. The middlemen of the buying and selling world. For example, travel agents selling airline tickets to the consumer.

International Air Transportation Association (IATA) Formed to regulate international air travel. Some basic functions are: security, safety standards, and appointment of travel agencies to represent member airlines.

Internet Protocol (IP) A common network communication language enabling communications between network computers, such as transferring data, using one another's computers and programming one another's computers remotely.

Internet Research The process of seeking, collecting, and analyzing data to arrive at information that aids decision-making with the aid of all the tools available through the Internet. It deals more with dynamic information rather than static information and is fast-paced, ever-changing, and evolving.

Internet Service Provider (ISP) A company in the business of providing Internet access to computer users who do not have a direct connection in exchange for payment of a monthly fee.

Interoperability The ability of systems or products to work together automatically.

Interstitials Special banner ads that pop up on the screen to catch the attention of the online visitor.

Intranet Web sites Web sites that are established over an Intranet set-up, which is basically an Internet within a business corporation. It is a private network in which access is determined by the owner.

Intranet A network that uses Internet technology and protocols and is housed within a business corporation or organization.

Invisible Interstitials Same as an interstitial, but they are invisible at first since they pop under rather than pop up on the screen as a regular popup.aka popunders.

IP Internet Protocol. Enables communications between computers, such as transferring data, using one another's computers and even programming one another's computers remotely.

LAN Local Area Network. A communications network that connects computers and other terminals within a geographically limited area (typically within adjacent buildings or complexes). A LAN requires a LAN server and allows resources to be shared.

LISTSERV Mailing list management software that runs on a variety of platforms, designed to scan incoming e-mail messages for the words "subscribe," "unsubscribe," and other housekeeping commands, and update the subscriber list automatically.

Location-Based Service   An information service that marries advertising, database systems, GPS technology, and advanced cell phone features.

Location-Based Technology   An information technology that supports location-based service which combines advertising, database systems, GPS technology, and advanced cell phone features. With this technology, a traveler who either knows where he is or where he is headed can input that information and find out where nearby restaurants, stores, theaters, etc. are located. On the other hand, a company, for example, could provide you with restaurant, gas station, hotel, or ATM locations via your cell phone, based on your current, GPS-tracked location.

Log File   Created by a Web server and contains every request received by the server from every user. Typically raw data requires extensive data manipulation and analysis in order to arrive at intelligent information.

Log File Analysis Software Needed to organize and analyze the records; it extracts useful information from the log files and generates reports from the analysis to the parties concerned.

Mailing List   A subscription-based e-mail discussion forum in which a list of people's e-mail addresses is used to send certain

messages or announcements to the subscribers at once.

Majordomo   One of the common types of E-mail discussion lists.

Management/E-CRM   Electronic Customer Relationship Management. The whole aspect of customer service is done electronically.

META Tag   An HTML tag that contains information about a Web page. It is a description of the Web page, key words, and the page's title.

Micro-browser   A miniature browser that can only traditionally view sites in HDML. It uses its own gateway, or software on the server to provide access to the wireless Web.

Moving Banner Ad   A banner ad that moves around the screen to try to stay visible to the eyes of the online visitor as the visitor looks at the different part of a Web page on the screen.

Multi-Channel Communications The utilization of a combination of the traditional media and the Internet technologies in marketing and customer service.

Network   Two or more computers connected for the purpose of data communication and management using a common language.

One-Stop Shopping Portal   Web sites that supply travel information as well as booking for all types of services ranging from lodging to airlines, from entertainment to transportation to allow consumers to get all their traveling needs taken care of at one place.

Online Pricing Special offers and prices given over the Internet and usually only available on the business' website. They are usually discounted or have special incentives.

Online Transaction The act of buying and selling a product and/or service over the Internet.

Open Architecture Networking A key underlying technical idea in which each network can be designed in accordance with the specific environment and user requirements of that network.

Opt-In E-mail Marketing A type of e-mail marketing that asks the target audience for permission for sending e-mail messages to them. It is in contrast to spam, unsolicited, mass e-mail marketing.

Opt-In Marketing/Permission Marketing See Pull Marketing.

Optical Fiber A thin, flexible cable containing a bundle of very fine, highly transparent, tubular glass fibers made of pure silicon dioxide, designed to transmit information encoded in pulses of laser light at very high speed (billions of bits per second) by means of internal reflection.

Outsourcing Paying another company to provide services which a company might otherwise have employed its own staff to perform. Example: having a technology company run and manage your technology service needs instead of doing it yourself.

Overrides Rewards presented to agents when they show exceptional sales performance.

Packet The unit of data sent across a network. In Internet technology, it is a "transportation vehicle" that the Internet uses to accomplish its communication tasks.

Paradigm A model, a pattern or a perspective, that is generally accepted by a particular discipline at a given time.

Partnership One of the important elements in traditional tourism and hospitality marketing. It is important for inter-related groups of businesses that serve the needs of the travelers to form partnerships to benefit each other. Example: Hotels partnering with airlines.

PayPal A Web-based service that enables users to send and receive payments electronically. PayPal enables any business or consumer with an e-mail address to securely, conveniently, and cost-effectively send and receive payments online.

PDAs Personal Digital Assistants. A small cellular-enabled device that has Internet access capabilities.

Peer-to-Peer System A network system in which every computer or workstation acts on its own and can communicate every other computer on the network, that is, each workstation has equivalent capabilities and responsibilities.

Platform-Independent
A network structure in which computers with different hardware and operating systems can still talk to each other, allowing free development of competitive hardware and software systems. The Internet is such a network.

Platform-Independent   Refers to one of the most important characteristics of the Internet which offers a communication platform that allows networked computers with different hardware and software configurations to interact and communicate with one another. The Internet, therefore, breaks the barriers of communications between computers that "speak different languages."

Plug-ins   A hardware or software required to be added to a larger system for displaying different types of audio or video messages.

PMS   Property Management Systems. It is a network system used in lodging industry to manage and integrate various functions of a property.

Popunders   See Invisible Interstitials.

Popups   See Interstitials.

Portal/Web Portal   A gateway or entrance to a room or space. A Web portal is a Web site that offers a broad range of services, resources, and links for various interests or for a specified area of interest.

POTS   Plain Old Telephone System. The all-analog telephone network system.

PowerWallet   The name for a type of digital wallets. It is encryption software for conducting online transactions. The wallets contain an online shopper's ID, payment information, shipping address, and more, and lets users use one wallet for any site on the Web.

Print Brochures   A print publication that is distributed, typically free of charge, to travelers who are interested in travel products and services.

Product-Oriented   Focusing on the product itself as the key selling point in a transaction.

Public-key encryption   A method of encryption for secure online data and information transaction. It uses an encryption scheme where each person gets a pair of keys, called the public key and the private key. Messages are encrypted using the intended recipient's public key and can only be decrypted using his private key.

Public-key Encryption   See asymmetric encryption.

Pull Marketing   Asks the target audience's permission to send marketing message or present message in such an attractive way to pull the audience towards it. aka Opt-in Marketing or Permission Marketing.

Push Marketing   A collection of Internet marketing techniques that is used to present and send data to the online visitor.

Push   Where target markets are clearly selected and companies push their marketing messages to individual consumers based on their predefined preferences.

QuickRent A system introduced by Alamo Rent-A-Car that allows online travelers to actually complete the whole rental process online.

QuickTime A special plug-in used to play audio and video messages. It was originally designed for Apple computers.

Random Moving Banner Ad A banner ad that moves around the screen continuously in random directions to draw the attention of the online visitor.

RealPlayer A special plug-in used to play streaming videos as well as audio messages.

Response Rate Percentage of responses generated from the target market.

Retailer Businesses that sell a product or service directly to consumers.

Rich Media/Media Rich Advertising Refers to any online ad that allows for transactions, streaming media, and interactive communication directly in the ad space without leaving the homepage where the ad is being placed. Rich media marketing tries to take advantage of one of the most powerful features of the Internet: interactivity.

ROI Return of Investment. The amount of return on the monetary investment made.

Sabre A Global Distribution System for travel information and reservation.

Search Engine An Internet searching tool that uses categories and classifications or spidering and crawling techniques to find the information the user is looking for.

Search Logic Logical techniques and methods used by search engines to search and organize information on the Internet.

Secondary Data Data that are collected for research purposes other than your own.

Server A host computer on a network, programmed to answer requests to download data or program files, received from client computers connected to the same network.

Service-Oriented Focusing on tailoring product/service to the needs and wants of the consumers and create values through customer service.

Smart Card Refers to a credit-card-size electronic device that includes an imbedded memory chip that can store data.

SMS Short Messaging Service. A feature that allows users to receive or transmit short text messages using a wireless phone.

Software Programs, applications, and protocols that make communication, publication, and transaction online possible.

Spamming Sending mass e-mails to people who have not indicated interest in receiving e-mails from you.

SSL Secure Sockets Layer. A protocol used to transmit private documents over the Internet.

Standardization The imposition of a standard. In technology, the adoption of a common technical standard so that communication between different media and compatibility of equipments can be facilitated. Lack of a standard can create confusion and incomparability.

Static Information Information that stays unchanged for a relatively long period of time. For example, texts and graphics provided by individual tourism companies and businesses.

Station Banner Ad A banner ad that stays on the same spot on the screen and never moves.

Stream Video A means of sending compressed moving images one-way over the Internet, at the user's request, that allows viewing in real time as it downloads over the Internet. Unlike video that is downloaded for subsequent playback, streaming video is stored in temporary files and deleted when the application used to view it is closed.

Streaming Media A technique for transferring data such that it can be processed at a steady and continuous stream.

Streamline Has information available in seconds for an always

up-to-date information source available to the consumers.

Suppliers The manufacturers and providers of products and/or services.

Symmetric Encryption Both the sender and the receiver use the same key for secure communication.

T1 A term introduced by AT&T to refer to a dedicated digital circuit provided by the telephone companies, capable of transmitting data point-to-point at the rate of 1.544 Mbps (megabits per second), containing 24 individual channels, each capable of transmitting voice or data at the rate of 64 Kbps (kilobits per second).

T3 A term introduced by AT&T to refer to a dedicated digital circuit provided by the telephone companies, capable of transmitting data point-to-point at the rate of 44.736 Mbps (megabits per second), used mainly by Internet service providers to connect to the Internet backbone and for the backbone itself.

Tangible Nature Consists of something that is physically there that you can touch, see, etc. Service is not of tangible nature because you cannot physically see or feel what you are purchasing .

TCP/IP Transmission Control Protocol / Internet Protocol. The basic communication language or protocol of the Internet. TCP converts data into packets that are sent across transmission lines to the next computer, whose TCP reconverts the packets into data it can read.

Telnet One of the first applications developed and made publicly available that would allow your computer to dial a phone number and would then act as a terminal to the computer contacted.

Third Party Travel Web sites Web sites owned by travel e-commerce businesses that offer similar services as the traditional travel agents, but typically without a physical storefront.

Top Level Domain TLD. Domain names are derived from a hierarchical system, with a host name followed by a top-level domain category. Some of the common top-level domain categories include .com, .org, .net, .mil, and .gov.

Traditional Marketing Media The old way of marketing your product or service, with the use of traditional media such as radio, newspaper, television, etc.

Traveling Public Consumers of travel products and services in the general public.

24/7 Office Refering to a company's Internet Web site that is always accessible and responsive with proper design and service.

Unique Selling Proposition (USP) An e-commerce business plan that defines what makes a business unique from every other competitor in a particular field and sorts out the precise niche the e-commerce business seeks to fill.

URL Universal Resource Locator. The Web site address of an information source; you can type in the address bar of a browser and go directly to the source.

Usenet A distributed bulletin board system. A bulletin board is a computer and associated software that provides an electronic message database where people can log in, post, and/or read messages.

Viral Marketing Refers to a process in which consumers voluntarily spread a message about a company, a product, or a service based on their own experience. It is the Internet version of word-of-mouth marketing.

Virtual Communities Communities based on the Internet and which only exist in cyberspace. People in the virtual communities do not necessarily know each other by real identity and they are bound only by common interests.

Voice Command Service Basic voice recognition technology.

VPN Virtual Private Network. A private data network that makes use of the public telecommunication infrastructure, maintaining privacy through the use of a tunneling protocol and security procedures.

Walking Brochure Another name for a Web-based wireless device. Information will be accessible anytime and at anyplace unlike regular print brochures.

WAN   Wide Area Network. It is similar to LAN in that it is also a network connecting computers to each other for sharing resources and speedy communication, but it differs in that it covers greater geographical distances than LAN.

Web Authoring Program
Programs developed for people who do not know HTML code but want to create documents readable by Web browsers. These programs convert whatever you type on screen into HTML file in the background, so that what you see on the screen is what you will get when the file is presented through a Web browser.

Web-based Wireless Device
A portable, hand-held device that allows Web access without physically connecting to the Web.

Webcasting   Simultaneous transmission of live or delayed audio or video programming over the World Wide Web to a group of Internet users, based on their individual needs or interests. The Internet counterpart of broadcasting via radio or television.

Web server   A computer capable of providing Internet access to Web-based resources and services in response to requests from client computers on which Web browser software is installed.

Wireless Internet/Web   Refers to a computer network scheme where there is no physical connection between sender and receiver but are instead connected by radio.

WML   Wireless Markup Language. WML is an XML language used to specify content and user interface for WAP devices. WML is supported by almost every mobile phone browser around the world.

World Wide Web   Also referred to as the Web. A collection of globally distributed text and multimedia documents, files, and other network services linked in the Internet and with hypertext technology create an immense electronic library from which information can be retrieved quickly by intuitive searches.

Worldspan   One of the four main GDS systems existing today.

WYSWYG   "What you see is what you get" interface. It means that whatever you type on your computer screen is what you will see and get when displayed on your screen or through a browser.

XbaseY   X is the data rate in Mbps: 'base' means 'baseband' as opposed to radio frequency and Y is the category of cabling. It is used to classify cables such as Ethernet.

XML   Extensible Markup Language. XML is similar to HTML. Both XML and HTML contain markup symbols to describe the contents of a page or file.

Index

223